Bigger than *Ben-Hur*

Television and Popular Culture
Robert J. Thompson, *Series Editor*

Bigger than BEN-HUR

THE BOOK, ITS ADAPTATIONS, AND THEIR AUDIENCES

Edited by

**BARBARA RYAN &
MILETTE SHAMIR**

Syracuse University Press

Copyright © 2016 by Syracuse University Press
Syracuse, New York 13244-5290

All Rights Reserved

First Edition 2016
16 17 18 19 20 21   6 5 4 3 2 1

∞ The paper used in this publication meets the minimum requirements of the
American National Standard for Information Sciences—Permanence of Paper for
Printed Library Materials, ANSI Z39.48-1992.

For a listing of books published and distributed by Syracuse University Press,
visit www.SyracuseUniversityPress.syr.edu.

ISBN: 978-0-8156-3417-1 (cloth)   978-0-8156-3403-4 (paperback)
978-0-8156-5331-8 (e-book)

Library of Congress Cataloging-in-Publication Data

Names: Ryan, Barbara, 1958– editor. | Shamir, Milette, editor.
Title: Bigger than Ben-Hur : the book, its adaptations, and their audiences /
edited by Barbara Ryan and Milette Shamir.
Description: First edition. | Syracuse : Syracuse University Press, 2016. |
  Series: Television and popular culture | Includes bibliographical references and index.
Identifiers: LCCN 2015037762| ISBN 9780815634171 (cloth) | ISBN 9780815634034 (pbk. : alk.
paper) |
ISBN 9780815653318 (e-book)
  Subjects: LCSH: Wallace, Lew, 1827–1905. Ben-Hur. | Christianity in literature. |
Wallace, Lew, 1827–1905—Film adaptations. | Ben-Hur (Motion picture : 1925) |
Ben-Hur (Motion picture : 1959) | Christianity in motion pictures. | Motion pictures
and literature. | Historical films—United States—History and criticism.
Classification: LCC PS3134 .B43 2016 | DDC 813/.4—dc23 LC record available at
http://lccn.loc.gov/2015037762

Manufactured in the United States of America

Contents

Illustrations

Tables

Foreword

Who loves *Ben-Hur*? Certainly not, by and large, professional critics and academics. Literature professor Leslie Fiedler thought it the second worst American novel ever written, surpassed only by the one that provided the source material for D. W. Griffith's *Birth of a Nation* (1915), Thomas Dixon Jr.'s *The Clansman* (1905). According to D. H. Lawrence biographer Harry T. Moore, the British novelist felt physically ill after watching the 1925 silent film version of *Ben-Hur*. In 1959, despite winning eleven Oscars—a record at the time—William Wyler's film version had a devastating effect on his reputation amongst the critical intelligentsia. Later, Wyler would suggest ruefully that some critics, particularly his former champions in the French fraternity, never forgave him for having directed *Ben-Hur*.

And yet, almost from the moment of its publication in 1880, *Ben-Hur* has proved to be a phenomenon of popular culture. The statistics are well known but still astonishing: by the end of the nineteenth century, it had sold more copies than any other novel ever written. The stage version, first performed in 1899, had totaled 6,000 performances across North America by 1920, earning the management many millions of dollars. There were two silent film versions, the second of which (directed by Fred Niblo in 1925) was Hollywood's most spectacular epic of the decade. There have since been an animated version (1988) and a television movie (2010), but, most famously, there was the 1959 film, which rescued the fortunes of MGM studios and whose takings in its first year of release accounted for nearly 10 percent of the U.S. film industry's entire earnings for that year (of a total of 534 films). Incidental Hollywood details have added to the work's legendary status. When Humphrey Bogart's private-eye character Sam Spade poses as a fussy collector in the bookstore scene in *The Big*

Sleep (1946), which was based on a Raymond Chandler novel, the work he feigns to be after is a rare copy of *Ben-Hur*. Later in the twentieth century, a reluctant 12-year-old named Steven Spielberg was taken to see the Wyler film of *Ben-Hur*. He was totally enthralled. Now an accomplished film-maker, Spielberg has said that at the time he had had no idea that a movie could be that good.

So what is it about *Ben-Hur* that has, in defiance of arbiters' approval, so appealed to the popular imagination? On the simplest level, *Ben-Hur* is a great adventure story that enriches its profusion of incident with variety and contrast. It is a great love story, but it is also a great hate story; it is a story of revenge but also a story of redemption; its action scales the highest peaks of imperial power but also scrutinizes the lowest level of a galley ship or a Roman prison. *Ben-Hur* is the story of an individual but also of a nation. It appeals to a reader's sense of spectacle, but the mood is predominantly contemplative, and the narrative carries alongside this momentum of action a strong moral, educative, and religious sense. In its account of a noble hero unjustly accused of a crime, punished and presumed dead, who rises again to eminence and seeks vengeance against his oppressors, one hears echoes of the romance novels of Victor Hugo and Alexandre Dumas. If you add to this array an over-arching religious dimension, you can gauge *Ben-Hur*'s potential appeal to an international audience, young and old.

Still, having all of the ingredients for popular success is not the same as having the skill to blend them into an irresistible whole. Yet, somewhat to his surprise, this is what Lew Wallace achieved. Wallace was fifty-three years old when the novel was published; he told his wife that he thought, with a bit of luck, *Ben-Hur* could earn them about fifty dollars per year in royalties. It had taken him five years to write his 500-page tale, during which time he became the governor of New Mexico. As governor, his responsibilities included asking Sheriff Pat Garrett to arrest Garrett's former friend, Billy the Kid.

Wallace's first novel, *The Fair God* (1873), occupied him for twenty years but made little impression on the literary world. With *Ben-Hur*, Wallace combined a Gospel story with his knowledge of the behavior of men in combat and under stress, which he drew from his involvement in the American Civil War, particularly his firsthand experience of one of its bloodiest encounters: the Battle of Shiloh. Wallace's war experiences gave an edge of authenticity to the scenes of battle and physical conflict in *Ben-Hur*. His campaigning against slavery as a young lawyer may also have given extra piquancy to his portrayal of Judah Ben-Hur's years as a galley slave.

Some critics have defended Wallace's literary style; in the Oxford World's Classics edition, for example, David Mayer claims that Wallace writes "effective, unornamented prose."[1] I don't think, though, a persuasive case can be made that the novel's popularity owes much to the quality of the writing. In aiming for archaic authenticity, Wallace often achieves only a kind of pompous piety that many subsequent plays and films about this period have found hard to avoid. There are too many appeals to the reader, who is constantly being "besought." Also over-frequent are attempts to imitate the language of two thousand years ago ("God of Abraham forefend!") and phrasing that sounds more quaint than compelling: one of the Wise Men does not simply wear sandals; sandals "guarded his feet." Particularly comical is the flowery dialogue, such as when Ben-Hur recalls his sister to the Roman commander, Quintus Arrius, in tones quite at odds with the desperation of his situation: "Her breath was as the breath of white lilies. She was the youngest branch of the palm—so fresh, so tender, so graceful, so beautiful!" he exclaims, before adding with leaden bathos, "she made my day all morning" (3:III). Yet such is the power of the narrative that readers can sweep past such infelicities. Why is this?

It seems to me that the novel has two great ideas, one of which was not especially unusual in the fiction of the time, and the other strikingly original. First, *Ben-Hur* is the story of an ordinary individual who suddenly finds himself at the center of extraordinary historical events. This story brings the period alive not as a remote episode in the past but as something being experienced by a person whose sensibilities are very like our own. Tolstoy did the same thing in *War and Peace* (1869), for example; Boris Pasternak was to do it again in *Doctor Zhivago* (1957). Wallace may not meet their literary height, but he deserves to be recognized as part of a tradition that stretches back to Sir Walter Scott.

More remarkably, though, Wallace chose to tell the biblical story from the perspective of a minor fictional character who has his own history. This character fills in gaps and margins of the main story to give it a new dimension. That is, *Ben-Hur* is a novel that shadows a classic and well-known narrative with a more prosaic one of its own that involves a lesser character on the sidelines of the main drama. Part of the fascination with *Ben-Hur* comes from the point at which these narratives intersect. Offhand, I cannot think of another major nineteenth-century novel that does this—certainly not so resonantly. This strategy anticipates Tom Stoppard's *Rosencrantz and Guildenstern Are Dead* (1966), a play that depicts the fate of two minor characters as they weave in and out of the plot of Shakespeare's *Hamlet* (1599), and Jean Rhys's *Wide Sargasso Sea* (1966), a novel that re-tells the story of Charlotte Brönte's *Jane Eyre* (1847) from the point of view of Rochester's mad first wife. A scene in Wyler's *Ben-Hur* perfectly portrays this strategy: during the depiction of the Sermon on the Mount, we see a small figure moving from left to right in the far background of the shot. Judah Ben-Hur, on his way to a meeting with Pontius Pilate, is too preoccupied with his own troubles to pay attention to the momentous event he is passing by. Indeed, he is unaware at this point that the man speaking in the distance is he who had saved Ben-Hur's life in the desert years before by giving him water. This awareness only dawns when Ben-Hur gives water to Christ on the march to Cavalry and makes the connection with the earlier event; it is one of the story's most superb epiphanies.

Although the popularity of *Ben-Hur* as novel and play was virtually unprecedented, the cinema was to provide *Ben-Hur* with its widest audience. I suspect that most people today know this tale essentially through its cinematic interpretations. Niblo's 1925 version remains highly regarded by both cinéastes and *Ben-Hur* scholars, perhaps because it sticks most closely to the original text, is genuinely spectacular in its set pieces, and has the advantage of being silent, so actors do not have to struggle with awkward and anachronistic dialogue. The fan magazine *Photoplay* ran advertisements that billed *Ben-Hur* as "the picture every Christian ought to see!" Yet as a writer in this magazine remarked, so should every Jew, Buddhist, and sun worshipper if the film were to have any chance of making its money back. (It did eventually show a profit, but it took a few years.) Film historians have tended to prefer Niblo's 1925 film to Wyler's 1959 re-make. I would concede that the earlier film's sea battle sequence surpasses the re-make in terms of excitement and compelling brutality. However, in all other respects, my allegiance remains with the Wyler film, which, more than any interpretation before or since, stimulated my love of the *Ben-Hur* story.

For someone like me with an interest in adaptations of literature to the screen, *Ben-Hur* exerts a particular fascination. Two major problems of adaptation immediately present themselves. How do you explain the motivation behind Messala's malicious treatment of his former close friend, Ben-Hur, when neither the novel nor the 1925 film version offers much of a clue? Also, how do you dramatize what happens after the chariot race, which rouses an audience to such peaks of excitement that anything that comes after is in danger of seeming anti-climactic? That certainly would not do for a film that concludes with the Crucifixion.

Wyler handles these narrative challenges with consummate skill in his 1959 adaptation. The reunion between Ben-Hur and Messala at the beginning of the film is superbly acted by Charlton Heston and Stephen Boyd. Both bring emotional intensity to the scene that, judging by the embarrassment and laughter that follows their initial embrace, seems to take both characters by surprise. It is well known that Gore Vidal suggested a homoerotic subtext to this relationship that would help explain Messala's subsequent vindictiveness toward his dear friend and (possible) lover. The rumor is that Wyler went along with this suggestion, provided that it was implicit rather than explicit, and that no one told Charlton Heston. The subtext works when Messala's remarks on his supposed view of the political situation take on erotic subtones, linking the personal and political undercurrents of his relationship to his one-time Jewish friend.

Politics is to the fore, however, when Messala grows incensed that his friend refuses to help him in quelling treasonous elements in the region. When the representative of imperial Rome asks the subjugated Judean to name others who have expressed hostility to Rome, Ben-Hur refuses. "Would I retain your friendship if I became an informer?" he asks. But Messala is insistent. "Either you help me or oppose me," he says. "You're either for me or against me, you have no other choice." In the context of the

1950s, this demand is instantly recognizable as the language of McCarthyism and the House Un-American Activities Committee (HUAC), the group whose dubious investigations of Communist infiltration had a devastating effect on the Hollywood community and whose activity Wyler loathed with every fiber of his being. By punishing Ben-Hur for a crime of which Messala knows he is innocent, a cynical political opportunist demonstrates that not even a close friend and pillar of the community is safe from persecution when treason is suspected. Political cunning is interwoven here with disparate notions of male friendship, and the force of this relationship is thrillingly brought to its logical conclusion in the chariot race. Wyler revised Wallace's original scene significantly when he decided that, in the 1959 film, Ben-Hur will not win the race so much as Messala will defeat himself: fearful and furious at the prospect of a humiliating defeat, he loses control of his chariot when he tries to lash his rival out of the race.

Immediately after the chariot race comes another master stroke by Wyler: a scene that is not in the novel or the 1925 film but vibrantly reinvigorates the narrative at a critical point where it might otherwise ebb. Summoning Ben-Hur to his tent, the dying Messala has one final card to play that will diminish Ben-Hur's triumph and forgiveness. Ben-Hur has been told that his mother and sister have died in prison. But Messala now reveals that they are alive and in horrible conditions. "Look for them in the Valley of the Lepers," he says, adding maliciously, "if you can recognize them." Messala tugs at Ben-Hur's clothes as he says his last words: "It goes on, Judah, the race is not over." Stephen Boyd is magnificent in this scene; he is vengeful and defiant as death approaches. His malice assures the audience and Ben-Hur that the chariot race has not been the culmination of his enmity with the hero. Further implied by this scene is the distance Ben-Hur still must travel in his spiritual journey. When he leaves Messala's tent and steps back into the arena, it is deserted. Wyler's framing demonstrates the hollowness of his victory; Ben-Hur is now a tiny figure in an empty stadium. The lesson is that, in a conflict fueled by hatred and revenge, there can be no winners.

With scenes like these, Wyler's 1959 film gives the novel's sprawling narrative a cogent dramatic structure. Pervasive imagery of water, stone, steps, blood, rings, gifts, and variations of light and dark resonate with cumulative force to take full advantage of the story's potential for contrast, conflict, ambivalence, and irony. Ben-Hur is a character who goes from the extremes of wealth and privilege to the extremes of poverty and suffering and then back again. He goes from Jew to Roman and then back again. His best friend, who saved his life when he was a child, becomes his worst enemy. A Roman commander, Quintus Arrius, who has the potential to become his principal oppressor as commander of the slave ship, will become his champion and father figure. At all points the film accentuates the narrative's dynamic polarities. As a man who has spoken out against violence, Ben-Hur is transformed through circumstance into a revenge hero; eventually he is in danger of becoming the thing he set out to destroy. "Hatred is turning you to stone," Esther tells him. "It's as if you've become Messala." Only his (initially inadvertent) involvement in Christ's destiny shows Ben-Hur, at last, the error of his ways. The film's conclusion appropriately emphasizes rescue of the innocent rather than punishment of the guilty: Ben-Hur's mother and sister are miraculously cured of leprosy. This structure parallels his gradual relinquishing of force in favor of forgiveness. On hearing Christ's last words on the cross, Ben-Hur tells Esther: "And I felt the sound of his voice / Take the sword out of my hand." In this act of renunciation, a prayer is answered and his family is restored. Making this point orthographically is the script that frames this speech as blank verse.

Wyler's *Ben-Hur* is the final installment in what I see as his unofficial trilogy on the themes of pacifism and revenge. His film *Friendly Persuasion* (1956) followed the fortunes of a Quaker family during the American Civil War. The story peaks when its pacifist hero (Gary Cooper) is confronted by a rebel soldier who has just killed his best friend and is about to kill him. After a struggle, the pacifist overpowers his assailant, snatches his rifle, and points it at the terrified youth before saying: "Go on, go on, get—I'll not harm thee." The last word is a moving reaffirmation of his Quaker faith and an explanation for his action. In my favorite of all Westerns, Wyler's *The Big Country* (1958), another pacifist, this one a greenhorn just arrived from back East (Gregory Peck), finds himself caught up in a feud over water rights between two warring families. He starts posing awkward questions about Westerners' apparent obsession with outmoded conventions of masculinity, honor, and confrontation. Wyler frames a prolonged yet inconclusive fistfight between the greenhorn and a hostile foreman (Charlton Heston) in an ironic long-shot that cuts the men down to size; the scene ends with the Easterner asking the foreman: "Tell me: what have we proved?" With similar elegance, intelligence, and even wit, Wyler's *Ben-Hur* builds to a comparable resolution that demonstrates the futility of violence. Its major themes—freedom from dictatorship, the evil of slavery, and the renunciation of force as a means to political ends—are as relevant as ever. Although on the surface it is simply a biblical and historical tale, *Ben-Hur* is better understood as a remarkably fluid text in its capacity to speak to an ever-changing modern audience about contemporary concerns.

NEIL SINYARD

Bigger than *Ben-Hur*

Introduction

The *Ben-Hur* Tradition

BARBARA RYAN AND MILETTE SHAMIR

As this collection goes to press, polarized reactions are greeting Metro-Goldwyn-Mayer's announcement of plans to film a new *Ben-Hur*. For some, this news merits a snort or shrug—another revival of a time-worn warhorse. For others, though, the announcement stirs keen interest: what will the dream factory conjure to outdo the epic that swept the Academy Awards in 1959? Such strong yet incompatible reactions are a reminder that the name "Ben-Hur" has long meant more than the novel General Lew Wallace published in 1880. Indeed, for more than a century, this name has circulated as an icon, connoting for some a profoundly spiritual or at least powerful experience, but signifying for others false piety, bad taste, and cheap thrills. This debate—the puzzle of what qualifies as art in modern times—will not be resolved in the essays that follow (although it will certainly be discussed). Essays gathered here are centered on more nuanced questions that readers and viewers ask about *Ben-Hur* as they strive to expand the context within which this favorite can be studied. Of particular interest are adaptations of Wallace's tale, which have swelled an audience that began with print but moved thereafter to theater and film. Jointly, these essays seek to recover and analyze the rich lineage Howard Miller has identified as the *"Ben-Hur* tradition."[1]

As the first collection devoted to this tradition, *Bigger than "Ben-Hur"* reminds readers that when Wallace's tale moved from print to stage, then to cinema and onward, it changed unpredictably. No adaptation was completely separable from religious concerns. Still, a fair few intersected

1

with those concerns at oblique angles. When homemakers klatched, for instance, over Ben-Hur coffee or automobile shoppers considered the Ben-Hur luxury sedan, the *Ben-Hur* tradition had more to do with commerce than with Christ. Realizing this, scholars have approached *Ben-Hur* from multiple directions, both religious and secular. Whereas New Testament and "third quest" specialists examined *Ben-Hur*'s portrait of Jesus, often through the door opened by film scholars, classics experts pioneered inquiry that moved away from Wallace's religious message to study instead his depiction of imperial Rome. As literary historians came on board, so too did theater researchers, American studies analysts, and students of adaptation, with each group bringing its own set of questions. In the foreword to this collection, Neil Sinyard suggests a source of this dynamism when he describes *Ben-Hur* as "a remarkably fluid text" of signal "capacity to speak to an ever-changing modern audience about contemporary concerns."[2] *Bigger than "Ben-Hur"* establishes a forum for analysts from a range of academic disciplines to investigate not just one tale in varied formats but also a tradition that, after more than 130 years, appears tireless.

Essays collected here are not for *Ben-Hur* scholars only. They offer insights to students of popular Christianity and Judaism; to scholars of reading, reception, and fandom; to those who investigate the United States' sense of the Middle East and of Zionism; to researchers who probe the intersection of education and entertainment on stage and on screen; to chroniclers of ways of imaging Jesus Christ, femme fatales, and masculine performance; and to many more. Holding all of this together is tradition. We conceptualize tradition as movement in and through time that powerfully evokes the past to feed the present and, by so doing, looks to the future. Our idea of the *Ben-Hur* tradition owes much to a thinker who is new to this corpus: Édouard Glissant. According to Alessandro Corio, Glissant conceptualizes modernity as "an uninterrupted movement characterized by continuity and rupture" that is "perpetually open to the unexpectedness of the event, and alert to the vertigo of the unimagined."[3]

Ethicists, anthropologists, and students of postcolonialism have found use-value in Glissant's delineation of "lived modernity" (*modernité vecué*). This phrase identifies certain social actors' inability to engage historical writing with the assurance of subjects of "mature" (sometimes called "evolved") modernity. The distinction is not between subjects who are or are not modern; rather, it lies between denizens of sites in which modernity originated and developed gradually over generations and of sites in which modernity was imposed with an abruptness Glissant deems "brutal."[4] He focuses on the European power/knowledge project that writes Caribbean history from colonizers' vantage. Widely applicable, however, is Glissant's observation that lived modernity is de-authorized in seats of power, yet generative of alternative narratives that draw on past events.

This understanding of generativity captures neatly Wallace's decision to romance God's Word historically and how negatively some power-holders of his day reacted. Wallace's formal education was limited. But this is no mark against his romancing because he did not write in competition with trained historians or biblical scholars. In an important discussion of Glissant's work, John Muthyala points out that lived modernity typically "overlaps with the preoccupations of matured 'modernity.'"[5] In the case of *Ben-Hur*, this overlap is recognized by scholars who ponder Wallace's creativity in relation to the labor of the German philologists known as "Higher Critics." Oft forgotten, though, is that Higher Critics compiled scholarly histories: the critical nub of mature modernity. Wallace contrastively wrote fiction that, though extremely well informed about facts, pursued unscholarly goals. Like the Higher Critics, he sought truth. However, his use of historical facts was less a disinterested search than a pragmatic marshalling that made sense to many of his contemporaries. Wallace's pragmatism meant that, in tandem with *Ben-Hur*'s religious interpretation, his tale shared thoughts on modern issues that were far from the Higher Critics' minds: the "woman question," ties between virtue and wealth, Jews' place in the present day, and much more.

Sensitive to such modern issues, as well as to *Ben-Hur*'s religious valences, authors of the essays in this volume recover ways in which certain social actors have explored the "living" of their varied modernities through Wallace's tale. Among these actors were democrats who looked to Rome for inspiration, Sunday-school administrators, the Jewish duo who moved *Ben-Hur* to Broadway, all who noted the 1925 film's attempt to "get Judas right," and a Scottish civil servant. Also living modernity through *Ben-Hur* were fans of its mother–son reunion, Christians who pondered a Jewish homeland, a "New Woman" whose script for the first feature-length film was rejected, and anyone who took libidinous delight, decades later, in Charlton Heston's bulging biceps. Contributors to this collection interpret Wallace's book, the script for the 1899 stage show, and feature-length films made in 1925 and 1959. Approaching these versions of *Ben-Hur* from varied academic realms, each contributor moves from discussing semiotic meaning to identifying impact that could be commercial, religious, sexual, pedagogical, artistic, emotive, civic, and more. In and through the research collected here, readers will descry a babel of reception cohorts. Some were mature in their modernities whereas others were not. All, though, were drawn to *Ben-Hur*.

To chart a modernizing tradition that accrues strength when iterations shift to new media, this volume follows a roughly chronological order. Four essays examine Wallace's tale-telling, six study adaptations, and a coda pulls reception research to material culture by surveying products to which manufacturers gave the name "Ben-Hur." By collecting these projects, we honor a tradition that includes the name of a cliff face in the Pyrenees and several U.S. towns, a school in Uttar Pradesh, a department store in Kentucky, a go-kart speedway in Indiana, and a baby in decolonizing Singapore. All of this, though, comprises just a fraction of what the name "Ben-Hur" has meant since a former Union army general and self-taught romancer dared to write the first U.S. tale to make a literary character of the historical figure whom tens of millions worship as the Messiah.

✦ ✦ ✦

A source text for Wallace's colorful life is his autobiography, published in 1906. Adding much to it is Robert E. Morsberger and Katharine M. Morsberger's well-researched *Lew Wallace: Militant Romantic* (1980). Still, many who love *Ben-Hur* know little of its creator. He was born in 1827 in Indiana to David and Esther Wallace. His father, the state's sixth governor and later a congressman, oversaw the last of the Native American tribes' removal from Indiana. Wallace's mother died of consumption when he was seven. Her loss would haunt him for the rest of his life. He did enjoy, however, a warm relationship with his stepmother, Zerelda, a prominent suffragist and temperance activist. Growing up, Wallace felt tugs from competing worlds. The military intrigued him. Also appealing was a career in law and public service, which his father encouraged him to pursue. Then there was the allure of art, music, and literature; Wallace displayed pictorial talent early in life, and he continued to draw and paint into old age. Visual sensitivity enhanced his prose but so did his musical gifts; he was a skillful violinist who enjoyed playing for friends and family. An ardent reader who would dot *Ben-Hur* with references to Shakespeare, Keats, Schiller, and Byron, Wallace attempted his first novel at sixteen. This juvenile effort was set among the *hidalgos* of Guadalajara yet ended in a crusade to Jerusalem; it anticipated themes and settings that would make "Ben-Hur Wallace" a household name.

In 1846 Wallace began his military career. Bored with law studies and "hungry for war," he raised a militia to fight under Zachary Taylor in the Mexican–American War.[6] Although he did not participate in any battles, Wallace established enough of a soldierly reputation to be asked later to muster regiments for the Union army. Having done so, he assumed command of the Eleventh Indiana regiment. During the first year of the Civil War, he rose to the rank of brigadier general. His rise ground to a halt, however, in April 1862 when controversial conduct in the Battle of Shiloh caused his removal from command. Perhaps to avert public criticism, the Union army top command blamed Wallace for the many casualties on that bloody battlefield. He would suffer long from the sense of having been slandered. Decades later, Ulysses S. Grant would seem to retract the criticism of Wallace. Grant's intervention was so ambiguous, though, that Wallace's good name was recuperated instead by *Ben-Hur*'s huge appeal.

That appeal was yet to come, however, as he drafted *The Fair God; or, the Last of the 'Tzins* (1873). Inspired by William H. Prescott's *History of the Conquest of Mexico* (1843) and enriched by Wallace's experiences south of the border, this romance imagines the Spanish conquest mainly from the Aztec point of view. Wallace used narrative techniques he learned from Prescott, James Fenimore Cooper, and Sir Walter Scott. By studying history and allowing his imagination to fill in the gaps, he honed skills vital to the Bible-extender he would soon compose.

In 1878 Wallace and his wife, the writer Susan Elston Wallace, moved to Santa Fe, where he served as governor of the New Mexico territory.

1. Lew Wallace, ca. 1885. Frontispiece to the Garfield edition of *Ben-Hur* (1892).

Despite broils with outlaws, Wallace was able to draft his Christly tale, mostly at night, as he switched "from the serious things of life to the purely romantic."[7] For many of his fellow Americans, though, these "serious things" *were* the stuff of romance; this is attested by the dozens of Western novels based on the Lincoln County Wars. Wallace was aware of such blurred lines; he ensured that his purely romantic extension of the ancient documents he cognized as "God's Truth" was backed up by the histories available at the time. He probably consulted several hundred sources to provide a meticulously realistic literary account of Palestine and Rome in the first century.

   Why did Wallace undertake the bold literary foray of romancing the New Testament? The opening pages of his autobiography state that he was not, and never had been, a member of "any church or denomination." He was careful, all the same, to add that he "believe[s] absolutely in the Christian conception of God." Some commentators have not credited this claim; they say he romanced the Bible to exploit the best-selling book of all time. This view still finds adherents.[8] But in 2003, Victor Davis Hanson countered that Wallace was working through the shame of Shiloh.[9] Still another explanation carries Wallace's imprimatur: *Ben-Hur* retorts to an agnostic's challenge about the Bible's historical validity.[10] The implication is that, for Wallace and the many, many readers his tale attracted, the "Revealed Word of God" revealed too little. The hunger to know more was not new, and *Ben-Hur* was not the first attempt to supplement the Gospels' lean reportage. It was the first, though—and among the most appealing— to be written by a romancer capable of fashioning a small mountain of historical facts into a thrilling tale without letting the realism swamp the generative power of his vivid pictorial gifts and ranging imagination.

◆   ◆   ◆

As Wallace's novel opens, Judah Ben-Hur is the pride of his Jewish household. He is unprotected, however, from imperial Rome's depredations because his father is dead. In his late teens (n.b.: adaptations would make him older), Ben-Hur becomes the target of a boyhood friend who seizes a chance to advance his ambition at the expense of the Hur household. Messala's selfishness rips Ben-Hur from his home, sends his mother and sister to prison, and casts the gently raised youth into slavery. Wallace lets readers know that although death came quickly to most of the slaves who were forced to row on imperial galleys, Ben-Hur is strengthened and toughened by it. Just one spark of humanity succors him during these harsh years: a Nazarene gives him water when he is near dying of thirst as he marches to the galleys.

Years of hard-labor enslavement induct the stripling into manhood. He holds on tight to his concern for his mother and sister; this concern provides his moral compass. Slavery ends for Ben-Hur when he earns the respect of a Roman who captains the galley. Quintus Arrius manumits and adopts Ben-Hur, and the Jew begins to learn Rome's ways. After Arrius's death, Ben-Hur quests on. In Antioch, he is tempted by pleasures of the flesh, but his love of home guards him from debauchery. Simonides, a faithful steward of Ben-Hur's father's fortune, helps him, as do the Magus Balthasar and Sheik Ilderim. Then, when the chariot race gives Ben-Hur a chance to best Messala, he bends his wealth, strength, and alliances to do so. He wins the race fully yet ruthlessly, considering this pitiless tactic: he uses his chariot as an attack weapon.

The hollowness of this victory becomes clear as Ben-Hur quests on, still seeking his mother and sister. A flair for subterfuge stands him in good stead. Embodying its peril to his rectitude, though, is the temptress Iras. Ben-Hur finds her attractive. But he also admires Simonides's daughter, home-loving Esther. Embittered by the loss of his family, he turns his leadership ability to rebellion against Rome. Jesus's reappearance saves him from the wrath that had made him hungry for war. The Nazarene preaches of a kingdom that Ben-Hur understands only in part. The quester is astounded, however, by Jesus's miraculous ability to heal his mother and sister of the leprosy to which they were exposed in prison. Finally, Ben-Hur realizes the meaning of the new covenant: Jesus will not reign as a sublunary king. This realization explains why he accepts Jesus as the Messiah, lays down his sword, spurns Iras, and starts Christian householding with Esther. Ben-Hur is last seen heading off to Rome. There, he will donate wealth to fund construction of the catacombs that will shelter his fellow Christians from imperial persecution.

This is a sketch of the tale that would become, with scores of repetitions and variations, an icon. Within a decade of the book's publication, *Ben-Hur* turned Wallace into one of the most admired U.S. men. This outcome could not have been foreseen when certain Protestant journals expressed indignation over his mix of the worldly and the divine. Sales soon picked up, however, in the United States, and then in much of the industrialized world. After President James Garfield stayed up nights reading *Ben-Hur*, he offered Wallace a diplomatic position in Turkey. Wallace ably filled this distinguished post from 1881 to 1885, and the experience provided material for his third and last novel, *The Prince of India* (1893). It was *Ben-Hur*, though, that made Wallace the sort of author who received fan mail from people reporting lasting conversion experiences after reading his work.

In an attempt to map this tale's unique cultural position, we identify pole-stars between which contributors to the *Ben-Hur* tradition have steered. One pole-star is a sentimental and romantic literary lineage from which Wallace drew and which he helped modernize. The second is a more disparate grab bag. It is dominated by the major adaptations to stage and cinema, but includes creative popular responses. As early as in Wallace's day, these creativities ranged from Ben-Hur tin snips to a buggy blanket. More recently, they include a Muppet's love for a film named *Ben-Hare* and a photoshopped image of Beyoncé-Hur.

◆   ◆   ◆

We consider first the sentimental and romantic literary lineage. Wallace's merger of secular aesthetics and sacred myth was key to *Ben-Hur*'s success. In this regard, however, he was far from working alone. The postbellum era was a time of huge ferment for the Bible and of marvelous artistic creativity in relation to it, over which subjects of lived and mature modernity tussled. While the Christian scriptures' value, as an historical record, came under fire, some conservatives closed ranks. But, as a spokesman for liberal U.S. Protestantism would reflect in 1911: "The change in the popular conception during the last half century was so great that the Bible might properly be called a genuinely new book."[11] This point is demonstrated by a chronicle of literary events that begins in the 1850s. In that decade, many novels preached openly. The one that pleased the largest audience was Harriet Beecher Stowe's *Uncle Tom's Cabin* (1852). Also crowd-pleasing was a tale that included Jesus as a character; J. H. Ingraham's *The Prince of the House of David* (1856) sold extremely well for decades with almost no advertising, as did its sequels. In the next decade, a French Orientalist discerned in the topography in and near Jerusalem a "fifth Gospel" that casts doubt on the Bible's truth to history. Ernst Renan's *Vie de Jésus* (1863) became a byword for infidelity but inspired other fictional biographies of Christ, including one by Stowe's no-less-famous brother, Henry Ward Beecher. Soon, another U.S. writer attracted readers by supplementing what the Bible reveals of heaven. Elizabeth Stuart Phelps's *The Gates Ajar* (1868) inspired a cigar, a tippet, a floral arrangement, and piano music before disappearing from the American literary canon in the twentieth century.

In the 1870s Bible-themed literature continued to find U.S. readers. The biggest crowd-pleaser at that time was the work of a minister, E. P. Roe; his greatest success was *Barriers Burned Away* (1877). As Roe composed the first of his twenty widely read novels, Herman Melville crafted a brilliant but unnoticed biblical work, *Clarel* (1876), which married a Holy Land pilgrimage to theological musings. *Ben-Hur*'s popular success was followed (though not matched) by international best sellers such as *Robert Elsmere* (1888) by England's Mrs. Humphry Ward and *Quo Vadis* (1895, translated into English in 1897) by Poland's Henryk Sienkiewicz. The century's final decade saw a deluge of religious fiction, including four novels "of the cross" by Florence Morse Kingsley and, most remarkably, *In His Steps* (1897). This novel by Kansas minister Charles M. Sheldon still ranks as one of the best-selling books of all time.

It is astounding that literary criticism all but ignored this corpus, *Ben-Hur* included, for most of the twentieth century. The glaring exception is America's (and, likely, the world's) most popular novel before *Ben-Hur*, *Uncle Tom's Cabin*. Part of the explanation for this scholarly imbalance is found in contours of literary critical scaffolding: the standard account is that *Uncle Tom's Cabin* and *Ben-Hur* inhabit different cultural epochs that are separated starkly by an internecine war. The timeline presented by most literary anthologies and college survey courses tells a familiar story: U.S. fiction enjoyed its first aesthetic and marketplace surge during the 1840s and 1850s, then dropped to a trickle between 1860 and 1865, and re-emerged after the Civil War as something quite new. If antebellum fiction was dominated by romantic and sentimental styles, the postbellum sort was shaped by realist sensibilities. If antebellum fiction was concerned with ideal forms and subjective sensations, the postbellum sort was committed to objectivity and empiricism. If fiction such as Stowe's and Nathaniel Hawthorne's was inspired by spiritual and/or religious truths, that of William Dean Howells and Theodore Dreiser scrutinized the growing regard for wealth and conspicuous consumption that defined the Gilded Age.

It is telling, therefore, that Dreiser would recall reading *Ben-Hur* as a child.[12] What the standard account fails to register, arguably, is the abiding importance of religious and spiritual themes in postbellum literature.

Much is lost by commitment to a grand narrative that assumes too simply U.S. secularization after the Civil War. Uncritical belief in the unequivocal triumph of realism ensures that a vibrant literary tradition of evangelical fiction (with huge crowd appeal) has rarely been a topic of study. *Bigger than "Ben-Hur"* encourages perspectives revisionary enough to augment comprehension of the twining of realism with romance—*and* of popular culture with religious, spiritual, and anti-religious concerns—that have shaped literature, theater, and film. This augmentation has value on its own. However, its value grows as researchers realize that this twining promises to continue to shape creative expression across many media in the twenty-first century.

◆   ◆   ◆

This discussion moves us to our second pole-star: the "pop" creativities of people who lived their modernities through *Ben-Hur*. Here again Glissant is helpful, specifically his interest in generativity. Take this example: When kidnapped Africans were brought to North America, some of them generated songs that we now know as "spirituals." All of the songs' lyrics are Christian. But the actor named most often is neither Jesus nor God; it is Moses. This example draws attention to powerfully productive ways in which a subject of lived modernity can find "a way of transforming" the historical narratives imposed on him or her "without"—a central concern for Glissant—"losing oneself."[13] Glissant conceptualized modernity as uninterrupted movement that is hallmarked by "real discontinuity beneath the apparent continuity."[14] Described in these terms, the *Ben-Hur* tradition is characterized by the continuous transmission of Wallace's quest saga over time. The tradition is unique in its openness to the unexpected—to the vertigo of what has not been heretofore imagined.

Attention to this duality significantly enlarges investigation of *Ben-Hur*'s influence on twentieth-century culture.[15] Consider the intervention of the duo who dared to move Wallace's Christly tale to Broadway. The play that Marc Klaw and Abraham Erlanger produced in 1899 rewrote the rules for who could (and should) attend theater. Howard Miller gauges the tectonic discontinuity of this action in his essay in this volume. Within a very few years, though, this rupture was naturalized as the stage version of *Ben-Hur* prodded mainstream, middle-class U.S. Protestants toward the blur of church and theater that only the wealthiest Christians had enjoyed previously. At the same time, this eye-popping play raised the bar for stage craft; famed, for instance, was its elaborate system of under-stage treadmills to help dramatize the chariot race. This production of *Ben-Hur* toured so widely that it reached a young William Faulkner in Mississippi. He said that the show was unforgettable "because it had live horses and a camel and I'd never seen a camel before."[16]

Next came the 1907 film. Though a minor effort in comparison to the feature-length films that followed, this "short" drove the Klaw & Erlanger show to new heights of splendor (e.g., the horses racing on stage grew more numerous). Nowadays, it is hard to see why theater magnates worried about Sidney Olcott's almost incoherent mélange of unconnected shots. Nevertheless, fearing a potential dent in profits, Klaw and Erlanger sued Kalem Studios for infringement. Their victory remains a legal precedent. In Glissantian terms, though, it marks something just as important: imposition of a modernity that quashes rupture to keep the existing power/knowledge structure in place. This modernity resides in a seat of power with the institutionalized authority to decide which versions of (in this case) *Ben-Hur* would be permitted. The court's decision against Kalem gave the Klaw & Erlanger *Ben-Hur* a firmer appearance of continuity with Wallace's book. In this respect, the court's decision papered over the play's capacity to cause conceptual or categorical vertigo.[17]

Suggestive in this regard is Ted Hovet Jr.'s observation that it was quite harsh for the court to order Kalem to pay $25,000 in reparations. He points out, correctly, that the Kalem project only did what Wallace's publishers had done, with no reprisal, when they issued (as a stand-alone) the part of Wallace's book that describes the chariot race. Students of Glissant will discern that what the court championed, in effect if not intent, is a sense of historical writing (in this case, Wallace's) that puts its faith in authorship, origin, and right deployments. It is no coincidence that these concepts recall the Higher Critics' search for the authors, origin(s), and rightful deployments of each Bible book. Hovet's point is that fragmentation was integral to *Ben-Hur*'s popular iconization. Indicating this are recitals at which certain episodes were favored but also creativities as material as a china pattern in which gilt horses race the perimeter of cups, plates, and bowls.[18]

This backstory for Kalem's decision to film *Ben-Hur* with no Jesus or Crucifixion does not make its truncation less draconian. Instead, the backstory exposes the copyright court's (somewhat brutal) imposition on what Olcott was really selling: not steeds galloping (his "short" shows less of the race than of the crowd cheering it), but rather a simulacrum of the press of bodies and clamor. These crowd scenes recall thrill-seekers who could not afford a ticket to the Klaw & Erlanger spectacular or who lived far from theaters big enough to stage it. Kalem tried to reach out to this market for financial reasons; the goal was not art. Students of early cinema, and especially of non-narrative cinema, can ponder how this "short" might have reshaped the Klaw & Erlanger show had it been allowed to continue.

When the show's final curtain descended, Hollywood was ready with offers for the film rights. Two essays in this collection probe what came next: versions of *Ben-Hur* that imposed significant changes on Wallace's plot and characters. However, only Fred Niblo's version was made. Generative indeed were the cinematic techniques with which he crafted the most pulse-pounding film action sequence yet seen: the chariot race. Some outcry was roused by the decision to cast a Mexican immigrant, Ramon Novarro, in the title role. But when much of the United States and large parts of the world enthused about this extension of the *Ben-Hur* tradition, Novarro's swoon quotient reshaped notions of Judaism, Whiteness, non-Whiteness, and maybe even of the United States.

The 1925 film's generative innovations paved the way for the 1959 remake that gave the *Ben-Hur* tradition all but overt geopolitical resonances. Against a backdrop of the Cold War, mounting oil interests, and creation of the state of Israel, William Wyler's film helped shape perceptions of U.S. interests in the Middle East. As Melani McAlister has argued, Wyler's Oscar-winning film (along with other grandiose biblical epics of the period) helped fortify U.S. self-conceptualization as a world power. This *Ben-Hur* also helped win support for a U.S. policy of "benevolent supremacy."[19] More overtly, the 1959 *Ben-Hur* is the one that scholars discuss most often in terms of its homoerotic subtext. Charlton Heston's vehement denial of this interpretation incited debate.[20] Irrefutable, however, is this *Ben-Hur*'s contribution to a gay fascination with toga films.

The 1959 film's effects were felt, yet reworked, by a children's cartoon version and an adult Canadian television version twenty years later. These versions remind analysts that the stamina of the *Ben-Hur* tradition owes much to the story's ability to appeal to all ages. It also owes much to the story's ability to delight receptors in varied social strata: from crowned heads of Europe to a teenager in a home for delinquent girls, from the White House to a social reformer who uplifted slum-dwellers, from an accused murderer to children in a remedial reading class, and many more (with quite a few ministers in between). This appeal depended, in large part, on continuity. Wyler made directorial decisions on the basis of his awareness of Niblo's work; Niblo had studied the Klaw & Erlanger play; and Klaw and Erlanger had learned, in their day, from magic lantern shows and amateur stagers who were performing even before Wallace set off on the first of several *Ben-Hur* lecture tours.[21] However, rupture can also be discerned: As each *Ben-Hur* builds on the last, and strives to top it, the results move ever further from Wallace's years of study toward treating his fiction as an historical narrative to rework. As we draft these thoughts, it remains to be seen whether the next film version wins more Academy Awards than Wyler's, or if it closes shop with the ignominy of the stage version attempted recently in London. This much, though, is certain: Whether the next *Ben-Hur* succeeds wildly or blunders badly, it will only be a matter of time before someone else steps up to give this favorite a new "spin."

◆   ◆   ◆

Early essays in this volume offer contextualized analyses of Wallace's novel. In the first, Eran Shalev discusses *Ben-Hur* in relation to the history of the representation of Rome in American letters. From the revolutionary era, Shalev demonstrates, Rome was a useful political symbol that was most frequently evoked as a model for the young republic. He argues that Wallace's Rome—the heartless and corrupt empire embodied by the anti-hero Messala—reflects the changes this symbol underwent in the course of the nineteenth century due to democratization, market revolution, and evangelical revival. Next, to investigate the status of belief in a quickly modernizing world, Milette Shamir focuses on *Ben-Hur*'s narrative structure. She contends that during an era in which secular knowledge and modern epistemologies exerted pressure on traditional religious worldviews to the point of crisis, Wallace's success lay in his ability to forge a compromise between the two by combining a masculine, progressive plot with a nostalgic, mother-centered one. Jefferson J. A. Gatrall then situates *Ben-Hur* and Wallace's less famous *The Boyhood of Christ* (1886) amidst the mass Sunday-school movement's use of imaginative tales. Of particular interest is the nineteenth-century U.S. pedagogy of the "Jesus novel," of which the well-researched *Ben-Hur* is by far the most popular exemplar.

As this collection continues, Hilton Obenzinger charts the transition from print to screen. He begins by showing how Wallace's tale was shaped by a venerable practice of linking America's manifest destiny with the Holy Land and the chosen people. He argues that, beginning with Wallace's book and peaking with the 1959 film, *Ben-Hur* fostered U.S. identification with the oppressed Jew turned "restored" superhero. This identification bespeaks support for U.S. global ambitions. Next, Howard Miller shows how the Klaw & Erlanger play helped erase one of the boundaries between the sacred and profane. Miller's labor-of-love archival research reveals how this erasure opened the gates to additional border-crossers, many of which proved popular. Cecil B. DeMille's *The King of Kings* (1927), for instance, owed much to Klaw and Erlanger's success. More recently, blockbusters such as *The Passion of the Christ* (directed by Mel Gibson, 2004), *Noah* (directed by Patrick Cederberg and Walter Woodman, 2013), and *Exodus* (directed by Ridley Scott, 2014) stand close to the theatrical arm of the *Ben-Hur* tradition.

The Klaw & Erlanger production of *Ben-Hur* closed in 1921. Thomas J. Slater's essay examines the first script written for the much-touted feature-length film made four years later. The reason his findings are startlingly unfamiliar is that June Mathis was fired from the film she had envisioned as her magnum opus. Slater's textured account of her "New Woman" attempt to turn *Ben-Hur* to spiritual, rather than religious, ends pairs neatly with Richard Walsh's probe of the film Niblo directed, after Mathis's departure, in terms of "getting Judas right." Walsh's analysis does not stop there, however; he also discloses how Niblo's *Ben-Hur* explores the Jesus film, biblical epic, and Christ figuration. These essays remind analysts why people whose modernity is "lived" rather than "mature" work with historical narratives to new ends: they use the past to promote futures they think better than the present day. Relevant here is Terry Lindvall's reminder in 2010 about the many early filmmakers who were ministers' sons.[22] Neither Mathis nor Niblo fell into that category. Both tried nonetheless to use *Ben-Hur* to preach from the screen, even if what they tried to preach differed formidably.

Some preaching still took place in book form. Barbara Ryan demonstrates how the *Ben-Hur* tradition can be tracked through quiet resistance to an amalgam of Wallace's book and Niblo's film that was published in 1941. That the resistance she discovers was penned by a Church of Scotland elder reminds us that some Christians have disapproved of *Ben-Hur*. John Buchan's disapproval exhibits, in Ryan's hands, a racial dimension that suggests unhappiness at the reality that Jesus was a Jew. Shifting topics, the next essay focuses on the 1959 film and its blend of transgressive sexual desire and religious sacrifice. By situating her analysis amidst cinematic presentations of Jesus's death as an erotic spectacle, Ina Rae Hark builds on inquiries that "queer" *Ben-Hur*. To bring the discussion to the present day and espy possible futures, David Mayer delves into omissions in *Ben-Hur* adaptations to construct a "wish list" for the next round. His acute reflections indicate how much generative potential remains to be tapped as modernizing processes continue. Finally, in the coda Jon Solomon surveys *Ben-Hur*'s presence on the consumer market. By listing dozens of uses of this name on for-profit products, Solomon deftly extends the tradition this collection recovers.

These essays, one and all, recover and probe generativities of lived modernity. In the tradition that *Bigger than "Ben-Hur"* analyzes, we discern an extraordinary case study of popular art's ability to shape faith (and its lack), affect, entertainment, and a sense of the past beyond the confines of one era or country. The essays that follow recover only a fraction of this "bigger than *Ben-Hur*" phenomenon. By recovering even this fraction, though, the essays lay groundwork for future recoveries on terrain that has not yet been mapped—far less, explored.

A Note on the Text

Because Lew Wallace's book has been published in many editions, languages, and countries, we chose to use a uniform citation system throughout this collection. The system is based on Wallace's organization of his tale into "books" that recall the Bible, rather than on page numbers. For example, when an author quotes a line from the fourth chapter of Book III in *Ben-Hur*, the citation appears as (III:4).

Ben-Hur's and America's Rome

From Virtuous Republic to Tyrannous Empire

ERAN SHALEV

*B*en-Hur enthralled late nineteenth-century U.S. readers. Its unprecedented success attests to the era's fascination with the novel's setting, classical Rome. Fascination with Rome was in no sense new after the Civil War. On the contrary, the classical polity played a central role in Americans' imagination as early as the founding era. In light of the century of American absorption in the history of Rome preceding *Ben-Hur*, the novel's "Romanness" follows a well-established tradition.

Ben-Hur's Rome, however, was in many ways diametrically opposed to the Rome that the American imagination of earlier generations had found so appealing. Revolutionary Americans and their immediate successors invoked the virtuous Rome of the early republic as a model for their own newly founded republic. The Rome of *Ben-Hur* was instead the tyrannous, corrupt, and bloodthirsty domain of the Caesars. Thus, the much later Rome that Lew Wallace portrayed was a far cry from the free and independent yeomen whom the revolutionary generation tried to emulate. It was a massive and corrupt empire that suffocated liberty and virtue. No less important to a generally evangelical, Christ-centered society, it was the Rome that crucified Jesus. The shift from the late eighteenth-century republican Rome to the late nineteenth-century tyrannous empire could not have been more extreme.

As opposed to the past, in which republican Rome was frequently recruited as a metaphor for the young United States, *Ben-Hur*'s Rome

18

symbolized an entity that was difficult to parse. Exploring it will help us better understand a watershed moment in Americans' changing perception of classical Rome. The results position Wallace's immensely popular novel in wider cultural contexts.

The Founders' Rome

The American Revolution, which witnessed the unyoking of the British crown and subsequent construction of federal institutions, enticed patriots to give free rein to their historical imagination. Revolutionary Americans were particularly fascinated by the Roman republic, the rural village that rose from rustic obscurity. Especially compelling were this Rome's virtuous citizen soldiers and unique republican system of government that gained world domination, only to morph into an autocratic Caesarian Empire and eventually succumb (centuries later) to barbarian invasions. Americans could not stop contemplating Rome's greatness. But in their attempts to enlist Roman history in their purposes they characteristically focused on Rome's earlier history, when it was a virtuous republic on the rise. In private moments and staged performances, American revolutionaries referred to venerated ancient Romans such as Brutus and Cato, who embodied the manly public virtue that neoclassicists so admired. They appealed to Rome's history for consolation, justification, and validation. Invocation of the inspiring examples of the ancient republic was a vital tool in the hands of American orators and writers, who held aloft the exempla of the virtuous ancients to emphasize their relevance to the American situation. The Roman model of sacrifice and self-effacement (exemplified by Cincinnatus, the retired senator who forsook his plough to save Rome and, having done so, at once took it up again) encouraged patriots as they crossed the Rubicon of independence. This model also consoled them when war tried their souls. When they created a novel federal system Rome was there to inspire them, even as their state-makers seemed to break every rule of classical wisdom. In short, the Roman republic exerted immense influence on the ways early Americans made sense of their revolution. Evidence of this influence is still abundant (if somewhat obscured by repeated use); for example, the founders of the United States chose to create a *res publica* whose legislative branch was a *congressus*, with its member *senators* residing in a Roman *capitol* in the form of a Roman temple.

Revolutionaries found the classics so appealing because they perceived the ancient republics, first and foremost Rome, as the origin and embodiment of some of their most cherished ideals. Modern scholarship frames this ideological bundle as "the republican synthesis."[1] Many patriots envisioned a society and government based on virtue and disinterested citizenship, the main sources of classical republicanism.[2] Unsurprisingly, a powerful ideal of many of the revolution's leaders and their followers was not a democracy (government still associated with mob rule) but an organic hierarchy led by patricians who would embody the classical (and hierarchical) virtues.[3] Thus republican Rome, more than any other classical polity, enticed late eighteenth-century Americans' political imagination and historical inquisitiveness.[4] Thinkers of that day perceived the relevance of Republican Rome—and the irrelevance of Greece, especially democratic Athens—to the American political condition as crucial. The ideal form of government for many Americans at that time was a republic governed by a mixed constitution and led by a "natural aristocracy."

Addison's *Cato*

To understand the nature and magnitude of the change in the representation of Rome in *Ben-Hur*, we may examine the most popular play in revolutionary America. Joseph Addison's *Cato* (1718) portrays Cato the Younger's last hours, as he was besieged in Utica by Julius Caesar, to dramatize the virtuous hero's dilemma before he chooses to commit suicide once his beloved republic is doomed.[5] Addison's neoclassical play was staged in an eighteenth-century public sphere defined by the refined sensibilities we now know as "Augustan." Accordingly, Addison intended the play to both delight and instruct in the realms of manners and character building, without necessarily carrying political overtones.[6]

Nevertheless, scholars writing about eighteenth-century American political culture have widely acknowledged the influence of Cato's image on radical Whigs.[7] The stern republican, faithful to his ruined republic to the bitter end, particularly appealed to American patriots who demonstrated intimate knowledge of Addison's play. As Fredric Litto pointed out in a seminal essay of the 1960s, this tragic drama was transformed during the revolution from a piece of genteel entertainment to a patriotic "instrument of political propaganda."[8] Patriots such as Nathan Hale, before his execution by the British, and Patrick Henry, in his "Liberty or Death" oration, appealed to their respective audiences by rephrasing well-known lines of Addison's belligerent hero.[9] Washington's lifelong intimacy with Cato, memorialized by the staging of Addison's play at Valley Forge in the dire winter of 1777, is a much discussed instance of the influence Cato's *fama* exerted on Americans in the thick of their first civil war.[10]

The most remarkable testimony to the appeal of Addison's play, and thus of ancient Rome, to American revolutionaries is Jonathan Mitchell Sewall's *A New Epilogue to Cato*.[11] Intended as the concluding section of Addison's tragedy, this classicized literary piece was first published with *Cato* in 1778. Literary historian John Shields speculates that this specifically American epilogue was performed many times during the revolution, possibly even before Washington and his men at Valley Forge.[12] Sewall's *New Epilogue* replaced the British ending in four of five printings of *Cato* in America between 1778 and 1793.[13]

Sewall's Americanization of Addison's allegory rests on a Manichean worldview that contrasts "heroic fortitude" and "patriotic truth" to "tyrannic rage" and "boundless ambition" in a cosmic battle which "mark'd all periods and all climes." In this battle Britannia occupies the role of the wicked, tyrannous Rome of Caesar, while "what now gleams with dawning ray, at home, once blaz'd . . . at ROME." The newly born United States was, for Sewall, the new republican Rome. Like the Roman Senate, the Continental Congress (i.e., the "aristocratic" branch of its successor legislature soon to be named the United States Senate) had armed a "virtuous few" to fight the "British Caesar." Leading these few, Sewall perorated, was a worthy candidate: "for a CATO," the American patriots had armed "a WASHINGTON."[14]

The identification of the two leading antagonists marked the beginning of an elaborate effort to assign Roman signifiers, all characters from Addison's play, to contemporary American figures. Washington represented Cato and the British monarch represented Caesar. Sewall also portrayed William Howe, the British general, as the cunning Decius, one of

Caesar's cronies. On America's side, "in Franklin and in generous DEAN shine forth / Mild Lucius' wisdom, and young Portius' worth." Continuing with his analogies, Sewall assigned Marcus, Cato's son, to another American general, because his image "blazes forth in [John] SULLIVAN!" And in General Nathaniel "Greene . . . we see . . . Lucius, Juba, Cato, shine." Ultimately, Sewall went beyond the *dramatis personae* to Roman heroes who did not take part in the play. For example, the fallen Bunker Hill hero Joseph Warren (who "like Pompey . . . fell in martial pride") led to Benedict Arnold (who crossed "Canadia's Alpine hills") being hailed as "a second HANNIBAL!" Villains were treated in the same way when Sewall linked Benjamin Church to the Roman traitor Sempronius, condemning them jointly.

Sewall's analogies in *A New Epilogue to Cato* demonstrate the length to which Americans went to explain their revolution as the reenactment of a classical spectacle.[15] Americans in the late eighteenth century found varied ways in which to represent themselves as latter-day Romans and their republic as the reincarnation of a classical polity. Rome, as Sewall's *New Epilogue* demonstrates, was so much on the minds of revolutionary Americans that it enabled them to convert the era's most popular play into a tale about the new American Rome. In the generations that followed, Americans would continue to appeal to republican Rome for inspiration and encouragement in their own republican task.

Rome, Jacksonian America, and the Second Great Awakening

Much changed in the American imagination before Wallace set his Christ tale in the late Roman Empire. For instance, as large as republican Rome loomed during the founding era, its central place in the American imagination was fundamentally shaken in the early decades of the nineteenth century. One blow was felt as educators began to re-examine the relevance of the classics in schools' and colleges' curricula. Weightier, though, was the blow dealt by Jacksonian Democracy. With the expansion of democratic practices and sentiment, ancient Athens, which the eighteenth-century neoclassical generation had maligned as an anarchic polis ruled by the mob, was suddenly seen as an attractive model. Republican Rome, on the other hand, came to be viewed as an anachronistically aristocratic and anti-commercial form that was of little use to a modern nation-state.[16]

As if democratization were not enough, "a massive outpouring of evangelical religious enthusiasm" from circa 1800 to 1840 further re-shaped Rome's place in U.S. culture.[17] The surge known as the "Second Great Awakening" constituted a double transformation: a dramatic rise in the number of religious adherents, which was even faster than the rapid growth of the general population, and a reversal in Americans' denominational affiliations. All Protestant churches did well in absolute numbers in this period. By 1860, evangelical churches comprised at least 85 percent of U.S. congregations, dwarfing Congregationalist and Episcopalian churches (formerly the largest churches in the eighteenth century).[18] Well before Wallace wrote *Ben-Hur*, evangelical Christianity had taken over the religious landscape.

A deep theological transformation accompanied these institutional changes. Americans, who had started discovering back in the eighteenth century that traditional Christianity did not satisfy them spiritually, "began looking elsewhere," according to Gordon Wood, "for solace and meaning."[19] They found it in droves in evangelical creeds that taught believers to acknowledge their sin before God, look on Jesus Christ (crucified, dead, and resurrected) as God's means of redemption, and see their faith in Him as savior as a way to reconcile with God. Evangelical sensibility included renewed emphasis on the Bible as the ultimate religious authority and conversion as the means to relate to God. Most significant, however, was Christ's redemption as the heart of true religion. Ideas about Rome shifted perforce as evangelism became, in Mark Noll's words, "the unofficially established religion in a nation that had forsworn religious establishment."[20]

Historians of religion have noted that by the 1840s, with evangelism in full swing, "preaching and worship increasingly centered on the figure of Christ."[21] The earlier understanding of a frowning and omnipotent God (a traditional Calvinist view readily distilled from the Hebrew Bible) may have suited the patriarchal ideal of the eighteenth-century family. But once old hierarchies began to collapse in the wake of the revolution, and new ideals arose related to Victorian notions of domestication and the mother as the center of the household, Americans found a loving and compassionate Christ more congenial than an angry God who held sinners over the pit of hell. As "awakened" Protestants increasingly emphasized Jesus's humanity, they became uneasy with the doctrine of predestination, which seemed to offend divine mercy. By the second third of the nineteenth century a new American religiosity, no longer centered on a wrathful father but on the loving son, had emerged: Jesus's martyrdom was now believed to be not only for a select band of Puritan saints but for humanity in its entirety. This universal call was embraced by evangelical Christians, who would no longer wait passively for conversion, sainthood, and salvation, as had earlier generations of reformed Protestants.

The remarkable rise of evangelism at a time when U.S. Christianity was still an overwhelmingly Protestant affair meant that millions of citizens now positioned Jesus at the center of their piety.[22] Americans were becoming fixated on a Jesus who was more of an intimate friend than an aloof deity and on "accepting Jesus as one's savior," which was the formula that became a virtual Protestant mantra and "cultural program."[23] Throughout the nineteenth century, for more and more U.S. believers, Jesus became a spiritual "person" with whom they wished to converse as well as obey and follow. Not all Americans had this wish, but it was felt publicly by a great many.

Henry Ward Beecher, the plenipotentiary minister of mid-nineteenth-century America, captured the zeitgeist because he found "the very genius of Christianity" not in its dogmas, rites, or institutions, but in Jesus's person. Beecher said he could still "gather a great deal from the Old Testament." However, he felt most "conscious that the fruit of the Bible is Christ. The rest to me is just what leaves are on an apple-tree. When I see the apple I know that there must have been a tree to bear that fruit; but after that I think of the fruit, and nothing else."[24] Confirmed by Beecher's popularity as a preacher for a sustained period, scholars have concluded that evangelical insistence on Jesus's person is "the main religious story in the first century of U.S. history."[25] Naturally, this recognition led to strengthened emphasis on the New Testament. Voicing this view, Alexander Campbell proclaimed that "we only aim at substituting the New Testament in lieu of every creed in existence whether Mahometan, Pagan, Jewish or Presbyterian." Eschewing factions, this co-founder of the Disciples of Christ explained, "we neither advocate Calvinism, Deism, or Sectarianism, Arianism, Socinianism, Trinitarianism, Unitarianism, Deism, or Sectarianism, but New Testamentism." This ardent, book-centered surge followed and paired inextricably with the "Jesus Christism" that asserted itself as a major cultural force during Lew Wallace's young manhood.[26]

With this dramatic remaking of the American religious landscape, and particularly the rise of Jesus's popularity, Rome not only became a less relevant political model, but it also came to be perceived as responsible for the murder of the son of God. In the late eighteenth century, as we have seen, the protagonist of the most popular play in revolutionary America was a virtuous Roman, and the newly United States was a modern Rome rising in the West. During the next few decades, though, the United States gradually yet decisively moved from a positive attitude toward Rome to one of ambivalence, if not outright negativity.[27] This shift explains why, by the closing decades of the nineteenth century, powerful cultural processes, from the rise of democracy to a commercial and industrial revolution and evangelization, created an atmosphere in which the depiction of Rome in Wallace's *Ben-Hur* was extremely negative.

Rome in *Ben-Hur*

Wallace set his novel in the Roman province of Judea, the biblical homeland of the Jewish people, among them the fictional Ben-Hur family. The intensive research, to which he devoted years, ensures his knowledge that "Judea" was originally the name of the southern kingdom centered around Jerusalem and ruled by kings from the House of David. By the time of the rise of Rome as an imperial power and the growth of its interest in the territories of the eastern Mediterranean, biblical Canaan (which comprised both historical Israel and Judea) was under the control of the Seleukid Empire, one of the successor kingdoms to Alexander the Great's short-lived empire. When Pompeius Magnus marched on Judea in 63 BC he conquered it with little resistance from the Jewish Hasmonean dynasty, who ruled the land as a free Jewish state from at least 110 BC. Judea subsequently became a tributary state to Rome under the Herodian family, a dynasty of client kings. At the time of the events told in *Ben-Hur*, around the year AD 30, Judea was already a formal Roman province under the prefecture of Pontius Pilatus.

The Roman Empire is not only the backdrop and setting against which Wallace's plot develops; more significantly, it is the most obvious political reality. As such, it is the force that dictates the unfolding of events in *Ben-Hur*: Valerius Gratus's fateful procession, Judah's enslavement and the travails of the protagonist's family, his gladiatorial training, his eventual triumph as a chariot driver, and his subsequent raising of a rebellion. This is obviously not the Rome that revolutionary Americans admired. Rather, *Ben-Hur* is pervaded by the militaristic, cruel, and arbitrary imperial Rome of the Caesars, specifically Tiberius Caesar Augustus.

To enhance *Ben-Hur*'s historical realism, Wallace mobilized multiple strategies to create a first-century AD world dominated by the Roman Empire. He allots much space to detailed descriptions that Romanize his tale of Christ. These descriptions range from his characters' cultural references ("by Pluto!" they exclaim), to the clothes they wear, to exhaustive presentations of urban views: all are Roman. Wallace also used temporal cues and historical events to situate his plot in ancient Rome: "In the time of which we are reading," he writes in the prologue, which refers to the birth of Christ, "Pompey entered Herod's temple and the same Holy of Holies, and came out without harm, finding but an empty chamber, and of God not a sign" (1:VII). *Ben-Hur*'s calendar is Roman, beginning with the city's founding ("the meeting just described took place in the year of Rome 747" [1:III]) and dating by imperial administrations ("it is necessary now to carry the reader forward twenty-one years, to the beginning of the administration of Valerius Gratus, the fourth imperial governor of Judea" [2:I]).

Throughout the book, *Ben-Hur*'s world is defined by a massive, tyrannous empire: "Rome did not wait for people slow to inquire about her; she came to them" (1:XI). Powerful, brutal, vengeful, and in turn hated and feared by its subjects, *Ben-Hur*'s Rome shares no qualities with the founders' revered republic. In Wallace's conspicuously corrupt and decayed Rome, the virtues that made possible the empire's rise are crumbling. Traditions are so shattered that the empire resembles the old Rome in nothing but name. As an example, Wallace refers to "the old religion [that] had nearly ceased to be a faith; at most it was a mere habit of thought and expression" (2:II). Another novelty is Rome's cosmopolitanism: "Nowhere else," the narrator reveals, "was there such constant assemblage of so many people of so many different nations; in no other city was a stranger less strange to the residents than within her walls and purlieus" (1:XII).

Shifts in habitual ways would not be so ruinous if the new mores were noble and inspiring; however, as Wallace shows in his characterization of Messala, they are debauched. Nineteenth-century Americans universally held that Rome had begun as a virtuous republic. History taught them, however, that Rome's territorial expansion had been accompanied by corruption that led to its decline and fall.[28] This corruption was well under way when Judah Ben-Hur's adventures begin, as is demonstrated when Messala tells him about life in the metropolis, revealing what really matters there: "Money," he recounts, "money, wine, women, games—poets at the banquet, intrigues in the court, dice all the year round" (2:II). Corruption by power was well understood in the civic humanist tradition of commenting on Roman history. Although neoclassical observers such as the American founders admired the early Romans' active yet disinterested citizenship, they knew that humans were too weak to preserve free republics indefinitely. Realization that such polities depended on the ascetic virtue of citizens and magistrates makes Messala's cynicism indicative not only of his own fall but of Rome's as a whole, because he speaks as its metonym. Against such corruption, the civic humanist worldview—which is sometimes called the "republican tradition"—idealized self-sacrifice and disinterestedness. Wallace and many of his nineteenth-century readers knew that corruption incessantly undermined virtue. Egoistic temptations of self-betterment were to blame, therefore, for the desolation of the admired early Roman republic and the rise of the heinous Caesarian Empire upon its ruins.[29]

No less objectionable to *Ben-Hur's* early readers—many of whom had witnessed the bloodbath of the disastrous U.S. Civil War—was the late Roman Empire's "love of games and bloody spectacles" and its "vast [gladiatorial] theaters, and . . . schools of fighting-men, drawn, as is the custom, from the Gallic provinces or the Slavic tribes on the Danube" (1:VII). All of these spectacles are shocking in Ben-Hur's eyes and to other

2. Ben-Hur and Messala in the Klaw & Erlanger theater production. From the Player's edition of *Ben-Hur* (1901).

Judean Jews. The virtuous Esther thinks Rome "a monster which has possession of one of the beautiful lands and lies there luring men to ruin and death—a monster which it is not possible to resist—a ravenous gorging with blood." Brutality so defines this empire, she adds, that she "cannot think of Rome as a city of palaces and temples, and crowded with people" (5:IX). This representation of Rome as a corrupt, oversized, and bloodthirsty polyglot reflects histories of Wallace's day. But it also reflects the language and sensibilities of late-nineteenth-century, post–Civil War America. Aversion to slavery and servitude is one of the novel's leitmotifs; these themes are evident, for example, in Simonides and Esther's fear of being sold into slavery.

Memories of the founding era also play their part in Wallace's *Ben-Hur*. Most striking is Wallace's decision to frame Judea's resistance to the Roman Empire in the most recognizable terms of U.S. political thought and culture. When discussing Rome's arbitrariness and tyranny, particularly the taxation of its provinces, the empire's subjects do not complain "of the amount of the tax" because, they admit, "a denarius is a trifle." Rather, it is "the imposition of the tax [which] is the offense." When Wallace's fictitious first-century Romans assert, "what is paying [tax] but submission to tyranny?" (1:VIII), *Ben-Hur* draws on *the* American political idiom of the revolution: The rebels fiercely opposed not the financial burdens associated with heavy taxation but the submission to arbitrary taxation levied by a faraway metropolis. They found this imposition as politically obnoxious and tyrannical as slavery. This insistence on provincial autonomy lay at the core of American revolutionary republicanism. Ironically, such thought originally stemmed from the example of Roman republicanism: *Ben-Hur*'s political logic assailed the Roman Empire in terms that owed heavily to a political language originating in Rome itself.[30] If, however, Judea was the equivalent of America resisting tyranny, what did oppressive Rome stand for?

The Empire Strikes Back

Ben-Hur's Rome surely has its less dark sides. Decent and virtuous, for instance, is the Roman whose adoption of the Jewish Judah Ben-Hur symbolizes the remnants of early Rome's appreciation of self-sacrifice for the greater good. Nevertheless, Rome's imperial tyranny, corruption, and militarism dominate the novel presumably because these traits repelled Wallace and his U.S. readership. By turning so vehemently against Rome, *Ben-Hur* broke from Roman models like the stern, suicidal Cato. However, it would be wrong to assume that *Ben-Hur* was the first significant statement against reverence for Rome. Throughout American history there were people who highlighted Rome's corruption to point out the obvious:

why emulate an empire that collapsed? Criticized too was the futility of appealing to an ancient and pagan polity as the model for a modern state in which Christianity played a large role. Various thinkers found reasons, well before Wallace wrote *Ben-Hur*, to abandon Rome as a political and historical guide to America's future. To take one salient example, Thomas Jefferson—an avid student of the classics—was skeptical about the benefits of looking to Rome's history for ideas on how to conduct American public policy.[31] Later thinkers loathed Rome's aristocratic oligarchy and/or attacked its slaveholding.[32]

Wallace's representation of the Roman Empire in *Ben-Hur* differed significantly from these types of critiques. Remarkably, his Rome came full circle in returning to a condition that American revolutionaries invoked in the years leading to independence. After the Stamp Act (1765), as the relationship between the metropolis and the North American colonies deteriorated with successive rounds of taxation, Americans began to abandon their view of Britain as a glorious, world-dominating Rome. This view had gained ground after Britain's victories in the French and Indian War (1754–63). During the revolutionary years patriots came to characterize the metropolis by conjuring the image of a different Rome: Rome of the corrupt tyranny of the most hated of Caesars.

This rapid deterioration in the representations of Britain from heights of glory to depths of tyranny and corruption is encapsulated in one patriot's letter from 1774. North Carolina's William Hooper elaborated a comparison of Britain and imperial Rome that other writers echoed. Writing as the Intolerable Acts were being passed, Hooper enumerated the causes of decay shared by the two empires: "The extent of the British dominion [like the Roman] is become too unwieldy for her to sustain. Commerce hath generated a profusion of wealth, and luxury and corruption. . . . Venality is at the standard it was when Jugurtha left Rome. . . . What strikes them [the British] as the glow of health, is but the flushing of fever. . . . Rome in its greatest luster was upon the verge of dissolution."[33] Similar statements, like that of John Adams in Massachusetts a year later, would repeat this sentiment: "Is not the British constitution arrived nearly to that point, where the Roman republic was when Jugurtha left it, and pronounc'd it a venal city ripe for destruction, if it can only find a purchaser?"[34] Evidently, at the same moment in which they viewed themselves as a pristine, republican, and new Rome, revolutionary Americans viewed Britain as an old and corrupt Roman Empire that they were about to replace.[35]

Revolutionary-era depictions of Britain as a tyrannous Rome were part of a civic humanist discourse in which corruption, virtue, luxury, and sacrifice formed the backbone of an intellectual paradigm that understood the present in terms of antiquity.[36] A century later Lew Wallace's civic humanist commitments, although discernible, were not as pronounced. Wrought by fast-paced democratization, a market revolution, and a sweeping evangelical revival, the republicanism of the United States had gone through shattering transformations during the first half of the nineteenth century. These processes, compounded by a horrendous civil war, transformed the moral and political economy of the expanding nation and thus its prevailing ideology. Consequently, by the time *Ben-Hur* was published, the stern civic humanism of the founding generation was irredeemably out of date—a neoclassical relic of a bygone world. The attitude toward Rome as a historical model followed these changes closely: from an earlier adoration of the stern early Roman republic, Wallace and his nineteenth-century readers scorned Rome's later imperial incarnation.

When eighteenth-century revolutionaries depicted a Roman Empire that was insuppressibly corrupt (with Britain in their minds), they were convinced that it was tottering and ready to succumb. But *Ben-Hur*'s first-century AD Rome, which symbolized the United States, was far from collapse. Historically, the empire of Tiberius (the one depicted in the novel) was at the height of its power and centuries from its eventual decline and fall. But if Wallace's Rome was not on the brink of collapse, its militarism was much more pronounced than the British Rome that the founders had depicted. Messala reveals the nature of the empire: this haughty, ironic, and derisive Roman sneers at his old friend Judah, "I am to be a soldier; and you, O my Judah, I pity you; what can you be?" The Roman continues: "Ah, the world is not all conquered . . . a campaign into Africa; another after the Scythian; then—a legion!" Judah listens while his boyhood friend continues in this vein, then replies full of pathos: "I wish I had not come. I sought a friend and find a [pause]." Messala snaps: "Roman" (2:II).

Wallace, like his protagonist, was ill at ease with the imperialistic militarism that he projected onto first-century Rome. In all probability this lack of comfort reflects the soul-searching of a veteran Union general turned author who had experienced the horrors of the Civil War. It certainly appealed to the evangelical Americans who read *Ben-Hur* avidly. They too despised the militaristic Roman Empire. Their fervor for *Ben-Hur* may also reveal their dislike of the imperial role the United States was about to assume on the world stage in the decades following the book's publication.

The ambivalence toward the Roman Empire that *Ben-Hur* reflects was short-lived. By the turn of the nineteenth century, with a new spurt of U.S. imperialism reaching out to Cuba, Puerto Rico, Hawaii, and the Philippines, Rome once again would become a model that most citizens viewed positively. Proponents of U.S. expansion would then embrace the image of the Roman Empire—not the republic—as a constructive historical precedent for what they conceived as their own rising imperial republic. Consequently Rome, as Amy Kaplan points out, could be found "everywhere" in turn-of-century America.[37] The United States would bask, for a while, in the glory of empire rather than feel compassion for the suffering and indignity of the provinces. Critics of imperialism were heard too.[38] A century later, chastised by a series of conflicted far-flung wars, this conflict continues. Now, as then, *Ben-Hur* stays current with the question, "are we Rome?"

Ben-Hur's Mother

Narrative Time, Nostalgia, and Progress in the Protestant Historical Romance

MILETTE SHAMIR

Many apocryphal anecdotes are told about *Ben-Hur*, which befits a work that some early readers regarded as near sacred. One anecdote involves the book's dedication. As biographers like to tell, Lew Wallace dedicated the first edition "to the wife of my youth." Unfortunately, this phrase led some readers to assume that Mrs. Wallace had died and others to suppose that Wallace had been married more than once. Not appreciating either assumption, Susan Wallace asked the publishers to append the words "who still abides with me"; they did so in subsequent printings.[1]

The dedication, with its strange decoupling of the "wife of my youth" from the living and present Mrs. Wallace, captures what many in the intellectual vanguard of the 1880s found suspicious, even off-putting, about *Ben-Hur*: the sentimental, nostalgic tone, the pseudo-biblical archaisms, the yearning for the past, and the disregard for the present. In New York and Boston, where literary realism was *au courant*, early reviews associated Wallace's first-century "Tale of the Christ" with a genre they regarded as obsolete. *The Century Illustrated Magazine* reminded its readers that "the historical novel is rather an anachronism nowadays." *The Atlantic Monthly* complained of the "inertia to be overcome in taking up a historical romance," even as it grudgingly lauded "the many ingenious devices [by which] the author does his best to remove the reader from his modern life."[2] As if by way of contrast, the *The Atlantic* reviewed Henry James's *Washington Square* in the same article. One can only guess what

James—who would in later years complain of the "fatal cheapness" of historical romances and call upon writers to "come back to the palpable present"—felt about this confluence.[3]

Outside the elite literary establishment, however, readers assessed *Ben-Hur* differently. Rather than a stale relic, they described the book as a "bold, imaginative experiment" and an "adventurous attempt" characterized by "novelty and daring."[4] Indeed, for such readers the novel was exciting precisely because of the journey back in time it offered. A month after the novel's publication, a friend in Indianapolis wrote to Wallace:

> I make my acknowledgements for the creation of your genius—for *"Ben Hur."* I would [rather] be *its* author than *Ivanhoe's.* . . . No book has ever swayed me more from the stubborn coarseness of my nature; and made me even as a little child. . . . Its newness, its vastness, its generous profusion of great and beautiful thoughts, and noble sentiments and sympathies have been to me like a voyage back to the flower-land of my boyhood. . . . It has been left for you to make me young again—to blot and wash out the blotted pages of the years of a grim battle with the world.[5]

The "newness" that enthralled this reader referred to *Ben-Hur's* power to reverse time in two ways: the novel did not merely transport the reader back to the cradle of Christianity, but also carried him back to his own childhood, wiping out with one stroke two thousand years of history and a lifetime of "grim battles."

In what follows, I take my cue from this letter's sentiments to argue that *Ben-Hur*, as much as it looked nostalgically to the past, is a distinctly modern book. Indeed, I argue that the novel is modern precisely for being nostalgic. *Ben-Hur* was published during what Paul A. Carter called the "spiritual crisis of the Gilded Age": a drastic destabilization of traditional Protestant worldviews as a result of their encounter with modernization.[6] An effect of this encounter was an intensified investment in the past, manifested as a desire to travel back in time to the moment "where it all began" to reaffirm the truth of the Gospels. Holy Land travel, interest in biblical archeology, and biographies of Jesus are some of the forms this journey took. This investment in the past was often expressed in personal terms as longings for childhood and home: "the flower-land of my boyhood" in the words of the letter quoted above. Often this investment was expressed as longing for a simpler and purer era when Christian truths still seemed self-evident. In postbellum print, both types of investment in the past frequently converged in the symbolic figure of the mother.[7] Wallace's "novelty and daring" lay in combining what I will call the "nostalgic mother plot"—a sentimental, regressive narrative—with a secular, future-oriented plot. The novel weaves the romance of Judah Ben-Hur's voyage back to Jerusalem to reunite with his mother and sister Tirzah with the linear and historical temporality of the *bildungsroman*. This bidirectional narrative structure—back to childhood and forward to maturity—allows Wallace to work through the tension between private piety and a secularizing public sphere. Historian Howard Miller has pointed out that "Americans in the late Victorian era and well into the twentieth century embraced many aspects of modernity without rejecting religion." He argues that "Lew Wallace's great novel, published just as this process was beginning in the U.S., can help us understand the peculiar way in which Americans resolved, for a time, the tensions of secular and sacred."[8] In this essay, I analyze the narrative means by which Wallace achieved this resolution.

The Narrative Crisis of the Gilded Age

For the first two-thirds of the nineteenth century, Protestant-American worldviews rested securely on the traditional Christian narrative with its set points of origin (Creation in the Jewish Bible and Incarnation in the Christian) and absolute point of closure (Final Judgment). This narrative proved remarkably able to accommodate the fast-paced transformations of the nation's first hundred years. Most Protestants, that is, were comfortable describing the passage between the beginning and the end of time in reference to the worldly concept of progress. This was true first and foremost of postmillennialists, who were especially adept in integrating their temporal narrative with the linear, future-oriented ones of more secular epistemologies. The most "commonly received doctrine" of the era (in the words of one clergyman in 1859),[9] postmillennialism relied on Revelation 20 to maintain that Christ's Second Coming would occur after the millennium, rather than before, as premillennialists believed. Under this dispensation, history could be perceived as a steady march toward the end of time, with religious as well as secular improvements marking the path. The various features of modernization—democratization, growing material prosperity, technological innovation—could be absorbed into the postmillennialist narrative as signs of the approaching kingdom of God. Historian James Moorhead offers as illustration the group of Protestants who, upon learning that the transatlantic cable had been completed, broke into song: "Jesus shall reign where e're the sun."[10]

Postmillennialism's fixed limit points and relatively facile integration of progress allowed Protestants to balance traditional religious values with the realities of modernization. But in the years after the American Civil War, this narrative became increasingly tenuous. Among the challenges it faced were the forceful intellectual paradigms of Darwinism and Higher Biblical Criticism. By unhinging the Protestant narrative's concept of origin, both shed doubt on this narrative's claim to absolute, exclusive truth. Evolution extended the past of the world to an obscure point long before Creation; Higher Criticism relativized and disenchanted the myth of Genesis and the Gospel account of Jesus. By questioning fixed notions of origin, these paradigms opened the way for doubt about the future.[11] Herman Melville pointed this out in the epilogue to his great faith-doubt poem "Clarel" (written during the same years as *Ben-Hur*): "If Luther's day expand to Darwin's year / shall that exclude the hope—foreclose the fear?"[12] Indeed, Darwinist thought did not only put hopes and fears of the Second Coming in question; it also spilled over into views of the social domain in ways that were difficult for religious believers to absorb. For instance, social Darwinism (as promoted by Herbert Spencer and others) clashed with Protestantism's view of early Christianity as the purest and highest form of life: if humanity "matures" socially and morally as well as technologically, how can first-century Christians be regarded as superior to the modern generation? In 1920, philosopher George Santayana would look back on this dilemma: "If evolution was to be taken seriously and to include moral growth, the great men of the past could only be stepping stones to our own dignity. To grow was to contain and sum up all the good that had gone before, adding an appropriate increment. . . . Jesus was a prophet more winsome and nearer to ourselves than his predecessors; but how could anyone deny that the twenty centuries of progress since his time must have raised a loftier pedestal for Emerson or Channing or Phillips Brooks?"[13]

This destabilization of the postmillennialist narrative helps explain the blossoming of alternative narrative schemes in the decades after the American Civil War. It is one way to account for the proliferation of apocalyptic narratives in which postmillennialism's trust in gradual progress ceded to premillennialist fantasies of a sudden and violent eruption of end time.[14] Little wonder, also, that when a full-scale anti-modern movement emerged in the early twentieth century with fundamentalism, it focused on creationism and the inerrancy of scripture—the restoration of absolute points of origin—as its *casus belli.* An altogether different challenge to the traditional Protestant narrative inhered in American realism's fascination with "the palpable present" (to reiterate James's phrase). The postbellum realist writers' embrace of the present as meaningful in its own right was symptomatic of a vision of secular modernity formed in opposition to the resolute Protestant narrative of the previous generation. This group's relative lack of interest in, or even disdain for, the *longue durée* was manifested also in their distrust of historical romance.

Most U.S. Protestants, however, were not ready or willing to embrace either the anti-modern denial of progress or the modern surrender of determined narrative bounds. This social and cultural mainstream was in search of a different narrative that would at once protect a reassuring vision of the past and offer a legitimizing view of progress. Such narratives had begun to be preached from pulpits across the nation as liberal Protestant theologians (such as Henry Ward Beecher, Phillips Brooks, and Charles A. Briggs) forged a synthesis between modern thought and Protestant tradition. Using Darwinism and comparable doctrines of evolutionary development to support (but also extend) traditional Christian beliefs, these theologians were "quite willing to open their worldviews to the logic and language of modern evolutionary science but not willing to abandon their traditional beliefs in the process."[15] Beecher's *Life of Jesus Christ* (1872) offers an example of the logic on which this group relied. In this book Beecher looks back at Christianity's origins even as he boldly imagines Jesus as Man; he asks, "has the world . . . no experience . . . which shall fit it to go back to the truths of the New Testament with a far larger understanding of their contents than they had who wrote them?"[16] Affirming the pure, foundational status of first-century Christianity, Beecher nevertheless endorsed progress by arguing that the modern reader has the experience and maturity that allows for a better understanding of these truths than was possible for the men who wrote them. Beecher thus managed to look backward and forward at the same time and to claim that the return to the moment of origin does not demand the sacrifice of progress. On the contrary, progress is what enriches, perhaps even enables, this return.

The compromises wrought by liberal theologians gradually spread to almost every Protestant denomination across the nation.[17] But their Janus-like logic was developed most effectively, I argue, within the growing subgenre of the Protestant historical romance. *Ben-Hur* was this subgenre's most influential and popular example.

"Since the Beginning"

From its earliest drafts, *Ben-Hur*'s main theme, intellectual interest, and emotional motivation involved a return to a point of origin. The manuscript came into being as a result of Wallace's fascination since childhood with the story of the nativity; as an adult, Wallace still remembered his mother reading it to him.[18] In the 1870s he wrote an account of the nativity, intending to publish it as a short book. This wish to return to the scene where it all began, beyond its obvious oedipal hue, implies awareness of mounting pressures on the Protestant narrative by secular perspectives. According to another anecdote, Wallace's decision to expand his version of the nativity story into what would become *Ben-Hur* was in response to a chance conversation he held in 1876 with fellow American Civil War veteran and renowned agnostic advocate Robert G. Ingersoll. It was in reply to the latter's "most outright denials of all human knowledge of God, Christ, Heaven, and the Hereafter" that Wallace decided to turn his manuscript into a full-fledged novel.[19]

Ben-Hur's opening account of the meeting of the three Magi on their way to Bethlehem cannot be read apart from Ingersoll's "outright denials." To foster "a conviction amounting to absolute belief in God and the Divinity of Christ,"[20] Wallace takes the reader back in time and imagines the three travelers against the primordial backdrop of the "Desert of Arabia," which was there "since the beginning" (1:I). The conversation among the Greek, Hindoo, and Egyptian Magi immediately turns to the question of origins, with each presenting his civilization as a fountainhead for humanity. The Greek argues that his society is the source for "things that bring to men their purest pleasures" (1:III); the Hindoo retorts by claiming for India "the primal foundation of religion and useful intelligence" (1:IV); and the Egyptian insists, "history began with us" (1:V). Wallace was no doubt informed in writing this scene by Higher Criticism's contextualization of the Judeo-Christian narrative in more ancient cultures. He stages this competition over origins to illustrate the failure of each ancient civilization to serve as anything but a false start: a mere prelude for saved humanity's (and his novel's) true beginning.

Moreover, the terms with which Wallace accounts for each civilization's failure bespeak the tension during his own era between a secularizing public sphere and private religious faith. The Greek laments that his society's overemphasis on reason clipped the wings off individual piety (1:III); the Hindoo bemoans his countrymen's fanatical adherence to religious texts, which "closed all the gates" to social progress (1:IV); and the Egyptian attributes to his society an unhealthy rift between private devotion to a monotheistic God and public worship of false idols (1:V). Thus, by the time Wallace narrates Jesus's birth, he has prepared the reader to regard the scene not only as the story's true beginning but also as a promise of future harmony between tradition and progress and between private belief and worldly "reason."

After this prelude in the desert, *Ben-Hur* moves away from the three patriarchs toward a maternal figure. In fact, considering Protestantism's long resistance to Mariolatry, Wallace devotes a surprising amount of attention to the mother of God. His Mary, with her "air of purity which only the soul can impart" and hands crossed "upon her breast, as in adoration and prayer" (1:VIII), recalls Roman Catholic iconography, although her blonde hair and blue eyes evoke the repertoire of saintly mothers in evangelical sentimental fiction. Her primary function, in any case, is to provide the reader with assurance about stable origins. Feminist theorists often point out that the mother's visibly active role in gestation (in contrast to the father's) means that culturally she connotes a connection to the past and a guaranteed relation to origins.[21] Indeed, Wallace's Mary functions as an unmistakable link in the chain that stretches from the House of David to Jesus. Not only does her fair appearance signal her biological relation to the golden-haired son of Jesse (Wallace is careful to attribute to Jesus the same fair features), but her exalted ancestry, inscribed on her very body, is alluded to several times (1:VIII-IX). In this way, Wallace deploys both sentimental motherhood and biological maternity to endow the story of the nativity with reassuring certitude:

> The apartment was lighted by a lantern enough to enable the strangers to find the mother, and the child awake in her lap.
>
> "Is the child thine?" asked Balthasar of Mary.
>
> And she who had kept all the things in the least affecting the little one, and pondered them in her heart, held it up in the light, saying,
>
> "He is my son!"
>
> And they fell down and worshipped him. (1:XIV)

By returning to his favorite childhood story, Wallace deploys literary means not only to affirm the nativity's status as "the beginning" (ruling out other options in the process), but also to emphasize this story's link to the Jewish biblical prophecy through the maternal figure.

When Wallace decided to continue writing beyond the scene in Bethlehem, the path the narrative should take seemed self-evident. As his best biographers describe, "as soon as the concept came to him, he saw the Crucifixion as the inevitable conclusion. The question was how to fill in the years between."[22] Although the story's beginning and end as set forth in the Gospels were precisely what Wallace aimed to mimic and validate, less obvious was the route the plot would take between these points. The main problem was the literary representation of Jesus, which Wallace overcame by placing Judah Ben-Hur's story at the center of the narrative and keeping Jesus in the background.[23]

However, "how to fill in the years" between the nativity and Crucifixion (as well as between Jesus's time and the reader's) created a second dilemma for Wallace; this one concerned the plot's temporal structure. On the one hand, to tell the story of Ben-Hur, Wallace modeled the plot on the *bildungsroman,* a narrative convention based on a secular, historical conception of time with a linear succession of events driven by the ideal of progress. The *bildungsroman,* in critic Franco Moretti's words, expresses "modernity's 'essence,' the sign of a world that seeks its meaning in the future rather than in the past."[24] The fact that in the *bildungsroman* the protagonist becomes an adult by leaving home, mother, and childhood behind implies a view of the past as an obstacle to progress. This is where the tension lay for Wallace: telling the story of the Gospels through this literary prism would mean prioritizing progress over tradition, perhaps even with the implication that Jesus too could be relegated to the historical archives. As an alternative, he could pattern his plot on a circular, religious temporality—a choice that several authors of popular Protestant narratives had made. Analyzing the way in which these authors "struggled to integrate the experience of America and American modernity into a narrative of spiritual salvation," Gregory S. Jackson describes the time frame they used in terms of a refusal of linearity and an encouragement to readers to exit historical time so that they could see themselves as "bearing the cross *with* their suffering Savior."[25] The problem with this kind of literary regression was its disavowal of progress; by utilizing it, Wallace would lose some of his novel's relevance to the present by encouraging escape from, rather than engagement with, modern life. This is the fault that *Ben-Hur*'s highbrow detractors found in the book.

What these detractors did not sufficiently acknowledge, however, was the complexity of the novel's temporal structure. In constructing *Ben-Hur*'s plot, Wallace in effect synthesized linear and anachronistic time. This combination allowed him to take the readers back to the era of the Gospels without losing touch with the present. A telling example appears in the last sentences of Book First: "But look forward, O reader!" the narrator exclaims, "a time will come when the signs will all proceed from the Son. Happy they who then believe in him! Let us wait that period" (1:XIV). This short passage is both proleptic and analeptic. In the spirit of postmillennialism, it can be understood as encouragement to look forward in anticipation of the Second Coming (with the act of reading the book itself assisting seekers to bear the wait or perhaps even contributing to the hastening of that day). But it can also be read as an instruction to the reader to look forward not to the end of time but to the end of the novel, in which case "a time will come" refers to the Crucifixion depicted in the last chapters—an event that had already happened in historical time. By obscuring eschatological and historical time, Wallace allowed his readers to inhabit both. As I will discuss next, he did not invent this twofold temporal scheme ex nihilo. His inspiration was the genre of historical romance.

Modernity, Nostalgia, and the Historical Romance

A feature common in many U.S. novels from the age of realism, beyond their interest in the "palpable present," is what narratologist Mark Currie calls (after Derrida) "archive fever." By this he means the tendency of modern narratives to progress into the future "through a continuous archiving of the present in order to relegate events to the past as quickly as possible."[26] Rather than return to a previous era (as historical romances do), novels touched by "archive fever" strive to turn the present into history by anticipating its memory. When Wallace's contemporary, Theodore Dreiser, wrote in *Sister Carrie* (a work one critic has called a novel of "anticipation" for its future-oriented vision) that department stores, "should they ever permanently disappear, will form an interesting chapter in the commercial history of our nation," he appears almost eager to push an existing feature of contemporary life—the large retail store—into the past.[27]

Ironically, this modern "archive fever"—as much as it may be construed as an investment in progress and a wish to propel time forward—tends to produce the opposite effect: nostalgia (Dreiser's intermittently melancholic tone illustrates this effect). As several scholars have argued, nostalgia is a by-product of a modern, secular conception of time. Cultures that regard time as linear and progressing toward an open-ended future tend to be nostalgic; cultures that regard time as cyclical or the future as redemptive do not. The current meaning of nostalgia, these scholars show, emerged with accelerated modernization in the nineteenth century. Initially linked with spatial dislocation—the term was first used in the seventeenth century to diagnose the physical ailment of soldiers and merchants who longed for home—"nostalgia" shifted its meaning in the next two centuries from the spatial to the temporal. As one commentator put it, "Odysseus longs for home; Proust is in search of lost time."[28] Because lost time, unlike a forsaken space, is irrecoverable, modern nostalgia is often deemed an incurable, escapist, and potentially paralyzing condition. Whether one indulges in fantasies of "a voyage back to the flower-land of my boyhood" (with Wallace's admirer) or withdraws in the imagination to by-gone eras (e.g., when Christ walked on earth), nostalgia constitutes a reaction to the fast-paced changes that characterize modern life.

The irony that attends narratives touched by "archive fever," then, is that as much as they express a desire to progress by turning the present into the past, they also incite nostalgia for the past and anxiety over progress. By the same token, as much as the literary establishment of the 1880s regarded historical romance as a nostalgic, old-fashioned, and obsolete form, the genre was, in fact, an *effect* of modernization. As critic Ian Duncan has argued, it is precisely the nostalgic, "romance" component of historical novels—the regression to mythical golden days, coupled with sentimental longings for origin, mother, and home—that signals the genre's inextricable engagement with the present. Romance is not "some shell the novel refused to outgrow," Duncan argues, but a "distinctive garment of its modernity."[29] Late-nineteenth-century realist novels and historical romances can thus be viewed as symbiotic rather than antagonistic genres—not just in the obvious sense that historical romancers, Wallace included, frequently utilized the conventions of realism, but because the realist novel pushed into the archives that which historical romance recovered as a space of nostalgic reprieve.

The view of late-nineteenth-century historical romance as simultaneously a product of and escape from modernity was most famously explored in *The Historical Novel* (1937). Georg Lukacs's anatomy of the genre argues that since the middle of the nineteenth century the historical novel had become calcified as a form, offering its readers little beyond a nostalgic refuge from the present. The class insurgency of 1848, he claimed, caused the bourgeoisie to reject its view of the past as a dialectic chain of events leading up to the present; instead, its members imagined the past as a land elsewhere, disconnected from the here and now. Based on this understanding, the historical novel "archeologized" the past, representing it as a static and anesthetized space (though quaint and lavishly treated) to which the reader could flee from the travails of modern life.[30] In Lukacs's chronology, *Ben-Hur* would be associated with this archeologized form. Certainly that is how literati reviewers regarded Wallace's novel and why they dismissed an author whose goal, as they described, was "to remove the reader from his modern life."

Finding little appeal in post-1848 historical romances, Lukacs devoted most of his study to the genre's earlier incarnations. In the early nineteenth century, he argued, historical novels did not flee from but intensely engaged with historical change. The fullest exhibition, Sir Walter Scott's works, are for Lukacs masterworks of historical dialectics that skillfully set against one another the private individual and public events as well as archaic social forms and emergent ones. Lukacs contended that Scott achieved these juxtapositions by creating an "everyman" protagonist who participates in the conflicts of his time but is not a central agent in them. This type of hero, he argued, allowed Scott to present a wide, all-encompassing perspective on historical forces while nourishing in his readers historical consciousness (i.e., an understanding of the link between the private individual and the changing events of that individual's era). Scott's novels also illustrated for Lukacs how the finest historical novels are necessarily anachronistic in the best sense of the term: they allow readers to understand present conflicts in relation to past ones. Rather than representing a flight to the past, Lukacs argued, Scott's historical novels brought the past to bear on the present. Their romantic, nostalgic backward gaze is not escapist but, on the contrary, a means of negotiating present strife.

Despite its post-1848 publication date, *Ben-Hur* is best read in relation to the model Lukacs associates with Scott's historical romances from earlier in the century. This is not simply because Wallace was indebted to the Waverley novels (though indeed he was, as several of his first readers recognized),[31] or only because he followed Scott in creating a protagonist who is a minor participant in a great historical transformation. Rather, *Ben-Hur* is best analyzed in relation to Lukacs's model because Wallace's nostalgic structure—his tale's return to the "original" time of Christ and what I call its "nostalgic mother plot"—represents eagerness to grapple with a present crisis rather than to seek asylum in the past.

"May a Man Forget His Mother?"

As Lukacs pointed out, Scott frequently placed his protagonists' coming-of-age plots in the context of ideological conflict, typically between residual feudalism and emergent humanist rationalism.[32] *Ben-Hur* offers a variation on this theme, dramatizing in stark binary terms the conflict between an old world of religious certainties and a new world of secular progress: the spiritual crisis, in other words, that marked the Gilded Age. Following the nativity story of Book First, Book Second takes us twenty-one years forward to allegorize that crisis through "the final quarrel between Roman and Jew" (2:I). We now meet the young Jewish protagonist Judah Ben-Hur and his childhood friend, the Roman Messala. Just returned from several years in the empire's hub, where "philosophy was taking the place of religion" (2:II), Messala reveals how his soul has darkened under this secular influence. The cynical Roman, Wallace makes clear, stands for the kind of faith-destroying material progress of which many postbellum Americans were wary. He urges Ben-Hur to grow up, leave behind his ancestral home, and join the "modern" world by seeking a career in Rome. In Messala's eyes, being Jewish amounts to an unnatural disavowal of progress: "What is to be a Jew! All men and things, even heaven and earth, change; but a Jew never. To him there is no backward, no forward; he is what his ancestor was in the beginning. In this sand I draw you a circle— there! Now tell me what more a Jew's life is? Round and round, Abraham here, Isaac and Jacob yonder, God in the middle" (2:II).

To counteract Messala's irreverent influence, once again Wallace summons a mother. Ben-Hur's mother, whose allegorical status is signaled by the fact that she remains unnamed, is drawn from several sources. She echoes the sentimental novel's emphasis on the mother's role in shaping a son's character through religious instruction and moral persuasion. A personification of the Holy City, Ben-Hur's mother is also linked with Holy Land travel literature, in which the encounter with the land of the Bible, especially Jerusalem, often provoked in the traveler memories of the "early teachings at our mother's knee."[33] But while representing sacred geography and domestic pedagogy, this character also serves as assurance of origin and a direct link to the word of God, much as Mary does earlier in the novel. Speaking to her son in ancient Hebrew, a language "almost lost in the land" but "cherished in its purity" (2:IV), Ben-Hur's mother lays out for him in detail his family tree, tracing his lineage, "kept with absolute certainty" (2:IV), all the way back to the book of Genesis. This narrative of origins is meant to persuade Ben-Hur to remain loyal to the past and to ignore the lure of modern Rome. Echoing Messala's geometrical imagery, Ben-Hur's mother explains to her son that human progress is an illusion: "If I were called upon to symbolize God and man in the simplest form, I would draw a straight line and a circle; and of the line I would say 'This is God, for he alone moves forever straight forward,' and of the circle, 'This is man—such is his progress" (2:V).

Having established this dialectic between the "circle" and the "line"— commitment to the past and the lure of the future—Wallace begins moving the plot of his novel in both directions at the same time. He follows the linear conventions of the *bildungsroman*: Ben-Hur leaves his home and mother behind, goes out into the world, faces challenges that test his moral fortitude and masculine prowess (the chariot race being the most famous), gains in maturity, wealth, and power, and eventually marries the virtuous Esther, ending up as a paterfamilias in the empire's metropolis. Moving from Jerusalem to Rome, from childhood to maturity, and from tradition to worldly success, this dimension of the novel tells the story of the triumph of progress.

Conventionally, coming-of-age plots move forward by what I referred to earlier as "archive fever": to advance toward the goal of maturity, both narrative and protagonist need to "archive" home, mother, and childhood. Ben-Hur recognizes this imperative when he says to his mother at the outset, "it is the Lord's will that I shall one day become owner of myself . . . a day of separation and therefore a dreadful day to you" (2:IV). Wallace departs from *bildungsroman*, however, because that day of separation is dreadful not only to mother, or just to mother and son, but to the *raison-d'être* of the novel: if the mother personifies religious faith that includes loyalty to origin and tradition, then choosing to separate from her would amount to abandoning God. Wallace's challenge, from this vantage, was to craft a *bildungsroman* that does not demand this sacrifice.

This challenge lies at the heart of historical romance. In Scott's novels, Ian Duncan explains, "the progressive, rationalist ethos of a narrative of socialization" means that childhood, associated with the romance mode, "is a condition to be outgrown or cured." But because "romance signifies the heritage of a cultural identity that is lost but ethically true" it cannot simply be left behind.[34] The historical romance thus actively seeks to preserve the mode of romance within the rationalist, progressive narrative. In Wallace's variation, the endangered but ethically true cultural identity associated with childhood and romance is that of religious faith. Just as Scott's formula involves weaving history with romance, Wallace's method is to work into the progressive, future-oriented *bildungsroman* an alternative plot that is defined by nostalgia for home and mother.

An important variation that this nostalgic plot introduces is that Judah Ben-Hur does not choose to leave but is forcibly torn away from Jerusalem, his mother, and his sister (since Tirzah represents home and tradition as much as the mother does). This plot also dictates that however far away he travels, his gaze remains fixed on Jerusalem. Whereas characters such as Dreiser's Sister Carrie forget mother and home as soon as they depart for the big city, Ben-Hur's defining attribute is his unceasing longings for lost space and time. His thoughts never wander from his mother and sister; to the contrary, his only desire is to return to them and to the world he was forced to leave behind. As a slave on a Roman galley in Book Third, he cries for "Mother and sister—house—home—Holy Land" (3:V), summing up nicely the metonymic chain of maternity, ancestry, place of origin, and faith. Yet even after his fortunes turn, when his bravery and virtue are rewarded by the Roman Arrius (in the tradition of the *bildungsroman*), his origins dominate his thought. In Book Fourth, he asks Simonides, "may a Jew forget his religion? Or his birthplace, if it were the Holy Land of our fathers?" (4:III). He expands on this theme in a conversation with Simonides's servant, Malluch:

> "May a man forget his mother?" . . . Malluch looked into Ben-Hur's face
> for a hint of meaning, but saw, instead, two bright-red spots, one on each

cheek, and in his eyes traces of what might have been repressed tears; then he answered, mechanically, "No!" adding, with fervor, "never;" and a moment after, when he began to recover himself, "If he is an Israelite, never!" . . . The red spots on Ben-Hur's face deepened . . ."It is not enough to say of her she was good and beautiful: in her tongue was the law of kindness, and her works were the praise of all in the gates, and she smiled at days to come. I had a little sister, and she and I were the family, and we were so happy that I, at least, have never seen harm in the saying of the old rabbi, 'God could not be everywhere, and, therefore, he made mothers.'" (4:IX)

Such unrelenting pining for home and mother—resonant with the familiar idea from sentimental fiction that mothers act as God's surrogate—is the force that, two-thirds into the novel, curves the plot back full circle. Book Six takes the reader back to Jerusalem to reveal that during the time in which Ben-Hur transformed from boy to man, his mother and sister have been imprisoned in a moldy cell in a Roman fortress. Described as "ghosts" of the past (6:IV), they have been almost literally "archived" by Messala, who scorns the religious tradition they represent. In their leprosy-ridden, deformed bodies, mother and sister now come to personify the horror of a past abandoned.

Hence, the last third of Wallace's novel is largely devoted to the project of return and recovery. The nostalgic mother plot leads Ben-Hur back to Jerusalem until, with Jesus's reentry into the story, Wallace brings his plot to its climax. Jesus heals the Hur women upon his triumphal entry into Jerusalem, which enables Ben-Hur to reunite, finally, with them. The fantasy of circling back time is thus doubly fulfilled: Ben-Hur is back at home and the ravages of time are literally undone as Jesus restores Ben-Hur's mother and sister to health.

The rest of *Ben-Hur* is anti-climactic in comparison; even the Crucifixion and Ben-Hur's conversion to Christianity are less emotionally powerful than the reunion scene. An epilogue wraps up the linear *bildungsroman* plot: Ben-Hur marries, becomes one of the wealthiest and most powerful citizens of Rome, and uses his wealth to build the catacomb of San Calixto, from which "Christianity issued to supersede the Caesars" (8:X). With these last plot details, Wallace makes the point that Christian belief and worldly progress can indeed be reconciled. The reader may recall how, in Book First, one of the Magi said that Egyptian civilization is divided between private devotion to God and idolatrous public practices. The novel's ending implies that, under Christianity, faith in Christ will be harmonized with worldly power. In a final temporal twist, the reader is also reminded that the Roman Empire, which throughout the novel represented secular futurity, has long been archeologized and relegated to the dead archives, whereas religion, associated throughout with the past, now stands for the living promise of a better future. The first words from Ben-Hur's mother, that God "alone moves forever straight forward," prove, in the final analysis, to have been prophetic rather than outdated: progress *is* possible and desirable, so long as it is propelled by faith.

As carrier of such comforting messages, *Ben-Hur*'s nostalgic mother plot managed to touch the hearts of its first readers, serving to affirm the relevance of religious faith in a fast-changing modern world. Letters from early readers frequently alluded to Ben-Hur's devotion to his mother and mentioned being particularly moved by the reunion scene.[35] A poem in honor of *Ben-Hur* (by an admirer of the staged version) included the following lines:

> We gaze upon these scenes and feel
> That we are living in those years,
>
> . . . .
>
> The *Mother love*, so great, intense,
> In all its depth is here revealed;
> And *lovers true*, in *other* sense,
> Make vows that are with kisses sealed.[36]

This poem celebrates Wallace's power to undo the passage of time and admires his gift for linking past and present. It recognizes, too, that a central theme in the novel is "the *Mother* love, so great, intense." The "mother love" is greater than romantic love or what the amateur poet calls love in that "*other* sense." The poet is correct in thus demoting romantic love: one of the ways in which Wallace links past and present is through the relatively minor figure of Esther and the derivative place she occupies in the novel. Esther signals the hero's maturation, in line with *bildungsroman* conventions: choosing the "good" Esther over the "bad" (albeit sexually alluring) Iras represents one of Ben-Hur's successful rites of passage in that his marriage to Esther evinces the achievement of manhood. In the context of the nostalgic mother plot, however, Esther functions not as an autonomous love interest but as a pale imitation of the real object. She does not *replace* Ben-Hur's incestuous passion for mother and sister—she is derived from that passion. She initially attracts Ben-Hur's admiration because she reminds him of home. When he woos her, he promises: "You shall be another Tirzah to me" (5:IX). As the family's former slave, Esther is the next best thing to marrying within the family. By joining Ben-Hur and Esther, Wallace reconciles the novel's two temporal modes to make palpable the idea that desire for a better future is tethered to loyalty to origin.

Wallace biographers often point out that Esther was named after Wallace's own mother, on whose knees he first heard the story of the nativity. Wallace would dedicate his next book, *The Boyhood of Christ* (1889), "to the soul of my mother, in the ultimate isles of the blessed." He dedicated *Ben-Hur*, we recall, "to the wife of my youth," much to the discomfort of Susan Wallace, who did not like being pushed to the archives. But perhaps she need not have been upset. In a novel in which mother and wife, circular time and linear time, and religious tradition and modern progress are so insistently interwoven, the past is never allowed to become obscure or irrelevant; it "still abides with me."

Coda

In this essay I associated the nostalgic mother plot with a particular moment in postbellum America when secular paradigms exerted pressure on the Protestant narrative to the point of crisis. That this plot remained central in *Ben-Hur*'s twentieth-century adaptations attests to the relevance of the compromises it offered for the next generations. The 1959 film famously ends with Judah Ben-Hur back in his ancestral home, surrounded by all three virtuous, maternal characters: mother, sister, and fiancé.[37] The 1925 film retains the novel's reunion of son, mother, and sister as one of its climactic scenes. As in the novel, this moment is ripe with

promise: the boyish Ben-Hur, having come of age, is about to find his call-
ing in Jesus and lead the way toward a better, Christian future. However,
this vision depends on a powerful moment of regression, made effective
by modern cinematic techniques. In visualizing the healing of Ben-Hur's
mother and sister, cameraman Karl Struss invented a new technique: he
gradually removed a series of camera filters from the lens so that with
each shot the women appeared younger and healthier.[38] The 1925 film
audience must have felt simultaneously awed by the miracle of Christ and
the marvels of modern technology. The technique allowed filmgoers to
inhabit simultaneously, like readers of the novel, the modern present and
the time of Jesus. Offering a visual corollary to *Ben-Hur*'s power to "wash
out the blotted pages of the years of a grim battle with the world" (in the
words of the letter with which this essay began), Struss's cinematic innovation charted for viewers a path to modernity without disenchantment,
much as Wallace's novel had years before for its readers.

Retelling and Untelling the Christmas Story

Ben-Hur, Uncle Midas, and the
Sunday-School Movement

JEFFERSON J. A. GATRALL

During the summer of 1894, the *New York Evangelist* conducted a reader survey to determine the "100 Best Sunday-School Books." After Sunday schools submitted lists of their favorite titles to the newspaper, the survey results were analyzed in such diverse venues as the *Washington Post* and *Sunday-School Library Bulletin.* To no one's surprise, *Ben-Hur* topped the final list, appearing on 91 percent of all submissions.[1] The Sunday-school movement's adoption of Lew Wallace's novel represents an important development in the *Ben-Hur* tradition. By the early 1890s, this tale of the Christ had secured a prominent place on the shelves of the Sunday-school library. Well into the next century, passages from *Ben-Hur* appeared on lesson plans internationally. The association between *Ben-Hur* and Sunday school was particularly strong in the United States. The American Sunday-School Union (ASSU), by far the largest organization of its kind in the country, was among the novel's most influential endorsers. Thanks to Wallace's scholarly energy, doctrinal minimalism, and well-publicized conversion, *Ben-Hur* dovetailed with the union's pedagogical approach to biblical subject matter. The union promoted his novel in teaching manuals and periodicals, and its British counterpart published an edition of the book in 1895.[2] At the same time, the book's status as a Sunday-school classic made it a target for the literati's barbs. A detractor quipped, for instance, on the occasion of Wallace's death in 1905, "nobody who went to Sunday-school could have escaped the story had he tried."[3] As concerned about literary achievement were supporters who tried to rebut the charge that *Ben-Hur* was a mere "auxiliary reading book for village Sunday schools."[4]

Wallace, for his part, embraced his position as a biblical authority for U.S. youth. His cultivation of an adolescent Christian readership is evident in two publications in particular: *The First Christmas, from "Ben-Hur,"* a stand-alone illustrated edition of the novel's opening nativity section that Wallace dedicated to "all the Sunday-school scholars in the world"[5]; and *The Boyhood of Christ*, first published as a short story in the 1886 Christmas issue of *Harper's New Monthly Magazine* and reissued three years later in book form. These follow-up works to *Ben-Hur* reveal very different sides of Wallace's biblical fiction. The nativity section from *Ben-Hur* approaches its source material in the manner of an imaginative biblical supplement. Wallace fleshes out the story of the wise men with detail-intensive descriptive sequences that range from differential racial portraiture to landscapes of the lower Jordan. In *The Boyhood of Christ*, his fictional surrogate provides teenaged visitors on Christmas Eve a lesson in Higher Criticism (i.e., the study of biblical texts using modern methods of source criticism). After testing the reliability of various ancient sources concerning Christ's early years in Egypt and Galilee, Uncle Midas reaches the surprise conclusion that "Christ had no boyhood at all."[6] This reduction is in stark contrast to the narrative expansiveness of Wallace's first and far more famous rendition of the Christmas story. Because they draw on the resources of fiction, these less-studied contributions to the *Ben-Hur* tradition intersect in different ways with Sunday-school's pedagogical goals and spiritual mission. Wallace's literary reputation was tethered to this mass movement, which boosted his book sales and his fame. But this relationship brought with it an increased burden of truth-telling that matched Wallace's rising cultural authority. In *The Boyhood of Christ*, he handled this burden by leaning on the realist promise of word pictures at the expense of fictional narrative and its suspect pleasures.

Lessons and Libraries

The Sunday-school movement, which was on the eve of its second century when *Ben-Hur* debuted, had always been preoccupied with making books available to children and young adults. In the 1780s and 1790s, first in London and then in Philadelphia, the movement's founders sought to reach poor, working-class youth who had limited access to formal education. For the first Sunday-school managers and teachers, the unruly behavior of poor, unsupervised children represented a "social problem" that derived from illiteracy and a concomitant lack of basic religious knowledge.[7] Because such behavior was particularly out of place on the Lord's Day, provision of the right reading material was a priority. Even as the U.S. wing of the movement took a decidedly evangelical turn during the next few decades, the nineteenth-century Sunday school—in contrast to its denominational successors—maintained the secular roots that kept its lessons free from the direct control of major churches.[8] With the help of a professional, non-denominational leadership and a vast volunteer labor force, the ASSU held a normative sway over the movement as a whole through its publishing arm, which produced and distributed books and periodicals that children and young adults could read in lessons and— boosted by a pioneering library system—at home.[9] Furthermore, with the ASSU's help, middle-class Protestant women who authored Sunday-school material could exert the kind of cultural authority on religious matters that was denied to them by official church hierarchies. Indeed, eighty-five of the 100 "best" books in the *Evangelist*'s survey were written by women.[10] Wallace's outsized authority among this cohort was enhanced by his career as a war hero and statesman, but it also owed much to perceptions of him as a Christian writer, rather than a spokesman for a particular church. As he emphasized in the preface to *The Boyhood of Christ*, "I . . . am neither minister of the Gospel, nor theologian, nor churchman."[11]

The Bible was the primary text of instruction in nineteenth-century Sunday schools, with other texts serving different pedagogical functions within and beyond the classroom. The educational goals of using the Bible and its supplements varied as the mission of Sunday schools evolved. The pedagogy of the first U.S. Sunday schools had hardly been innovative in the history of Christian education: teachers used the Bible to teach children to read. In pre-revolutionary common schools in America, the Bible had likewise served as a standard primer—a practice that survived until the 1820s in some rural areas.[12] Gradually, though, the two school systems, weekday and Sunday, diverged. On the one hand, with the rapid growth of the public school system, juvenile illiteracy grew less pressing.[13] On the other hand, state educators succeeded in de-emphasizing and eventually banning the Bible in public schools, leading to what many perceived as a grave neglect of religious education.[14] As one concerned writer asked, "where else shall the religious instruction be imparted to the children who attend the common schools unless in the Sunday-school?"[15] The Sunday-school movement emerged as a mainstream, centrally administered schooling option for Protestant, Catholic, and even non-Christian families.

In 1872, at the National Sunday-School Convention in Indianapolis, ASSU representatives and representatives from major church organizations approved the International Unified Lesson System. For the next forty years, this curriculum was almost universally employed in ASSU schools and was widely adopted by U.S. Presbyterian, Methodist, and other denominational schools. British and Canadian Sunday-school organizations also adopted and contributed to the regularly revised lesson system, which consisted of a comprehensive course of study that covered both the Old and New Testaments and was spread over seven-year cycles. Emphasis was placed on uniformity so that on each Sunday in a given year of the cycle, children from schools in different countries and from all grade levels (with some exceptions for infant and advanced classes) would study the same biblical story.[16] Despite the limitations of a volunteer workforce and once-a-week schedule, Sunday schools thus offered by the end of the century a common educational experience for millions of children. Sunday-school scholars from novice to advanced grades learned in a setting modeled on the public school about subject matter that they would not otherwise encounter.[17]

The International Unified Lesson System permitted little flexibility in the scheduling of core biblical readings (a problem that contributed to its eventual overhaul). However, Sunday-school teachers could integrate supplemental readings in any number of ways. In the evangelical spirit of the Second Great Awakening, many early ASSU leaders hoped that primary contact with scriptures—unadorned with catechisms, rote interpretations, and other sectarian overlays—would provoke deep emotional responses in children and so prepare them for conversion (annual statistics on conversions were scrupulously compiled).[18] As Anne Boylan writes, the later adoption of the lesson system coincided with a shift in emphasis away from sudden conversion experiences to a gradual, multi-year process of religious growth in line with leading theories of education from the common school.[19] For teachers and their students, texts backed by the authority of churches yielded to a modern network of supplements produced by professional writers and scholars. These "lessons-helps" ranged from children's stories, including a large body of tales devoted to overseas missionary work, to modern biographies of Jesus, to biblical archaeologists' latest research.[20]

Within the lesson system, teachers turned to *Ben-Hur* for scholarly yet morally stimulating passages related to specific incidents from biblical history. In a manual for "kindergarten lessons," for example, one writer suggests Wallace's "word-picture" of the wise men's journey as an "inspiration" for teachers as they prepare their renditions of the story for the classroom.[21] For senior classes devoted to the Crucifixion, the author of another manual argues that the description of the scene in *Ben-Hur* is the best "in fiction," whereas the descriptions in the versions of *Lives of Christ* by Alfred Edersheim (1883), John Cunningham Geikie (1877; revised 1891), and William Hanna (1876) are "the best in Christological literature."[22]

Also of interest to Sunday-school teachers was Wallace's fictional reworking of the ten lepers' healing (Luke 17:11–19). In their regularly updated "notes" on the international lessons, P. N. Peloubet and M. A. Peloubet recommended *Ben-Hur*'s "vivid" account of leprosy. They also pointed teachers toward the relevant entry on leprosy from William McClure Thomson's *The Land and the Book* (1859), a staple Sunday-school resource, as well as to a contemporary account of the disease in South Africa.[23] In an anthology of Sunday-school stories by different authors, Edward Everett Hale (a celebrated author of the day) incorporated lengthy excerpts from Wallace's leprosy subplot. Hale remarks that aside from the ten canonical lepers, there are two extra lepers in the novel—Ben-Hur's mother and sister—"whom the Saviour cures" and who are not among "the ungrateful."[24] Wallace's loose reworking of this Gospel episode renders the Christian themes of compassion and gratitude accessible to impressionable young readers by incorporating fictional characters along-side their biblical models. It also provides a historically and medically sound portrait of leprosy and its stigmatization in ancient Jewish society. From the standpoint of Sunday-school pedagogy, Wallace's treatment of lepers contributed to the development of a child's moral character and knowledge-base.

Teachers were further exposed to *Ben-Hur* during their training. Here, Wallace's word pictures proved more valuable for their scholarly under-pinnings than for their aesthetic appeal. The proper training of volunteer Sunday-school teachers, who were often blessed with more "heart-power" than "head-power," was a perennial issue for Sunday-school movement leaders.[25] The renowned Chautauqua Assemblies in upstate New York were initially designed as a summer training session for Sunday-school teachers.[26] Wallace was a frequent guest lecturer at the assemblies, and he most likely watched Chautauquans staging tableaux from his tale. Cer-tainly he would have heard his legendary research ethic being vaunted as a model to emulate. As the authors of one Sunday-school manual explain, Wallace did not even need to travel to the Holy Land to work up his book's "accurate and realistic descriptions"; instead, "he had nothing but the printed page and the map."[27] Paul Gutjahr singles out the high esteem in which Sunday-school teachers held Wallace's exhaustively researched descriptions of the Holy Land.[28] For national leaders and teachers-in-training, as well as for students in advanced and adult classes, *Ben-Hur* served as a sort of literary atlas of biblical geography.[29]

For Sunday-school pupils, *Ben-Hur*'s influence was arguably stronger outside the classroom than during lessons. Like other popular works of religious fiction, such as *Pilgrim's Progress* (1678) and *Uncle Tom's Cabin* (1852), Wallace's novel earned the "Sunday-school" moniker by being fea-tured prominently in the movement's libraries, rather than in its lesson plans. In the 1820s and 1830s, when books were still prohibitively expen-sive for many U.S. households, the Sunday-school library developed into an essential aspect of the movement's mission. Libraries enabled teachers to promote and regulate the reading habits of children and young adults, thus extending the process of learning from Sunday through the rest of the week. Books were usually lent to young readers for two weeks, initially as rewards for good attendance but eventually under a free lending system, complete with card catalogs, due date slips, and overdue notices.[30]

Books entered library collections, however, in a somewhat less democratic spirit than when they were loaned out. In *How to Conduct a Sunday School* (1905), a long-term superintendent recalled offering his pupils the chance to pick the first two purchases for a new class library: "They selected *Ben-Hur* for the first book."[31] In fact, though, careful selection of books was a major responsibility for Sunday-school movement leaders. In addition to the Bible, tracts, sermons, and hymnbooks, libraries made available a range of secular material, especially biographies and histories, in which the lives of great men and women could be studied. Furthermore, in keeping with the movement's increasing centralization during the last decades of the century, manuals and journals devoted to the Sunday-school library were established, and regional and national committees formed to compile lists of approved books. An 1896 article in the *Sunday-School Library Bulletin* recommended that superintendents divide their collections according to grade levels. Significantly, *Ben-Hur* is the first work of fiction assigned to the "senior grade," where it sits alongside such multi-tome behemoths as Washington Irving's *Life of Washington* (1855–59), Johann Heinrich Kurtz's *History of the Christian Church* (1860), and Lord Macaulay's *History of England* (1848).[32] As for selection committees, in keeping with the ASSU's non-denominational inclusivity, the Ladies' Commission of the American Unitarian Association published an influential list annually, and the ASSU issued regular amendments to its lists through the *Sunday-School Times*.[33] Needless to say, the ASSU promoted vigorously (and foremost) its own books and children's magazines to the thousands of Sunday-school superintendents across the nation.[34]

Such lists were not incidental; libraries formed a large part of the Sunday school's early appeal because school libraries were rudimentary and free public ones were still uncommon. As one of the historians of this movement writes, a Sunday-school's library once served as its "principal attraction" for new recruits, so much so that some children joined two schools "in order to obtain each week two library books."[35] Inclusion of fiction in Sunday-school libraries nevertheless proved contentious until at least mid-century. As members of the Massachusetts Sabbath-School

Society Board argued, fiction was inherently untrue and thus "injurious" to the young mind. Additionally, any book of otherwise true narratives that demeaned itself with the occasional imaginary one roused real concern on these grounds: "If it is known that a Sabbath-school Society has published *one* such [novel], what security have the churches that all its publications are not mere religious *fictions*."[36] In practice, however, the popularity that novels enjoyed in Sunday schools challenged the priority that selection committees assigned to nonfiction. Even early libraries tended to make room for at least some works of imaginative literature: not just popular children's tales but also novels as evangelical as Daniel Defoe's *Robinson Crusoe* (1719).[37] That *Ben-Hur* was given out as a reward for attendance derives from a tradition of recruitment almost as old as the Sunday-school library itself.[38] This is not to underestimate the extent to which religious attitudes toward fiction in the United States changed over the course of the nineteenth century. As the books listed on the 1894 *New York Evangelist* survey suggest, religious fiction was openly acknowledged as the most popular fare in a Sunday-school library.

A recurring line of commentary has attributed *Ben-Hur*'s popularity to its success at overcoming resistance to fiction among certain kinds of rural and Protestant readerships. Critic Stewart Holbrook framed this thought memorably when he said that *Ben-Hur* entered "the homes of Hard-Shell Baptists and Methodists and other non-novel-reading sects."[39] Although valid, this commentary can be rendered more precise by emphasizing that *Ben-Hur* was a late, decisive blow in a protracted and insidious offensive in which Sunday schools had assumed a leading role for more than half a century. On loan from the Sunday-school library, *Ben-Hur* indeed reached many of these Baptist and Methodist "homes."

The direct role of the Sunday-school library in *Ben-Hur*'s reception nevertheless faded as the institution itself went into decline. Faced with the low purchase price for books and insurmountable competition from the burgeoning public library system—which commanded far greater resources and reached a far wider readership—the Sunday-school library quickly became obsolete. By the turn of the century, a sense of crisis over the library's fallen reputation pervades the writings of the movement's leaders: The Sunday-school library that had once filled "many homes with most of [their] reading material" had "lost much of its importance" as its books had sunk in popular impressions to the level of a "caricature" that dismisses this print with a "contemptuous sneer as synonymous with literary trash."[40] This was the context in which obituaries of Wallace alluded to "Sunday-school reading." Offering one such allusion in *Ben-Hur*'s defense, a friend of Wallace's (who was an author himself) rebuked the "sneer" that had been "repeated since his death" that *Ben-Hur* is "a classic only for the provincial church-goer, the village class leader and Sunday-school superintendent."[41]

The Jesus Novel

The rationale behind conservative resistance to religious fiction is not difficult to understand. Authors of Jesus novels—works of historical fiction in which Jesus appears as a character—devised unauthorized, crowd-pleasing plotlines for the holiest of figures. In portraying Jesus, these novelists intervened directly in the realm of the sacred. Professional writers had no more inherent claim in this protected space than did their readers and critics. Most Jesus novelists were acutely aware that their fictions risked charges of blasphemy. Unlike other novelists in this tradition, Wallace did not resort to a prefatory note to defend his intentions in writing *Ben-Hur*.[42] Yet in private conversations with his publisher, he did address the possibility that his tale of the Christ might offend Christian readers; he even offered to "pull" the book rather than risk that outcome. Wallace was wise to worry: early reviews remarked the "bold" nature of his undertaking.[43] For example, a *New York Times* reviewer commented on how "daring" Wallace had been in deciding to tackle "sacred narrative." Gospel paraphrases, the reviewer observes, were traditionally written with a "devotional character" in mind. Yet *Ben-Hur* appeared to serve "no religious purpose": "The point . . . to be considered is apparently whether propriety is not offended . . . by the intermingling of so many chapters of fiction with the sacred history."[44]

Such questions haunted the dozens of Jesus novels that were written in Europe and the United States over the course of the nineteenth century. Harriet Martineau's *Traditions of Palestine* (1830), which the author herself deemed "audacious," was the first of the independent French, British, and

U.S. works of the 1830s and 1840s to mark the emergence of this genre, which continues to enjoy a worldwide readership.[45] By the close of the nineteenth century—in large part because of *Ben-Hur*'s international success—Jesus novels were being published in Germany, Spain, Sweden, and Poland.[46] That novelists were authorized to represent Christ was not a given in any of these national literatures; rather, each novelist's authority was established, or countermanded, in the act. Authors of Jesus novels had to engage publishers, mollify censors, please critics, and gain audiences. Church officials, the Christ figure's traditional guardians, were often outsiders to this process. With the singular and important exception of denominational Sunday schools, the Jesus novel had no sanctioned function within the major churches of Europe or the United States. Clergymen and theologians could and did write Jesus novels, notably William Ware's *Julian; or Scenes in Judea* (1841), Joseph Holt Ingraham's *The Prince of the House of David* (1855), Franz Delitzsch's *One Day in Capernaum* (1871; English translation 1887), and Edwin A. Abbott's *Philochristus: Memoirs of a Disciple of the Lord* (1878). Yet so did socialists, atheists, and Jews. In *As Others Saw Him* (1895), for instance, the Anglo-Jewish writer Joseph Jacobs portrays the "rabbi of Nazareth" from the perspective of a fictional Pharisee who casts his vote for crucifixion in the Sanhedrim with a clear conscience. Two of the most successful French examples of the genre— Eugene Sue's *The Silver Cross* (1850) and Ferdinando Petruccelli's *The Memoirs of Judas* (1867)—likewise reach pointedly non-Christian conclusions: the first with the humiliating death of a misunderstood champion of the proletariat, and the second with a botched execution (Judas saves his "friend" from execution only to watch him die, a broken man, three years later).[47] State churches, depending on the country in question, had varying means to influence each step in the chain of a given novel's production, distribution, and consumption. Censorship proved especially effective in orthodox Russia. Although *Ben-Hur* was permitted to appear in translation in 1888, the first Russian Jesus novels were not published until after a 1905 decree permitted freedom of worship in the empire.

More Jesus novels were published in the United States, which lacked a state church, than in any other country during the nineteenth century. Certain broad differences can be observed between U.S. Jesus novels and their European counterparts. Whereas Jesus novels on both sides of the Atlantic drew on common and often heterodox sources for their biblical geography, historiography, and ethnography, U.S. authors were more prone to harmonize such scholarship with mainstream doctrine on Christ's divinity. They were also more likely to target their novels at adolescent audiences. In "The Sunday-School and Modern Biblical Criticism" (1894), Charles Briggs, a Presbyterian theologian, argued that Higher Criticism's textual methods should be taught to youth through the international lessons, including the study of ancient manuscripts and the laws of their transmission, even if this meant that the "truths and facts" of Holy Scripture would be put to the test.[48] These views made Briggs, whose church had earlier tried him for heresy, an outlier among Sunday-school educators. However, cutting-edge biblical scholarship from Germany and England did reach U.S. readers, albeit in an attenuated form, through *Ben-Hur* and similar novels. These novels were, in this respect, a popular byproduct of scholars' quest for the historical Jesus.

The stakes surrounding Jesus novels were high no matter where they were published in Christendom, with authors potentially extolled as defenders of the faith, denounced for blasphemy, or both. A number of novelists, writing in the wake of *Ben-Hur*'s spectacular popularity, managed to strike a deep evangelical nerve among audiences, and they did so in a quicker manner than Wallace. In 1894, the *Detroit Free Press* asked its readers to submit fictional "lives of Christ" for a contest, with the winner to be awarded a $1,000 prize. The editors received 377 manuscripts. Florence Morse Kingsley's *Titus, A Comrade of the Cross* (1895)—the winning entry, published in an inexpensive edition for Sunday-school use—sold 200,000 within weeks. In a prefatory announcement, the novel's publishers explain that the goal of Kingsley's novel was the instruction of "young readers" who were already "believers in Christ." *Titus* was not designed to convert. Rather, its role in children's continuing religious growth was to "make the life and teachings of Christ as real . . . as if he lived and taught in our streets at the present day."[49]

Across the Atlantic, reception of Marie Corelli's *Barabbas: A Dream of the World's Tragedy* (1893) was as divisive as that of Jesus films like Martin Scorsese's *The Last Temptation of Christ* (1988) and Mel Gibson's *The Passion*

of the Christ (2004). Corelli's novel incorporates the most graphic (and pro-
lix) descriptions of the Crucifixion in nineteenth-century fiction. Her long-
time publisher was so appalled that he turned the book down. *Barabbas*
would nevertheless become a sensational best seller, going through seven
editions in its first seven months alone and fifty-four by the time of Corelli's death in 1924. This Jesus novel's opponents were as fervid and organized as its supporters. For example, when the outraged board members
of one city library voted to remove all of Corelli's books from the shelves,
deeming them "cheap and sensational," the board's chairman resigned
in protest. So hostile were literary critics, Corelli instructed her new publisher not to send them review copies for any of her subsequent novels.[50]
By contrast, she found considerable support among Anglican clergymen,
many of whom saw in *Barabbas* a recipe for England's salvation. Whereas
Wallace's tale won early support from President James Garfield, Corelli
received the enthusiastic backing of Prime Minister William Gladstone, a
moral crusader then in his fourth term in office.[51]

Within the literary tradition of Jesus novels, *Ben-Hur* achieved a
higher and more enduring level of success than did any of its competition
at home or abroad. In terms of form, Wallace did not so much revolutionize the Jesus novel as exploit its conventions for maximal rhetorical effect.
Like most Christian Jesus novels, *Ben-Hur* is structured as a conversion
narrative in which the Nazarene makes dramatic yet ephemeral appearances before potential followers, the genre's true protagonists. With Jesus
in the background, novelists were free to develop subplots beyond the
limits of sacred narrative, mixing events from profane history with episodes of their own creation. Wallace gambled correctly that even a small
number of encounters between his eponymous heroes would suffice to
consecrate his novel as a whole with Christ's presence. Some shadow of it
is felt even in Antioch, a place not named in the Gospels, where Ben-Hur's
conflict with Messala reaches its famous climax in an orgy of pagan spectacle and violence. This shadow explains why one Sunday-school manual
recommends Wallace's portrayal of the Grove of Daphne in Antioch for
a lesson on the rampant idolatry that led to the captivity of Israel under
Hoshea's reign (2 Kings 17:6–18)—a biblical event 400 miles and seven centuries removed from Wallace's setting.[52] As for "The Race," it was surely

the chapter from *Ben-Hur* read most often in Sunday schools. Scoffing yet plausible is one contemporary critic's recollection (with a telling gendered slant) that "no church entertainment was complete unless the local amateur elocutionist let herself go on the chariot race."[53]

Like the authors of scholarly Lives of Jesus, a closely related literary genre, novelists supplemented core Gospel events with material from non-canonical sources. The Christmas story represents one of the most venerable genres of the traditional Gospel paraphrase. Indeed, the nativity section of *Ben-Hur* was originally intended as a separate tale.[54] When published as part of a lengthy novel, this section is clearly a modern work of historical fiction. In the nativity section, which opens the novel, Wallace transforms seven verses from Matthew into a novella-length narrative through the aid of biblical geography, ethnography, astronomy, and comparative religion, among other academic disciplines. It is significant that the narrator's first words display extra-biblical erudition; for instance, he employs a contemporary Arabic name—"Jebel es Zubleh"—for a mountain near the Jordan River's base. With this gambit, Wallace reverses the linguistic methods of such biblical archeologists as Edward Robinson, an authority cited in the prefaces to several Jesus novels. Through cutting-edge excavation techniques and the etymological analysis of Arabic place names, Robinson, in 1838 and again in 1852, uncovered long-lost sacred sites and their ancient Hebrew names across modern-day Palestine. These recovered places and familiar names made their way into tourist guides for Holy Land travelers. In contrast, Wallace uses a contemporary Arabic name known to specialists to defamiliarize the ancient setting of a venerable biblical tale. He then introduces his first characters, the Magi, with literary portraits that accentuate their ethnic and creedal differences: thus the "Egyptian" wears a "kufiyeh" and "the Hindoo" a "turban," whereas "the Greek" is "bareheaded" (1:I-III). These characters' names—Balthazar, Melchior, and Gaspar, respectively—derive from Latin church tradition.

Jesus's curtailed presence in Jesus novels enabled novelists to be selective in choosing which stories from the Gospels to subject to fictional expansion. Unlike the authors of scholarly Lives of Jesus, Jesus novelists were not under any obligation to gauge the historical reliability of individual Gospel events. Nor were they obliged to harmonize all four Gospels into a unified, comprehensive biography. To the contrary, novelists—not bound by the documentary strictures of historiography—were free to invent actions for the historical Jesus to perform, from surprise appearances to fabulous new miracles. The principal criterion for the inclusion of any event in a Jesus novel is not whether it may have happened but whether it can be persuasively pictured. Jesus novelists thus relied less on the purging of mythic elements from Gospel narrative than on a proliferation of supplemental *realia*.

Nevertheless, some of these novelists' omissions did at times reflect the controversial excisions of Higher Criticism. This finding is relevant to Wallace's telling, and untelling, because Gospel claims about his Judean birth and genealogy were early casualties of the quest for the historical Jesus. Matthew and Luke open with patrilineal genealogies revealing Jesus's direct descent from David, a king of the tribe of Judah, whereas his birthplace in both Gospels is Bethlehem, the city of David. In contrast, nineteenth-century biblical scholars such as David Strauss exposed the mythic underpinnings of the Gospel accounts of Jesus's infancy. Strauss's *Das Leben Jesu* (1836) was widely read and hotly debated in the English-speaking world via an 1846 translation by a young George Eliot, who was still writing under her given name Marian Evans. Afterward, in *Vie de Jésus* (1863)—perhaps the only scholarly Life of Jesus of that century that could match *Ben-Hur* in terms of international sales—Ernest Renan stated outright that "Jesus was born at Nazareth, a small town of Galilee."[55] Writing in these scholars' wake, Wallace lavished his formidable erudition on a biblical episode that was under increasing critical pressure. A number of novelists instead followed the lead of Higher Criticism by eliding Jesus's Bethlehem birth. Karl Heumann's *Jeshua of Nazara* (1888), aptly subtitled "A Novel Grounded on the Result of Historical Research," begins in Nazareth.[56] An alternative option, used by novelists such as Martineau and Delitzsch, was to open with exhaustive descriptions of the hills of nearby Capernaum, the presumed center of Jesus's adult ministry and a site of great interest among nineteenth-century archeologists.

Unlike in the Christmas section of *Ben-Hur*, Wallace adopts a more critical approach to the project of narrating Jesus's early years in *The Boyhood of Christ*. Wallace's biographers understandably reserve little space for discussion of this work, as it does not appear to have garnered critical attention at the time of its publication. As a piece of metafiction, though, *The Boyhood of Christ* offers valuable insights not only into Wallace's creative process but also into his evolving public persona. In his second "tale of the Christ," Wallace re-centers his narrative emphasis from the fictional to the historical, whereas *Ben-Hur*'s extravagant plotlines give way to a more contemplative portraiture. Both shifts coincided with Wallace's emerging status as an internationally recognized biblical authority. *Ben-Hur*'s triumph in Sunday schools throughout the English-speaking world attested to the depth and scope of this authority, as did his lectures across the United States. In a sociological sense, Wallace's professional stature cannot be reduced to the formal innovations of his fiction any more than can, for example, Tolstoy's or Zola's be to theirs (two contemporaries who also took advantage of the novel's rise as a serious literary genre to become cultural authorities on a global scale). Still, analysis of the forms of *Ben-Hur* and *The Boyhood of Christ* can provide clues as to how Wallace surmounted the ostensible shortcomings of fiction by emphasizing its pictorial truths, particularly those truths of interest to U.S. Christian audiences.

In *The Boyhood of Christ*, the story's protagonist receives unexpected visitors on Christmas Eve. The narrator describes Nan and Puss as "more than girls, yet not quite young women."[57] They arrive from a neighboring dance "to hear Uncle Midas talk."[58] As others follow in their tread, by the end of the evening the old storyteller has won over the entire dance party for his audience. Yet rather than retelling the original Christmas story or reading aloud the relevant section from *Ben-Hur*, Uncle Midas settles on the question of what Christ had been like as a boy. He focuses on a ten-year period—from the flight into Egypt to Jesus's precocity at the temple in Jerusalem—that is not discussed in the Gospels. Such gaps in the Gospel record were popular subjects of speculative narrative among historians, novelists, and even literary forgers. In *The Unknown Life of Jesus Christ* (1894), for example, a major work of modern apocrypha, Nicholas Notovitch "translates" into French an allegedly ancient Tibetan account of Issa, a Jewish prophet who wanders through India between the ages of thirteen and twenty-nine before returning, fatefully, to his homeland. Within a few years of Notovitch's work, Jesus's tomb happened to be discovered in the city of Srinagar. In this counter-tradition, Jesus wanders through India after descending alive from the cross, a version of events proposed by Ghulam Ahmad, the founder of the Islamic movement Ahmadiyya. To this day, one can visit Jesus's Kashmiri tomb.

Uncle Midas, in comparison, proves reluctant to tell any tale that does not stand up to critical scrutiny. He instead guides his teenaged audience through a lesson in Higher Criticism. To transpose this approach to a Sunday-school context, Nan, Puss, and their peers resemble senior-grade scholars, with Uncle Midas as their eccentric yet engaging teacher. As he explains, the "authors of the four canonical Gospels were not biographers in the modern sense of the word" because "[i]n their great anxiety to get large facts set down imperishably they overlooked the small." Thus they elided such trivial details as "whether [Christ] had blue eyes or black, or was fair or dark, or tall or short, or lean or fat." In the early church, certain "men of sanctity," having enough time at their disposal to round out Christ's terse official biography, attempted to supply such "missing data."[59] Although Uncle Midas does not say as much outright, such guesswork was the modus operandi adopted by virtually all nineteenth-century Jesus historians and novelists (including Wallace in *Ben-Hur*). Renan, most notoriously, likened his *Vie de Jésus* to a "fifth Gospel" as if it could somehow supersede the canonical four. Yet even he admitted that his work was part "divination," part "conjecture."[60] Uncle Midas is more circumspect in his biblical revisionism; he confines himself to two apocryphal texts, the Infancy Gospel of Matthew and the Infancy Gospel of Thomas.[61] These non-canonical Gospels, both of which narrate Jesus's marvelous deeds in Egypt, are among the oldest extant accounts of his boyhood. After a close reading of several representative episodes from each, Uncle Midas rejects these Gospels' portrayals of the boy Christ as improbable and even impious: such early Christian apocrypha represent no more than "religious literary curiosities" and belong on the same shelf as the "Koran and the Mormon Bible."[62] The author of neither Infancy Gospel provides insight into Christ's character, Uncle Midas adds, although he concedes that the first one, a "devout old romancer,"[63] does at times spin a good yarn.

After this withering exercise in Higher Criticism, Uncle Midas is left with nothing to retell. Lest his audience leave disappointed, though, he embarks on a different task: how best to picture Christ as a boy. Throughout *The Boyhood of Christ*, Uncle Midas provides extended ekphrases of his favorite Renaissance paintings, including Carlo Dolce's *Ecce Homo* (ca. 1650), a work renowned for the kind of humanism to which Wallace aspired in his literary portraits of sacred figures. In the deluxe edition of *The Boyhood of Christ* issued by Harper & Brothers in 1889, reproductions of these paintings appear alongside the words with which Uncle Midas lovingly recreates them.[64] The task of picturing Christ posed unique challenges. Uncle Midas criticizes the supernatural flourishes of certain image traditions from the modern vantage point he adopts in relation to the Infancy Gospels: "The old painters, called upon to render this childish figure on canvas, would have insisted upon distinguishing it with a nimbus at least; some of them would have filled the air over his head with cherubs."[65] This criticism makes it more intriguing that although Uncle Midas refrains from telling a story where the Infancy Gospels had failed, he does attempt a literary portrait of Christ as a boy. Without overstepping the bounds of portraiture or genre painting, he permits himself the luxury of a few "outside facts" and "permissible touches of fancy":

> The boy's face comes to me very clearly. I imagine him by the roadside on a rock which he has climbed. . . . His head is raised in an effort at far sight. The light of an intensely brilliant sun is upon his countenance, which in general cast is oval and delicate. Under the folds of the handkerchief I see the forehead, covered by a mass of sunburnt blond hair, which the wind has taken liberties with and tossed into tufts.[66]

As the opening lines of this protracted portrait suggest, Uncle Midas does commit himself on such issues as Jesus's hair color. As I have argued elsewhere, his "delicate" and "blond" Jesus corresponds with *Ben-Hur*'s half-Jewish, half-Greek Jesus: a modern, racially inflected Christ type.[67]

More importantly, at the end of his impromptu Christmas Eve talk, Uncle Midas foregoes telling a story to paint a word picture instead. In

Ben-Hur Wallace had done both to a superlative degree. He integrates lengthy pictorial sequences into plotlines across the Eastern Roman Empire, from the wise men's journey along the lower Jordan to Ben-Hur's chariot race in Antioch. In *The Boyhood of Christ*, Wallace's conspicuous resistance to fiction is readily explained by his choice of subject matter: whereas the Christmas story that he retells in *Ben-Hur* is canonical, the Infancy Gospel of Matthew and the Infancy Gospel of Thomas are not (Higher Criticism likewise deemed the infancy stories unreliable from a non-canonical perspective).

Wallace's preference for pictures over stories in his later work may also reflect an increased burden of truth-telling that accompanied his rising cultural authority. Uncle Midas does not wish to mislead his young guests; therefore, he is scrupulous about pictorial details such as the "handkerchief" on the young Christ's head. The plausible basis for the handkerchief is ethnography of first-century Palestine. In the works of such contemporary biblical historians as Frederic Farrar and Franz Delitzsch, for example, the historical Jesus wears an ancient Hebrew equivalent of the modern Arabic keffiyeh.[68]

In the context of nineteenth-century literary styles, the perceived truth-value of pictures had long been central to the rhetorical strategies of literary realism. In the realist novel, plotlines that bear no direct relation to extra-literary events gain a semblance of reality from being set in geographically specific and pictorially simulated locations. Using the terms of Wallace's contemporary, Charles Sanders Peirce, novelists mobilize three types of signs to produce their ostensible portraits and landscapes: *icons*, which share some resemblance "in quality" with their objects; *indices*, which bear a "correspondence in fact"; and *symbols*, which relate to objects by means of convention.[69] Peirce uses the example of maps to clarify how indices differ from icons. A map, while mimicking a terrain's planar quality in an iconic sense, is not useful unless it also carries a "mark of known locality"; the index, not the icon, connects the map to a specific terrain, one that is contiguous with others within the interpreter's "experience of the world."[70] To extend Peirce's semiotic to *Ben-Hur*, Wallace deftly appropriates the indices of Christian iconography and biblical geography to underwrite the surface realism of his word pictures, whereas the word pictures themselves are symbols masquerading as icons.

In the case of Jesus, who is described at length from Ben-Hur's perspective during his baptism in the "river Jabbok," Wallace weaves pictorial flourishes and the odd modern touch with indices of ancient genealogy (7:V). In early and medieval Christian iconography, a given Christ image is recognizable only to the extent that it bears the markings of the "True Face." In Peirce's terms, what distinguishes an Eastern Orthodox "icon" from a mere painting of Christ is not its iconicity, which both image types share, but the former's indices, that is, a series of discrete, invariant traits that correspond point by point with those of the *mandylion*, or "Holy Cloth." As a perfect imprint, the mandylion represents a Peircian index in the most robust sense: the Holy Cloth and the True Face, as sign and object, correspond through direct physical contact. The legends of Veronica's Veil, Abgar's Cloth, and the Shroud of Turin offer differing accounts to corroborate this miraculous contact.

For his portrait in *Ben-Hur*, Wallace draws on a related medieval tradition: the letter from Lentulus to the Roman Senate, which purports to be a firsthand written description from the scene of Jesus's trial. According to the proconsul Lentulus, Jesus has "bluish-gray eyes," an "abundant beard," and a "faultless nose and mouth"; he also has hair the color of "ripe hazelnut," which is parted in the middle "after the pattern of the Nazarenes."[71] Wallace's Nazarene has "dark-blue" eyes; a soft "beard, which fell in waves over his throat to his breast"; "a delicacy of the nostrils and mouth"; and long, parted hair, "auburn in tint, with a tendency to reddish golden" (7:V). Neither in *Ben-Hur* nor elsewhere does Wallace acknowledge Lentulus's letter as a source. The apocryphal text is precisely the kind of pious fiction that Uncle Midas would have shelved away alongside the Infancy Gospels. Be that as it may, *Ben-Hur* does not simply paint the Nazarene on a blank canvas. Rather, through a set of long-familiar traits, Wallace's omniscient narrator indicates that the "stranger" whom Ben-Hur sees on the riverbank is Christ (7:V).

A similar conflation of icon, index, and symbol occurs in Wallace's literary landscapes. As one final example, Messala imprisons Ben-Hur's mother and sister in the Tower of Antonia in Jerusalem, where they contract leprosy. Not only does Wallace depict this tower and its environs in an exhaustive descriptive sequence, but in the deluxe 1892 Garfield edition of the novel, which incorporates dozens of photogravures and hundreds of hand-drawn illustrations of Holy Land sites (and also includes a letter from President Garfield to Wallace), a photograph with the caption "Tower of Antonia" appears alongside the text.[72] Notably, however, this photograph exists somewhat apart from the novel in that it functions neither as source material for, nor as an illustration of, Wallace's word pictures. What most directly connects image and text, or icon and symbol, is the place name (index) common to both. In the Garfield edition, moreover, the illustrator sketches two maps of the lower dungeon from the Tower of Antonia; Ben-Hur's mother and sister are hidden in a top secret cell, number VI, which is missing on one map but revealed on the other. The index separates the real image from the false even where both are sheer fantasy.

Wallace visited the Holy Land for the first time only after *Ben-Hur* was published. Most readers of his tale, including most Sunday-school scholars, had likewise never seen the land where Jesus walked. With Wallace's word pictures on one side (symbols), supplemental images on the other (icons), and place names on both (indices), the Garfield edition served as an effective substitute. For countless readers in the United States and abroad, Wallace and his publisher recreated the Holy Land in all the wonder of its presence.[73]

By the turn of the twentieth century, Wallace's pictorial virtuosity was on full display in the lesson plans of Sunday schools as much as it was in Harper's numerous illustrated editions of his biblical fiction. Ultimately, the fortunes of his word pictures faded as more modern media began to appropriate their imagistic allure. In the long-running Broadway production of *Ben-Hur,* Jesus was portrayed (with Wallace's approval) by a 25,000-candlepower light[74]: a rough equivalent of the Pauline *lux de caelo* for the industrial age. In the film adaptations, the Nazarene's face became subject to the kind of image ban that Wallace daringly transgressed. In Fred Niblo's *Ben-Hur* (1925), for instance, Jesus is reduced to

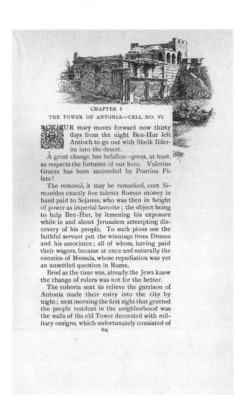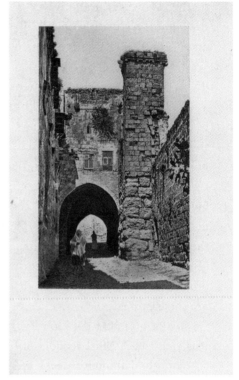

3. Illustration and photograph of the Tower of Antonia from the Garfield edition of *Ben-Hur* (1892).

the illuminated arms of an uncredited actor, whereas in William Wyler's 1959 version the actor standing in for the Nazarene is shot from behind. In Steve Shill's 2010 *Ben-Hur* miniseries, Wallace's Jesus at last turns his face toward the camera.

In Wallace's lifetime and in a different medium, his word pictures of the Nazarene and of Palestine grounded his imaginative plotlines in historical and even sacred reality. The picture compensates for the license of fiction. Wallace thus responded to the traditional evangelical objection to the novel as a narrative of falsehoods by fortifying *Ben-Hur* with truths of a non-narrative kind. He was convinced that his word pictures were adequate to their referents. While writing *Ben-Hur*, Wallace labored to become "familiar with . . . history and geography" of the land his fictive creations traveled through: "I must be able to paint it, water, land, sky, in actual colors." When he finally reached the Holy Land in 1883, he traced Ben-Hur's path all the way to Jerusalem, testing the accuracy of his tale's descriptions at every step. He was pleased to find that there was no need "to make a single change to the text of the book": everything was just as he had pictured it.[75]

Holy Lands, Restoration, and Zionism in Ben-Hur

HILTON OBENZINGER

As *Ben-Hur* approaches the Crucifixion scene and a description of the catacombs of Rome, a young Jew makes his way by foot, alone, up a rough road. He does not have "the vexed anxious expression which marks a man going forward uncertain of the way, but rather the air with which one approaches an old acquaintance after a long separation." After moving off "the beaten track" to the summit of the mountain, this traveler "comes to a dead stop, arrested as if by a strong hand" to take in the vista. "Then one might have seen his eyes dilate, his cheeks flush, his breath quicken, effects all of one bright sweeping glance at what lay before him." With this breath-quickening prospect, the narrator pauses to reveal that the "traveller, good reader, was no other than Ben-Hur; the spectacle, Jerusalem" (6:III).

In Lew Wallace's day, a "good reader" of Holy Land travel books would easily recognize the "old acquaintance" in this scene: when nineteenth-century Americans journeyed to where Jesus had walked, a dramatic first sight of the Holy City typically elicited tears and prayers. Like other Holy Land travel accounts, *Ben-Hur* invites the reader to perceive the sacred past beneath the profane present: to peer through the surface and read the hidden text of a palimpsest. What the traveler looks at, Wallace reports, is "not the Holy City of to-day, but the Holy City as left by Herod—the Holy City of the Christ. Beautiful yet, as seen from old Olivet, what must it have been then?" The reader joins Ben-Hur to make "the survey at leisure," regarding the same view that has been seen since "by a great variety of persons, under circumstances surpassingly singular." The narrator

74

remarks that Roman, Islamic, and Crusader conquerors had stood at this high place. More recently, though, the vista had been seen by a conqueror of a different sort: "by many a pilgrim from the great New World, which waited discovery nearly fifteen hundred years after the time of our story." According to Wallace, the lofty view is even more charged because no one has stood at this prospect "with sensations more keenly poignant, more sadly sweet, more proudly bitter, than Ben-Hur" (6:III). In this story of injustice, revenge, conversion, and restoration, the boy-turned-man, who was once ripped from his family, has finally come home.

At this point in the novel, the U.S. reader strongly identifies with the Jewish hero. Particularly evocative are "the pleasures and griefs of patriotism common to every Jew of the period" that impel Ben-Hur's—and his people's—yearning for restoration. Most overtly, his sister and widowed mother await "restoration to all they had lost—home, society, property, son and brother!" (6:II). I argue that Wallace's identification of the United States with ancient Palestine, and the U.S. citizen with the "restored" Jew, functions as justification of U.S. nationalist expansionism. Although in Wallace's America Jews were often marginalized, *Ben-Hur* invites readers to identify *ancient* Jews as patriots resisting the Roman emperor in God's name, just as American colonists had resisted King George III.

Most of the Jews in Wallace's novel will be spiritually lost, however, because they do not follow Ben-Hur's path to Christ; by mocking Jesus before the Crucifixion, they earn the scorn doled on them by late-nineteenth-century U.S. Christians. That is all the more reason, though, for Christian readers to sympathize with the newly converted Jews whose rebellion against the Roman Empire reaches a spiritual level: the Holy Land's sacred geography is now within the heart and available to all nations. An emergent universal religion rises from Rome's catacombs to overcome the vicious pagan empire. Like the fallen people who have been restored (as Christians) to help create a new empire of sublime holiness, Protestant Americans can assure themselves that they stand at the vanguard of a *moral* empire: "out of that vast tomb Christianity issued to supersede the Caesars" (8:X).

Eran Shalev argues elsewhere in this volume that although Rome was traditionally regarded as a forerunner for the United States, by 1880

Americans regarded the Roman Empire with ambivalence. Amy Kaplan initiated this discussion. "Wallace offers America a way out of the bind of how to be like Rome while avoiding its decline," she explained in 2009.

> The redemption promised by Christianity represents a new benevolent empire that abjures force and revenge. It is an anti-imperial empire, as the United States would represent itself throughout the twentieth century and indeed down to the present. Roman absolutism and Judean nationalism are subsumed and transcended by Christian universalism, which is a figure for America.[1]

Ben-Hur promotes this impossible notion of a good colonizing empire that is also anti-colonial by Americanizing the Holy Land and the narrative of Jewish restoration.

◆   ◆   ◆

Americans long imagined their land as the New Israel and its settlers as the New Jews. Although *Ben-Hur* became an international best seller, it resonated in a particular way for U.S. readers because it draws on a complex set of commitments and anxieties concerning America as a new Holy Land. A crucial aspect of early English settlement was a profound sense of providential destiny spun as a narrative of biblical parallels— even re-enactments—within a larger account of Christ's return. Cotton Mather coined the term "Christianography" to describe a practice of reading typological meanings of prophetic destiny in the American landscape. This practice involves a figural overlay, or yoking, of biblical locales and characters with the New World's geography (and destiny).[2] The ways in which citizenship, territory, and sacred text were conflated became an important component of the settler-colonial imagination, particularly in affirming the United States' divine mission, whether in the form of the "city upon a hill" or the more secularized manifest destiny.

The doctrine of Jewish restoration, which saw the return of the oldest nation to its glory, was a crucial element in this sense of destiny. Belief in Jewish restoration was so widespread among eighteenth- and nineteenth-century thinkers, whether radical deists or conservative biblical literalists, it was "endemic to American culture."[3] Belief in Jewish restoration paralleled or reinforced the notion that the settlers of the New Israel in North

America would also be restored, so to speak, in that their colonial presence would be made "natural" by God's approval: if the old Jews could be restored to their nation, then surely the new, typological ones settling the North American continent could be restored as well. In this way, the nationalism of America's settler society was given religious significance.

At the time of *Ben-Hur*'s publication, there was a growing trend to modify the doctrine of Jewish restoration to reinforce support for Jewish settlement in Palestine. Premillennialists shifted the narrative, asserting that apocalyptic destruction (in such scenarios as the advent of the Antichrist and the battle of Armageddon) would *precede* Christ's return and his rule during a thousand years of peace. The postmillennialist narrative saw the Second Coming taking place *after* Christian perfection had achieved the thousand years of peace. The change from post- to premillennialist doctrine meant that Jews did not need to convert to return to the Holy Land; once Christ saved the chosen people from total destruction, Jews would worship him as the Messiah as part of the overall end-days scenario.

A dramatic enactment of such a vision of parallel restorations is found in a Mormon elder's journey to Jerusalem in 1841 (although additional narratives in the *Book of Mormon* and doctrines of the new religion made the figure of the two Holy Lands even more complex). In one of the earliest official acts of the Latter-Day Saints, Elder Orson Hyde travelled to the Holy City to hold a ceremony announcing Jews' imminent restoration to the old Holy Land and the Latter-Day Saints' simultaneous ascent in the new one. In Jerusalem he prayed that God "would not only revolutionize this country [Palestine], but renovate and make it glorious" along with the new Zion in North America.[4]

The modern Zionist movement was only in its infancy at this time: *Ben-Hur* debuted just before Jewish settlement in Palestine began to accelerate in 1882. Nonetheless, the ways in which Wallace dramatizes links between the Holy Land and Christian-defined Jewish nationalism helped to create the grounds for U.S. support of that incipient colonial movement, regardless of the version of the Jewish restoration doctrine to which readers adhered. At the same time, aspects of Wallace's life before and after writing the book aided in his fictional creation and extended its ideological impact by underscoring how deeply entwined the narrative of Jewish restoration was with America's settler-colonial dynamics. Although I focus mainly on the novel in this essay, I also draw on Wallace's biography to unpack aspects of U.S. settler-colonial nationalism and widespread support for early Zionism.

As one columnist wrote in the *Nation* after Wallace's death in 1905, *Ben-Hur*'s influence was expansive: "Superintendent, pastor, and stray visitor, called on for a few remarks, reminded everybody at least once in three months that the most vivid picture of the Holy Land in the time of Christ was in 'Ben Hur.'" Wallace's attention to detail was particularly appreciated by the devout: his novel's "descriptions of Palestine and its religiosity won it eager readers," the columnist asserted, "among the millions who were bred to regard novels as hell broth."[5] One of Wallace's favored tactics was to bring the reader within the narrative setting. For example, in *Ben-Hur* he describes the Holy Land as follows:

> Nowadays, travellers in the Holy Land looking for the famous place with the beautiful name, the King's Garden, descend the bed of the Cedron or the curve of Gihon and Hinnom as far as the old well En-rogel, take a drink of the sweet living water, and stop, having reached the limit of the interesting in that direction. . . . [T]he travellers glance at the Mount of Offence standing in rugged stateliness at their right hand, and then at the Hill of Evil Counsel over on the left, in which, if they be well up in Scriptural history and in the traditions rabbinical and monkish, they will find a certain interest not to be overcome by superstitious horror. (6:V)

Readers as imagined travelers often were "well up in Scriptural history." However, the details of Palestine's geography and the ethnography of ancient Jews, Romans, and others were crucial for establishing the verisimilitude of Wallace's sacred fiction.

Wallace later described the "painstaking" nature of his labor to achieve realistic accuracy: "Of the more than seven years given the book, the least part was occupied in actual composition. Research and investigation consumed most of the appropriated time." He devoted himself particularly to geographical accuracy: "I examined catalogues of books and maps, and sent for everything likely to be useful. I wrote with a chart always before my eyes—a German publication, showing the towns and villages, all sacred places, the heights, the depressions, the passes, trails, and distances." Wallace remembered, later, how his years in Constantinople as the U.S. ambassador allowed him "to visit Jerusalem and Judea, under the most favorable circumstances possible." While there, he was able to confirm "the accuracy of the descriptions given in *Ben-Hur*." As he wrote in his autobiography:

> Then I went to the top of Olivet and saw the identical stone, as I thought, upon which my hero sat when he returned from the galley life. . . . At every point of the journey over which I traced his steps to Jerusalem, I found the descriptive details true to the existing objects and scenes, and I find no reason for making a single change in the text of the book.[6]

Such realism and accuracy helped to create a sense of ownership in readers steeped in religious sensibilities. Paul Gutjahr, summarizing the effect of veracity resulting from Wallace's attention to detail, explains why "readers felt they were acquiring accurate information about first-century Palestine." Though exciting, indubitably, in many descriptive scenes *Ben-Hur*

> became more than a simple adventure tale. Readers could learn things about the time in which Jesus lived and point to the educative qualities of the book as a reason for reading it. They could also point to the obvious historicity of the book's setting as a reason to believe in the historicity of the figure of Jesus.[7]

Although informed by research and respect for scripture, Wallace's book never purported to be anything but fiction. This allowed *Ben-Hur* to escape the need for confirming human testimony; instead, archaeology and other sciences were called upon as unimpeachable witnesses. Once readers perceived the basis of the book as accurate, they could confirm the mythic knowledge through the extension of their imaginations. By drawing readers in with a "you-are-there" sense of realism, Wallace's effort to replicate the past helped to instill a sense of common possession because the author and the reader share the imagined scene.

Wallace's completion of the novel during his stint as the territorial governor of New Mexico made the associations between the United States and the Middle East even more intriguing. He noted the resemblance between the New Mexican landscape and the landscape of the Middle East, writing in a report: "the Rio Grande Valley is more nearly a duplication of the region of the Nile than any other of which I have knowledge." Never having traveled overseas at that time, Wallace had no direct knowledge of the Nile. Still, his biographers believe that the Southwest "helped Wallace's sense of place" while he wrote *Ben-Hur*.[8] Long afterward, a member of a surveying team told his relatives that he remembered Wallace sitting around campfires in New Mexico and spinning tales of the three kings and other moments from the novel.[9]

Wallace's wife Susan makes the comparison between the Southwest and the Holy Land explicit in her book, *The Land of the Pueblos* (1888):

> There was much to remind us of Bible pictures; the low adobe houses, the flocks with the herdsman coming to drink at the shallow stream, the clambering goats in scanty pastures high up the rocks, shaking their beards at the passing strangers, the kids bleating by their mothers, the Mexican women, straight as a rule, carrying water-jars on head or shoulder, like maidens of Palestine. Now and then an old black shawl, melancholy remnant of the gay rebosa, shrouding an olive forehead, suggested the veiled face of the gentle Rebecca.

Susan Wallace does make distinctions between the visual impacts of New Mexico and the Middle East, drawing on widely held racial categories: "The lofty presence, the high eagle features of the Jewish race, the lustrous eyes of the Orient are not here," she told her readers; "nor is the barren magnificence of New Mexico more than a suggestion of the land once the glory of all lands."[10] Even negative comparisons give weight, however, to the possibilities of parallel landscapes and peoples.

◆   ◆   ◆

Wallace did not rely only on scrupulous research and associations of U.S. geography with the Middle East. He also used *Ben-Hur*'s thick descriptions to heighten identification with the Holy Land through popular narrative styles that had not previously been deployed in religious literature. As a columnist for the *Nation* described it in 1905, *Ben-Hur* has "an elaborated manner which is gorgeous with Oriental imagery" that Wallace combined with the Bible, Edward Gibbon's history of Rome, and historical romances such as *The Count of Monte Cristo* (1844). At the same time, *Ben-Hur* is "the gilded vehicle for characters and incidents which make a dime novel about bandits and beauties seem dull and lifeless." Uniquely then, this tale of the Christ

> gives us Crimson Dick, Old Sleuth, Jesse James, and the Queen of the Outlaws combined with the strongest religious influences; it is as edifying as a prizefight in a Young Men's Christian Association—unrestrained excitement and profound piety.

The "hair-raising adventure sensation in every five pages," which thrilled readers, set Jesus within the secular frame of detective stories and cheap Westerns—genres against which conservative Christians would rail otherwise.[11] *Ben-Hur* echoes other popular genres too: Judah Ben-Hur's capture recalls Indian captivity tales, whereas his bondage in the galley echoes slave narratives and brings to mind early nineteenth-century accounts of Americans captured by North African (Barbary Coast) corsairs. Ben-Hur's rise from captivity also evokes Horatio Alger novels such as *Ragged Dick* (1869): a poor-but-good boy succeeds because of luck and pluck. That association is furthered by the fact that Ben-Hur becomes the richest man in the Roman Empire: an appeal to the Gilded Age Gospel of wealth equating with God's beneficence.

Still, it is the Western dime novel that resonates most powerfully with *Ben-Hur*. Blake Allmendinger's essay "Toga! Toga!" draws on John Cawelti and Will Wright's analyses of the Western as a genre to point out *Ben-Hur*'s similarities.[12] Wallace set his tale at an epochal juncture of history, the clash between "civilization" and "savagery," with the charioteer as the hero who achieves revenge and then, after his conversion, redemption. The law-abiding people of the town are the Jews, whereas the "savages" or bandits are the Romans, with Ben-Hur as the hero caught between the clashing spheres. In the formula Western, the honest citizens of a small town are set upon by a large landholder or by bandits; typically, the hero saves them through reluctant though regenerative violence. The hero is drawn to the schoolmarm-type woman represented in *Ben-Hur* by Esther, a modest, loyal Jew. He is tempted by the saloon seductress: in *Ben-Hur*, the worldly Egyptian Iras.

Unlike most Westerns, though, Wallace's tale works—quoting Margaret Malamud—to an "archetypal 'vengeance' plot: the word 'vengeance' appears more frequently than just about any other word in Wallace's novel." Swearing vengeance when his sister and widowed mother are dragged off to prison, Ben-Hur threatens revenge when he believes they are dead; indeed, he races against Messala for vengeance. In addition, when he trains Israelite troops to fight Rome in anticipation of the uprising he expects Jesus will lead, it is for revenge as much as liberation. Malamud points out that "the key moment in the Western is the struggle or contest between hero and villain, the showdown usually being a gunfight. In *Ben-Hur* it is the violent confrontation between Ben-Hur and Messala in the chariot race, a cathartic act of violence, which leaves Ben-Hur ready to embrace Christianity."[13] Ben-Hur is raised to a higher level by his conversion to the spiritual path from a life of vengeance and brute violence.

Nevertheless, Wallace does exhibit some ambivalence toward this division of civilization from savagery. As Malamud observes, "Roman Judea is a frontier where the oppressive might of Rome clashed with the moral uprightness of its colonized Jewish inhabitants. The Romans are irreligious outsiders who reject the Jewish way of life . . . military overlords who have mastered the tools of violence."[14] In the divide of settler-colonial conquest, however, the Jews, as the native people, should be the violent savages while the Romans represent carriers of civilization. Wallace reworks this schematic by making the Jews, as proto-Christians who believe in the true God, the bearers of a finer civilization who fight for freedom against a colonizer.

Wallace's representation of oppressed Jews bearing the future of human civilization makes possible the idea of a good colonizing empire that is at the same time anti-colonial. In the context of postbellum America, such logic will allow, for example, conquest of the Philippines according to the rationalization that it was God's will that Anglo-Saxon conquerors uplift the natives.

◆   ◆   ◆

The convergence in *Ben-Hur* of Holy Land narratives with U.S. expansionism had roots in Wallace's experiences. Born in 1827, he witnessed many dynamics of U.S. development, including narratives of settler-colonialism and the early moments of settlement in Palestine. As governor of New Mexico he saw more than just landscapes that were similar to Palestine; he also saw, from a position of great responsibility, a complex frontier of clashing peoples and cultures: descendants of the original Spanish settlers, as well as Pueblo Indians, Apaches and Navajos, all of whom suffered from (and responded to) the violent lawlessness of Anglo settlers vying for control of land and resources. But before his 1877–80 stint in New Mexico, Wallace grew up in Indiana, the son of the governor, when Indian wars still raged in the region. As a young man, he fought in the war against Mexico, fully embracing manifest destiny; later, he fought for the North in the Civil War and served on the tribunal that condemned the plotters of Lincoln's assassination. All of this information is well known; oft forgotten, however, is that despite joining the U.S. war against Mexico in 1846, Wallace fought with Benito Juarez against French colonial rule in 1865. In 1873 he published *The Fair God*, a novel about the Spanish conquest that indicates an ambivalent attitude toward conquistadors and Aztecs.

Wallace began writing his first novel long before he participated in the U.S. war with Mexico. His inspiration for the book was William H. Prescott's *History of the Conquest of Mexico* (1843). Wallace's rendition was a Walter Scott–style novel about Hernán Cortés's incursion, which he presented as a translated manuscript written by an Aztec convert to Christianity. Adumbrations of *Ben-Hur* can be seen when the narrator in *The Fair God* refers to the crowds of people "made swift by alarm and curiosity" racing ahead of Cortés "like Jews to the Passover." In addition, Cortés exclaims upon entering Tenochtitlán, the Aztec capital, that "true Christian in a land of unbelievers never beheld a city like this. . . . I care not if you number Antioch and the Holy City of the Sepulchre among them," neither could "be put in comparison with this infidel stronghold."[15]

More deeply anticipative of *Ben-Hur* was Wallace's ability to tell the story mainly from the Aztec point of view. As his biographers note, *The Fair God* bespeaks awareness of how "Juarez's struggle against Maximilian parallels the earlier conflict between Aztecs and Spaniards." Robert and Katharine Morsberger remark that Wallace wrote from a romanticized native vantage point despite the increasing ferocity of U.S. militarism against aboriginal Americans: while he "was completing *The Fair God*," they explain in *Lew Wallace: Militant Romantic* (1980), "the United States had embarked on a program of conquest of the Indian lands" in which native peoples fought "a defensive war, comparable to the Aztec defense of Mexico." The Morsbergers add that although Wallace would "direct operations against the Mescalero Apaches in New Mexico . . . his sympathies in *The Fair God* are primarily for the Indians and against the conquerors, even though *The Fair God* was published at the height of the Indian wars and just three years before the battle of the Little Big Horn."[16]

Wallace could fight to dismember a country and then join in the battle against foreign, imperialist domination of the same country. He could identify with resistance to empire and then go to war against Apaches who fought colonial control by an encroaching empire. In anticipation of *Ben Hur*, he was able to be a soldier of expansion—a U.S. conquistador—while taking the unusual position of identifying with those who resisted the expansion. Paradoxical as these shifting viewpoints may seem, it is an aspect of colonial consciousness: the ability to romanticize the defeated indigene as a noble relic of the past and to absorb the native as a component of the new society's cultural makeup. Seen from this vantage, the natives' defeat enriches the colonists' subjectivity, as expropriating the land enriches the colonists' objective conditions.

After writing *Ben-Hur*, Wallace continued his practice of shifting perspectives: as U.S. ambassador to the Ottoman Empire, for example, he pleaded for the fate of Jewish refugees from Russia and Rumania in Jerusalem. He also "directed the attention of the State Department to the subject of Jewish colonization," although he simultaneously defended the reputation of the empire's sultan, whom he had befriended beyond his diplomatic role.[17] Later, he published *The Prince of India; or, Why Constantinople Fell* (1893), a novel about the Islamic conquest of the Byzantine Empire that demonstrates the same ability to embrace vantage points that were uncommon among U.S. citizens, including that of a Moslem conqueror. When war broke out with Spain in 1898 Wallace enthusiastically supported what he first perceived as a war to support liberation from

Spanish colonial rule. However, as the United States moved to annex the Philippines after Spain's defeat, he joined Mark Twain and others to protest the annexation of the newly liberated colony and the counterinsurgency war that was waged against the Filipino independence movement. Wallace could entertain the idea of a benevolent intervention yet quickly switch to the vantage point of the indigenous people once the United States took the role of new colonial master.

◆   ◆   ◆

Although *Ben-Hur* was unusual because it featured Jews and depicted Jewish nationalism as heroic, it was not the first non-Jewish novel to do so. George Eliot's *Daniel Deronda* (1876) revolves around a search for identity that leads a well-mannered, decent Englishman—the title character—to discover that he is a Jew. Eliot presents Jews as fully embodied, sympathetic characters, rather than stereotypes like Fagin and Shylock. Deronda awakens to his racial essence by meeting Jews, and he becomes drawn to a fully articulated expression of Zionist aspirations. In the words of the visionary character Mordecai, Jews should take on "again the character of a nationality" to revive "the organic centre" of their peoplehood with "a land and a polity."[18]

Mordecai echoes Lord Palmerston and other Christian Zionists, but with this difference: conversion has nothing to do with the vision of restoration in *Daniel Deronda*. Instead, Eliot advances something closer to a dominant strand in Jewish Zionism: a romantic racialism in which "the Hebrew blood which has maintained its vigor in all climates" will flower to "redeem the soil from debauched and paupered conquerors." This characterization makes Arabs in Palestine usurpers of a purer, more original past who must be supplanted by Jews who return to bring progress to a backward land. This vision expresses sacred nationalism's progressive role as it seeks "to found a new Jewish polity, grand, simple, just, like the old—a republic where there is equality of protection, an equality which shone like a star on the forehead of our ancient community, and gave it more than the brightness of Western freedom amid the despotisms of the East."

Through Mordecai's vision, Eliot puts into words a theme that would become persistent in the growth of political Zionism: employing as a model the settler-colonial development of the United States, which commemorated its centennial at the time of *Daniel Deronda*'s publication. Mordecai argues for the possibility of mass Jewish settlement in Palestine with the observation that it has been just "two centuries since a vessel carried over the ocean the beginning of the great North American nation." That seemingly impossible colonial project having taken root, "[t]he people grew like meeting waters—they were various in habit and sect—there came a time, a century ago, when they needed a polity, and there were heroes of peace among them. What had they to form a polity with but memories of Europe, corrected by the vision of a better?"[19]

Wallace may have read Eliot's novel, or at least her advocacy of a Jewish nation resuscitated by way of settlement circulated through Anglophone culture. In 1891, a Chicago businessman, Methodist Episcopal lay worker, and Christian Zionist wrote the first U.S. petition to support Jewish colonization of Palestine. "Why not give Palestine back to [the Jews] again?" argued William E. Blackstone in "Palestine for the Jews." "According to God's distribution of nations, it is their home, an inalienable possession, from which they were expelled by force. . . . Why shall not the powers which under the treaty of Berlin, in 1878, gave Bulgaria to the Bulgarians and Servia to the Servians now give Palestine back to the Jews? . . . Let us now restore them to the land of which they were so cruelly despoiled by our Roman ancestors."[20] Although Blackstone couched his petition to President Benjamin Harrison in secular, humanitarian terms, he was the author of *Jesus Is Coming* (1878), an immensely popular tract advocating premillennial theology, especially the need for Jews to return to the Holy Land as a condition for Christ's Second Coming.

With publication of Theodor Herzl's *Der Judenstaat* (1896), the manifesto to will a Jewish settler nation into existence, the modern Zionist movement took its ideological shape. *Ben-Hur* appeared in the midst of this ferment at a key juncture in the origins of a narrative of national restoration through settlement. In this narrative, support for Jews in the old Holy Land became a seemingly natural extension of national renewal for all forms of Western nationalism, whether British or American, but especially for the new nation that was already redeemed in North America.

In the scene with which this essay began, where Judah Ben-Hur climbs a hilltop to view Jerusalem, Wallace describes how his protagonist scans the city. Ben-Hur notes one by one all of the buildings and land-marks until "he singled out the palace of Herod." The narrator then asks, "what could he but think of the King Who Was Coming, to whom he was himself devoted, whose path he had undertaken to smooth, whose empty hands he dreamed of filling? And forward ran his fancy to the day the new King should come to claim his own and take possession of it." In Ben-Hur's fantasy the multitudes of Israel would then "sing rejoicing because the Lord had conquered and given them the world" (6:III). He has not yet learned of the spiritual conquest of the new, Christian dispensation; he still imagines the Jewish Messiah as the political leader who will over-throw the Romans.

Here Wallace pauses, steps out of the narrative to reflect on the nature of dreams and reality, and comments at the end of his reflection: "Let no one smile at Ben-Hur for doing that which he himself would have done at that time and place under the same circumstances" (6:III). Susan Wallace thought that this passage was so important that she excerpted it from the book (minus the concluding reference to Ben-Hur) to place it at the end of the autobiography that she completed for her husband after his death. Wallace began his autobiography with a declaration that he was a Chris-tian; however, he asserted sporadically in that book, and in other writings, that he avoided theology and doctrines. He owed no loyalty, he professed, to any Protestant denomination, he did not go to any single church, and he learned to believe in the Bible's truth through the force of imagination as he wrote *Ben-Hur*. This profession makes his meditation on dreams, in the midst of his tale of the Christ, a means to grasp his structure of belief:

> Men speak of dreaming as if it were a phenomenon of night and sleep. They should know better. All results achieved by us are self-promised, and all self-promises are made in dreams awake. Dreaming is the relief of labor, the wine that sustains us in act. We learn to love labor, not for itself, but for the opportunity it furnishes for dreaming, which is the great under-monotone of real life, unheard, unnoticed, because of its constancy. Living is dreaming. Only in the grave are there no dreams. (6:III)

Here, Wallace appealed to popular commonsense attitudes about the rela-tionship of will to action. By attaching the Gospel story (at least, glimpses of it) to a thrilling tale of loss, revenge, national resistance, and restoration, he brought Jesus into the secular realm of daily life. He projected a popular un-churched Christianity that could serve almost as a civil religion, and he promoted a religiosity as spectacular entertainment that heralded a consumer culture available to all. The Pope praised *Ben-Hur* at the same time as many Jews enjoyed the then-unusual figure of a muscular Jewish hero at the center of the story. The novel's imagined revelation added to the sense that U.S. providential destiny and Jewish restoration were parallel dreams that could be achieved by self-promise: they could be willed into existence.

◆ ◆ ◆

As Wallace's book became the steadiest seller of the nineteenth century, other Americans explored the implications of merging sensationalism, spectacle, nationalism, and religiosity. *Ben-Hur*'s blurring of the boundaries between the sacred and the secular led to an enormously successful stage production that opened in 1899 and was produced by Abraham L. Erlanger and Marc Klaw, who were both Jewish. Six decades later, another Jew, William Wyler, directed the 1959 film version of *Ben-Hur* starring Charlton Heston. Wallace's novel anticipated Jewish restoration; Wyler's film was released after restoration had become a fait accompli and the state of Israel had been established. In many respects the screenplay departs radically from the book (e.g., no Iras as temptress to complicate the romance). However, the basic story of injustice, revenge, and redemption remains, along with the key scenes of slavery in a Roman galley, the chariot race, and the fragments of various Gospels. The film does not need to draw as heavily upon the Holy Land travel book as Wallace did for a realist depiction of the terrain and sense of historicity. In fact, most of the Holy Land shown in the film is depicted in close shots of narrow Jerusalem streets and domestic interiors or in spectacular shots of imperial action and tableaux of Gospel events. Viewers of this film, just like readers of the novel, are expected to be so familiar with the Bible's account of Jesus that key moments or allusions are all that are needed. The cinemascope epic, grandiose and inescapable, saturates viewers with immediacy and realism to provide an even more imposing sense of portentous accuracy than Wallace's book. As in the book, though, Jesus is mainly viewed from the back or from great distance to conjure the sacred by discrete vagueness.

In *Epic Encounters: Culture, Media, and U.S. Interests in the Middle East, 1945–2000* (2001), Melani McAlister offers a perceptive study of the 1959 *Ben-Hur* as well as the other biblical epics that were very popular in the 1950s, such as *The Ten Commandments* (1956), *The Robe* (1953), and *Quo Vadis* (1951). "Like the Holy Land images of the nineteenth century," she writes, "epic films promised historical and religious knowledge, combined with the promise of 'views' and spectacle." Wyler's *Ben-Hur*, however, does not focus on the typical, studied view of Jerusalem, as Wallace's novel had. It does set most of its action there; even the chariot race has been moved to the Holy City, providing a vista of mountains in the background overlooking an immense amphitheater. McAlister observes that the "moral and political logic" of the film is constructed "through the organization of space" in three broad categories. Imperial spaces of excess and power are mostly staged with wide shots, such as the imperial palace. Slave spaces concentrate on galley scenes, and a third type of space, dominated by indoor scenes or close-ups of ordinary Jews, "is best described as 'nationalist' space" because "it represents the democratic character of the anti-imperial opposition, as well as promise and hope of freedom for the Jews who struggle against Rome."[21]

Using these spaces, Wyler's *Ben-Hur* presents the narratives of empire and resistance within the context of the early stages of the Cold War. If the brutal empire is imagined as the Soviet Union, the Jewish national resistance alludes to the material presence of the recently born state of Israel, which could be embraced by the new constructions of "Judeo-Christian" heritage and Western powers. The fact that Heston, already having played Moses in *The Ten Commandments*, projected U.S. masculinity as the Jewish hero emphasized the conflation of Hebrew, Christian, and American; that Heston's love interest, Esther, was played by Israeli actress Haya Harareet underscored the bond between the United States and the new state. McAlister also shows how the film complicates the imperial resistance dynamic even further. In the 1950s, the United States saw itself as offering "benevolent supremacy" to aid the newly emerging former colonies of Britain and of other receding empires against the ascendancy of the Soviet Union. Like other biblical film epics of the time, Wyler's *Ben-Hur* seems to equate "Hebrews/Christians with Americans and atheistic or idolatrous

Romans/Egyptians with communists." At the same time, though, Wyler's *Ben-Hur* "invites an interpretation of 'the people' as the formerly colonized peoples of the third world."[22]

The alliance between Ben-Hur and Sheik Ilderim is even more central in the film. In a scene unlike anything Wallace wrote, the sheik hands Ben-Hur a Star of David to wear during the chariot race, declaring that it should "shine out for your people and my people together, and blind the eyes of Rome!"[23] Today, given Israel's continuing occupation and expansion, it is hard to imagine Arabs supporting Israel. But in the 1950s an idea that Israel, newly independent from British rule, could be an ally of other anti-colonial struggles while opposing the Soviet Union was still being promoted by Israeli and Western governments, despite Israel's collusion with the British and French against Egypt in 1956.

Leon Uris's *Exodus* (1958), published just a year before Wyler's biblical epic, also became a huge best seller, and a film version starring Paul Newman was released in 1960. As novel and film, *Exodus* established a popular U.S. narrative for the creation of the state of Israel: it employed a Zionist interpretation of Jewish history along with allusions to America's frontier history. Here too the Western genre plays a role (no surprise given that Uris was the screenwriter for *Gunfight at the O.K. Corral* [1957]). Within a short period of time, these cultural performances formed a constellation of interlocking narratives invoking the frontier, resistance to empire (whether Roman, British, or Soviet), the benevolence of settler-colonial societies, and the new, secularized spirituality of the Judeo-Christian heritage. Simultaneously, Heston's heightened masculinity created the image of a heroic Jew conflated with America's rugged individualism. "Living is dreaming," Wallace wrote (6:III). Yet it is also clear that dreaming—at least as mythic narrative—is living.

"In the Service of Christianity"

Ben-Hur and the "Redemption" of the American Theater, 1899–1920

HOWARD MILLER

Most Americans today know Lew Wallace's novel *Ben-Hur: A Tale of the Christ* because they have seen all or part of the epic 1959 film adaptation, including its exciting chariot race. Some even know that there is a silent cinematic adaptation from 1925 in which the chariot race is even more thrilling. Almost no one has read the actual novel, and even fewer recall seeing the stage version of *Ben-Hur* that toured the United States, Canada, England, and Australia from 1899 to 1920, was seen by at least ten million people, and earned upwards of $20 million.[1] Hailed as the most stupendous theatrical event of that time, the show traveled in special trains of at least nine cars, which were filled with dozens of horses, a few camels, a cast and crew of between 200 and 350 people, and tons of costumes, scenery, and stage equipment.[2] The extravaganza toured almost every state that had a theater large enough to accommodate its gargantuan requirements. This "mighty play," without precedent or peer, was "the wonder of the age."[3]

Debuting during the last days of the nineteenth century, the stage version of *Ben-Hur* was hailed as the culmination of the best of one century

I would like to express my deep appreciation to my research assistant, Dr. Milanne S. Hahn of Austin, TX, who graciously performed with consummate professional skill the thankless task of digitizing the microfilm of the scrapbook. The research for this essay could not have been done without her assistance.

and a "beacon" into an even better one, in which it would set the standard for theatrical excellence.[4] *Ben-Hur* did have a singularly important effect on U.S. theater and the society that supported it. Its transcontinental tours provided a shared cultural experience for a nation that was still, even in the early twentieth century, healing from the wounds of the Civil War. The sheer size and magnificence of the production raised the bar for staged spectacle. In addition, *Ben-Hur*'s huge profits helped finance the early twentieth-century syndicate war in which the play's producers, Marc Klaw and Abraham Erlanger, fought for control of the U.S. theater.[5] This duo also spent upwards of $1 million to enlarge and improve the facilities of the nation's theaters. Most importantly, for the purposes of this essay, their adaptation of *Ben-Hur* weakened the traditional opposition to the stage by U.S. Christians, thereby substantially enlarging the U.S. theater audience.[6]

In the last decades of the nineteenth century, millions of religiously scrupulous Americans read their first novel by braving Wallace's "tale of the Christ." In the first decades of the following century, still more of them overcame serious religious objections to the theater by going to see the stage version of *Ben-Hur*. The American Tract Society set forth the main reasons behind this Christian opposition to the theater. The theater, the society declared, is a "school of vice and debauchery" that wastes valuable time. Because theaters in that age were typically located among corrupting temptations like saloons, gambling dens, and houses of ill repute, the society argued that they introduced the unsuspecting to even worse vices. To them, theatrical entertainment "dissipates the mind" and destroys "all taste for serious and spiritual employments," and the stage supports a community of "licentious play-actors." Many Christians, but especially evangelical Protestants, rejected in particular any suggestion that a stage actor could "impersonate" the son of God on stage. This conviction was behind the uproar in San Francisco in 1879 when the dramatist Salmi Morse staged a "Passion play" complete with Jesus's death on the cross. The performance, directed by a young David Belasco and starring James O'Neill as "Christus," caused a near riot that ended with several arrests, including that of O'Neill, who was still wearing a halo.[7]

Furor over the Passion play notwithstanding, by the time *Ben-Hur* premiered, religious opposition to the theater was not as virulent or uniform as it had been twenty years earlier. By 1899, Americans had seen Wilson Barrett's *The Sign of the Cross* (1895) and Hermann Sudermann's *John the Baptist* (1898) on stage. In the first decade of the twentieth century U.S. theaters were virtually awash in religious dramas: after an adaptation of Henryk Sienkiewicz's *Quo Vadis?* (1900) there was Paul Heyse's *Mary of Magdala* (1902) and Maurice Maeterlinck's *Mary Magdalene* (1910), plus Hugo von Hofmannsthal's *Jedermann* (1911), which was a revival of the medieval morality play, *Everyman*.[8]

Still, Klaw and Erlanger knew that if they were to recoup their enormous investment in Wallace's tale of the Christ, they must convince U.S. Christians, especially evangelicals, that the play posed no danger to their religious sensibilities. To this end, they devised an extensive and energetic marketing campaign under the direction of Charles Towle, their business manager, and Edward B. Cooke Jr., their advance agent. Following the example of the great touring railroad circuses, the producers of this "sacred circus" marketed *Ben-Hur*, in part, by providing voluminous press releases for local newspapers that sometimes appeared months before the opening show.[9] As they traveled with the company, Towle and Cooke seized any opportunity to add "zip" to their campaign by writing a locally focused "zinger" article.[10] Although the size of the firm's advertising staff is unknown, it was this staff's job to persuade Christian Americans that it was safe to join the theater crowd to see *Ben-Hur*.

The most obvious and direct way in which the publicists reassured the potential Christian patron was simply to repeat the reassurance. Reassurances appeared in virtually all promotional material of any length. A representative example, published in the *Galesburg Republican Register* in 1914, promised the religiously scrupulous that witnessing "the picturesque, realistic presentation of the men and the times of the period when Christ was upon earth" would dispel any reservations they might have about the play. "All is reverently shown, and not the slightest offense is given to any one's religious beliefs or prejudices." Instead, the Christian will find in the performance "the power and the mercy of the Saviour."[11]

The public relations team also tried, frequently with humor, to demystify the process of attending the theater for first-time patrons. They wrote articles providing all sorts of advice: how to wait in the long ticket lines that were common when "the sacred circus" came to town (what to wear, what to bring to sit upon and to eat while in line); how to avoid the lines by reserving tickets; how to get transportation to the performance; and so forth.[12]

Klaw & Erlanger publicists also developed a narrative about the play's history that demonstrated how from the start the hand of God had been upon Lew Wallace, his novel, and the eventual theater adaptation. This origins narrative reminded the public that Wallace had himself converted to Christianity in the process of writing his tale of the Christ.[13] Furthermore, the narrative honored evangelical Christians' reservations about the stage representation of the son of God by reminding the public that, sharing those reservations, Wallace had denied for twenty years continuous permission requests to stage his novel.[14] Wallace did not relent until Joseph Brooks, who became the play's stage manager, proposed that a radiant shaft of light represent the "Christ spirit."[15] Christian reservations about a human representing Jesus on stage were thus firmly embedded in the origins narrative of the staged *Ben-Hur*. Publicists also insisted that when Klaw and Erlanger engaged William S. Young to write the script, they chose an artist who "saturated himself in Wallace's writing style" and who, "under the spell of the son of Man," had produced a drama suffused with a "religious exaltation seldom found even in a church."[16] Overall, the publicists represented the theatrical company as being a good and faithful steward of the awesome responsibility of bringing *Ben-Hur* to the stage.[17]

In the course of the play's long run, the narrative of its origins became at least implicitly providential. A 1917 press release declared that the play had succeeded for eighteen years because the spirit "of the Christ," present from its beginnings, had given this production "immortal life." Providential claims were advanced for various parties: after Wallace "wrote better than he knew," William Young, "who humanized the characters for the stage[,] gave them more lasting life than he realized," and "Klaw & Erlanger, who conceived the magnificent idea of making the production from the novel," were said, also, to have "plan[ned] better than they knew."[18]

But even more was needed to sell Protestant America on the wicked stage. Klaw & Erlanger publicists further assured the scrupulous Christian that in *Ben-Hur* he or she would find not just a play but—even better—a play that was a sermon. A recurrent theme in the publicity campaign was that the dramatized version of Wallace's novel presented its lessons as effectively as any ordained minister of the Gospel could proclaim them in church. Sermons can be "preached by the action of a play just as potently as from the pulpit," stated one release.[19] The publicists declared repeatedly that people learned most effectively—and enjoyably—when as many senses as possible were engaged. Klaw and Erlanger's unexampled scenery, costumes, music, lighting, galley fight, and chariot race constituted a sensory spectacular that delivered, in the words of one release, "a sermon in varied speech."[20]

This was the work of an experienced New York City public relations team. Around the United States, reviewers enthusiastically embraced the assertion that the staged *Ben-Hur* was even more effective than a well-crafted sermon. The play's scenes of Jesus ministering and healing were "more enduring than a sermon spoken from the pulpit" because of the remarkable realism, declared one reviewer in the *Terre Haute Star*. Additionally, added a reviewer from the *Waterbury Republican*, the play, unlike a minister, caused "the saint and the sinner to sit side by side," each "lost in silent contemplation of the stage and the wonderful scenes disclosed." A *Utica Press* reviewer even suggested that the clergy could *learn* from the play. In the last act of the play, Judah becomes an evangelist who shares with his friends the "good news" of Jesus's miraculous ministry. As the review describes, the actor did so "with an earnestness and dramatic emphasis" that made the scene "vivid and almost real." This reviewer hoped that local preachers might put such "earnestness" and "emphasis" into their "pulpit utterances." Following this thread, a reviewer in Oregon turned the Klaw & Erlanger assertion that the play was as effective as a sermon into an indictment. The stage version of *Ben-Hur* would do more, advised the *Portland Guide*, to teach people "to lead good lives" than "the combined church sermons of Portland in a year."[21]

What were the lessons that the play taught as effectively as a sermon? A Klaw & Erlanger release in the *Nashville Banner* in 1906 described them in detail. This "sermon on Christianity, contained in an interesting play," taught of faith in Christ's "life and works and deed" and of "the love of the Christ for the world, of his power to forgive, to heal, and to save." In addition to these religious lessons, *Ben-Hur* exemplified "the beauty of a son's love for mother and sister" while it demonstrated in the character of Esther "the priceless jewel of modesty and virtue" (in Iras, it exhibited "their opposite").[22] Press releases counseled that lessons so valuable amounted to conversion-like experiences with lasting impact: "From the prologue to the final scene, you are awe-struck, touched, ennobled." As the troubles of life "dwindle to insignificance," the "reason and power of the religion of kindness" sink into the viewer, "never thereafter to be eradicated."[23] The result can be the end of religious uncertainty as the play "points out how doubt can be resolved, how unfaith can give way to faith, and rest succeeds unrest." In addition, it makes audiences believe that "the ambitions and aspirations, the longings and desires of earth can be put aside" as the faithful await "what reward comes to those who will only trust."[24]

Klaw and Erlanger even went so far as to assure Christians that church leaders, Catholic and Protestant, had approved their production. According to one press release, the Episcopal Bishop of New York, Henry Codman Potter, called *Ben-Hur* the "most impressive spectacle" he had ever seen. He added that it was performed with such earnestness and sincerity that it exerts an influence "which is most commendable and which I heartily endorse."[25] Already, Cardinal James Gibbons, the Roman Catholic Archbishop of Baltimore, had deemed this production the "mightiest play ever penned."[26] The publicity campaign (and follow-up reviews) emphasized that the play, alone among the many religious dramas of the period as having been vetted carefully by the pulpit, "has its sanction."[27]

In all of these ways, the Klaw & Erlanger public relations team helped America find its way to the theater, or at least to the theatrical production of *Ben-Hur*. Yet marketing did not stop there. Despite frequent references to Cardinal Gibbons's endorsement of *Ben-Hur*, publicists subtly assured their largely non-Catholic market that the play was a thoroughly *Protestant* sermon. Perhaps because of the near-riot that attended the opening of Morse's Passion play, promotional material for Klaw & Erlanger's *Ben-Hur* insisted that this dramatization had nothing in common with the Catholic Passion play tradition. Wallace "dreaded" any "suggestion of a 'passion play.'"[28] In accordance with his wishes, the Klaw & Erlanger dramatization had been "thoughtfully constructed so as to remove it from the domain of the so-called Passion Plays."[29]

Finally, publicists emphasized that *Ben-Hur* would not be performed on Sunday. In fact, *no* Klaw & Erlanger productions played on the Christian Sabbath. The firm's publicity material regularly stressed this point as part of their sustained effort to assure scrupulous Christians that *Ben-Hur* posed no threat to their religious sensibilities.[30] Quite the contrary, one release asserted: *Ben-Hur* attracted "as to a place of worship, hundreds of thousands who seldom, if ever, set foot within a theater."[31]

◆   ◆   ◆

Assurances from the Klaw & Erlanger publicity team had impact because, during the twenty years of the play's run, millions of Christians, Protestants, and Catholics alike found themselves attending the theater for the first time. Possibly to their surprise, much of what the first-timers saw would have appeared very familiar to them, especially to those who were Protestants. Reviews suggest that to many the dramatized version of Wallace's novel seemed, at least for an evening, to transform the theater into a Protestant church. A reviewer from 1906 thought that an audience in Rochester, New York, "resembled an immense church gathering," whereas another review of the same performance called the audience a "congregation."[32] This claim grew so familiar that one critic reported (perhaps in jest) that certain confused theatergoers asked to be shown to their "pews" instead of to their seats.[33]

Christian first-timers were the audience members most likely to notice that their evening in the theater unfolded in much the same way as a Protestant worship service. In those days, such services usually began with an invocation in which the minister prayed that God would be present in the service and his power upon it. The focus of the service that followed was a sermon that proclaimed the "good news" of the Christian Gospel and its implications for daily life. These services concluded with a benediction in which the minister commended the congregation to God's care and challenged the faithful to go forth to spread the good news they had heard that day.

Klaw & Erlanger's *Ben-Hur* began with a very dramatic invocation. Although an orchestra sat in the pit, the play had no traditional overture. Instead, in a darkened theater, music by Edgar Stillman Kelley, which was described as "oriental," "barbaric," "weird," and "strange," established "a deep reverential air" while the curtain rose on the misty, barren desert as the Magi gathered at dawn to begin their journey to Bethlehem. At this prelude's dramatic climax, a point of light appeared in the sky above the wise men. It grew, shimmering, until its radiant light flooded the theater. According to theatergoers, the effect was stunning.[34] One press release compared Kelley's prelude to the overture to Richard Wagner's *Parsifal*, which functions in that opera as "the forecast, a prophecy." The prelude to *Ben-Hur*, the release explicated, prophesies the coming of "the Christ Spirit," which then pervaded the entire production that followed.[35]

The Christian first-time theatergoer might also have agreed with the Klaw & Erlanger publicity team's assertion that *Ben-Hur* was, in the final analysis, a sermon. The firm's publicists had unknowingly exploited a shift that had spread wildly among religious Americans during the last quarter of the nineteenth century. During those years, Christians in general and evangelical Protestants in particular were taught that the Gospel could be conveyed not only in the spoken and printed word but also in visual images. As Protestants adjusted to this shift in their personal and corporate religious expression, a consumer market emerged for mass-produced images. These images urged Protestants to embrace the rich visual experience that ministers had previously denounced as an idolatrous violation of the second commandment's prohibition of "graven images" and/or a "Romish" perversion of true Christian worship and spirituality. Protestants purchased "illustrated lives of Jesus" and stereopticon slides on spiritual and religious topics. Meanwhile, they heard sermons preached by ministers who increasingly adopted stage rhetoric and techniques. Ministers gave these sermons in sanctuaries that grew to resemble, in form and function, aspects of theaters.[36]

This Protestant embrace of visual culture had important implications for the best-selling religious novel of the day. Beginning in the mid-1880s,

4. A scene from the prelude in the Klaw & Erlanger play. Photograph appeared in the Player's edition of *Ben-Hur* (1901).

visual adaptations of *Ben-Hur* began to appear. After productions of *Ben-Hur* in pantomime and tableaux vivants proliferated, Wallace chose to authorize one such production late in the decade. It was performed often, with his permission, in churches and commercial theaters.[37] A few years later, the world's leading stereopticon manufacturer produced a seventy-two-slide set of the novel accompanied by a lengthy epitome (or script). The company failed to secure Wallace's permission for any of these products; as a result, he took them to court and won.[38] Nonetheless, *Ben-Hur's* visuals remained so alluring that the leading U.S. stereopticon painter also produced a set of slides that illustrated *Ben-Hur*.[39] Finally, in 1899 Wallace and Harper & Brothers published an illustrated edition of the novel.

◆   ◆   ◆

An American who attended a performance of *Ben-Hur* in the early twentieth century could already have encountered its "sermon" in a variety of visual forms. Critical opinion agreed that the staged version of *Ben-Hur* was, overwhelmingly, a visual experience. Perhaps the most frequent observation made about the play was that it was not a traditional drama in which script and acting were all-important. According to one critic, the actors were just part of the scenery because their lines were about as important as those in grand opera (which is to say, hardly at all). *Ben-Hur* was thus not a traditional play, America learned, but a series of living pictures: a "visual feast."[40] The gorgeous sets and sumptuous scenery, extraordinary music, state-of-the-art technical mechanisms, and miraculous lighting effects were what made this stage version of the "tale of the Christ" so powerful.

The culmination of this spectacular achievement was the play's final scene. In it, the "Christ spirit" of the invocation returns to replace the "Messala spirit" of the great race. Jesus cures Judah's mother and sister of leprosy on the Mount of Olives while jubilant palm-bearing followers make their way to Jerusalem on the first Palm Sunday. Jesus is, of course, not shown in person. Instead, the phosphorescent light used in the prologue to represent the Star of Bethlehem reappears, representing "the Christ spirit" as a pure shaft of radiant light that sweeps across the theater until it rests on the lepers' rapturous, upturned faces. This final lighting effect was, apparently, even more powerful than that of the Star of Bethlehem at the beginning of the play.[41] The production ends with the reunited Hur family, surrounded by several hundred members of the costumed company and assembled on the Mount of Olives, singing loud hosannas to the miracle-working Nazarene.

The Mount of Olives scene was the "benediction" to the dramatized *Ben-Hur*. Reviews repeatedly used this term to describe the play and its effect on the audience. The ray of light "lingers lovingly in benediction" on the face of the miraculously healed women, one Illinois reviewer reported, "and then softly steals away."[42] This was not the only audience that interpreted the final scene as a blessing. In Denver in 1903, a reviewer wrote that this scene's effect "is that of a benediction" that left the audience "awed and full of reverence" even as they made their way home.[43] In Des Moines, an audience that had just "cheered vigorously" for the chariot race "sat spell-bound" for a full minute at the play's conclusion.[44]

This change in scene was a point of severe tension for the Klaw & Erlanger production. Everyone knew that the chariot race was thrilling, but this posed a deep risk to the religious message that justified even a conservative Christian buying a ticket to the show. Klaw and Erlanger took great pains to assure America that the "sermon" that produced this reverence and awe was much more important and powerful than the spectacular race that almost immediately preceded it. Nevertheless, the company produced massive amounts of material on the thrilling race and the costly mechanical innovations that made it possible.[45] But promotional literature still insisted that the play's spectacular elements never overpowered its spiritual core. Local reviews frequently referred to audiences' enthusiastic reaction to the chariot race.[46] Apparently men stood on their seats and cheered. This emotionalism had to be tamed, however, or at least subdued, before the play could move toward its benediction ending. As has been noted, the "Christ spirit" that had been present in the play since the invocation of Kelley's prelude returned in full force with Messala's defeat. "The chariot race stirs up the blood," said a Connecticut reviewer in 1904, "but the people watching and hearing seem to be subdued by the mightier prevailing influence" of the divine presence. *Ben-Hur* is a play "to make men better. It must inspire greater reverence for things sacred."[47]

In early twentieth-century America, making men better and more reverent was the prescribed responsibility of the church and of women. Therefore, the thrilling chariot race was always described in thoroughly masculine terms in press releases that bristled with statistics and discussions of intricate machines, striving men, and lunging horses.[48] In contrast, the Mount of Olives scene was usually described in traditionally female terms: "The whole scene is so bathed in beauty and perfumed with poetry in the form of strains of haunting music that the jaded imagination is stimulated and refreshed by contact with it."[49] The gendering of the "Christ spirit" and "the Messala spirit" that is so evident in the stage play originates in the novel. The "Christ spirit" triumphs over the "Messala spirit" in Judah Ben-Hur when the young man, deeply affected by his years of observing Jesus's ministry, confronts Iras after he has defeated Messala in the race. As the Egyptian begins to taunt him, Judah feels his "hope of vengeance" finally leave him as the memory of "the man with the woman's face and hair," now "in tears, came near enough to leave something of His spirit behind" (8:VI).

The story of a vengeful Jew's change of heart proved immensely popular. The Klaw & Erlanger publicists insisted that the play's financial

success was not because of the chariot race and other riveting achievements, but because this production remained true to the spiritual essence
of Wallace's novel. One early release, published in San Francisco, stated
that "while the play was highly spectacular and splendidly mounted,"
this fact alone "failed to account for its popularity." Instead, the play's success "was doubtless due to the religious character of the drama, which,
through the wide reading General Wallace's book has received, evidently
obtained a firm hold on the people."[50] Throughout the play's run, publicists insisted that it had not subordinated the spiritual to the spectacular.
Rather, the play remained, at heart, an affecting sermon with vital lessons to impart.[51] Regarding its success, concluded one review, the play
"deserves all the good things which come to it for the much good that
comes from it."[52]

A play is not usually reviewed in terms of how much good comes
from it. But just as publicity material emphasized that Klaw & Erlanger's
Ben-Hur produced *results*, reviews detailed its *effect* on its audience.[53] The
evangelical worship services that dominated Wallace's America were also
intended to affect worshippers and produce a result: the conversion of
souls. The evangelical Christian was taught to believe that every human
contact was important because it involved the possibility of converting
an unbeliever. One publicity release was couched in similar language:
it assured the public that every appearance of the play would be like a
"first night" performance because the entire company was "alive" to the
"possibilities for good" that could come from any and every performance.
The cast intended, one and all, to be faithful stewards of this God-given
responsibility.[54]

These assertions carried a clear message: *Ben-Hur* was church-like.
However, even the most theatrically illiterate first-timers would have
known that, at some point, one was supposed to applaud a theatrical performance. But when to applaud in a theater that has become a church?
Especially when the performance includes a thrilling race that is followed by the appearance of the son of God? In 1907 a reporter for the
Toledo News-Bee wrote that the audience's "dearth of applause" confused
regular theatergoers who believed that the first-timers did not know
when to applaud. The regular theatergoers therefore sought "to rally" the

first-timers "into a vigorous encore." This reporter recognized that a very real problem existed: the audience was "composed chiefly of people who had never been in a theater before" and for whom *Ben-Hur* was not a play. It was instead "a powerful sermon." The play had "made its way into the innermost parts of their souls," the reporter realized. "But applaud a sermon? Why not? No one knows, except that custom forbids it. Hence the silence."[55]

This quandary aside, reviewers and publicists noted the ease with which the Christians who attended the theater for the first time to see *Ben-Hur* learned to comport themselves in this new environment. Some commentators began to speak early on in the play's run of a *Ben-Hur* audience that was uniquely composed of a large number of Christian novices in the theater.[56] By 1908, though, a reviewer in Missouri attributed a surprisingly refined discrimination to a Kansas City audience who received the performance with "proper reverence, as well as a critical discernment." After the final curtain, this "'Ben-Hur' audience" left the theater "inspired by a sort of religious awe that seemed to find expression in a subdued, quiet and reverential attitude."[57]

Reports like this one explain why the play "converted" many ministers to the theater. In 1909, a New York City reviewer reported that *Ben-Hur* "attracted a great many clergymen who had heretofore warned their strait-laced parishioners that the box office stood at the gates of hell." As these clerics were converted, "the lid was lifted off the theater as a proscribed amusement."[58] A few years earlier in 1906, a Chicago minister who had attacked the theater because of its corrupting influence was persuaded by Charles Towle to attend *Ben-Hur*. A press release issued to a newspaper in Lincoln, Nebraska, said that this play proved to be a revelation for the minister because it demonstrated to him how "the stage may be given over to uses wholly worthy, commendable and which cannot fail to exert the greatest possible blessing on mankind."[59]

These converts to the stage endorsed the play and, in many cases, preached sermons on its sermon. For instance, a Presbyterian in California preached on "'Ben-Hur,' the Book and the Play," focusing on "the influence which both had had upon the world." The *Oakland Inquirer* reported that Reverend E. E. Baker "told his hearers that perhaps the best conception of the life of Christ" could be gained not from a sermon but from a play, where one could personally witness "the tragic events of the life of the greatest character that the world had ever seen." Testifying willingly to the overwhelming effect that *Ben-Hur* had had on him, Baker made no apology "for having shed tears as the greatness of the tragedy passed before his eyes." Six years later, a group of eight ministers attended the play in Chattanooga; two immediately announced that they would preach on "its capacities for doing good." For one of these ministers, Reverend Dr. J. W. Backman, *Ben-Hur* was his introduction to the theater. He proclaimed that he had admired "every line of it" and appreciated especially the audience's "impressive" reverence.[60] His pastoral colleague, Reverend Dr. Ira M. Boswell, added that "the man or woman who sees the play and does not feel an uplifting influence" is simply "beyond being uplifted."[61]

It is not surprising that, having embraced the theater, Protestant clergy immediately sought to reform or even "redeem" it. They believed that in *Ben-Hur* God had provided the ideal instrument for this important task. Virtually all who discussed the impact of the popular drama on U.S. culture in general, and on the theater in particular, agreed that *Ben-Hur* was playing a crucial role in at least mitigating the traditional Christian hostility to the stage. In 1907, Gertrude Dalton, the actress who played Esther in the 1907 and 1908 touring companies (she also taught Sunday school), observed that "old fogey notions" about "the immorality" of the theater that clerics had once preached were a thing of the past.[62] The Klaw & Erlanger publicists made frequent reference to the way in which *Ben-Hur* had "reconciled church and stage."[63] Chiming in was a reviewer in Cincinnati who argued in 1907 that the play "has reached millions of people, learned and unlearned, upon all of whom it has acted as an elevating and refining force."[64] In Cleveland another reviewer saw the play as an avenue by which Christians who had wanted to experience the theater could do so because "many who don't attend" are "always looking, hoping for an excuse." All these people need, he charged, "is a plank on which to walk from their consciences to their desires."[65]

One Little Rock reviewer made a less derisive argument in 1908. For this critic, the theater provided "a common ground on which the regular theater-goers and those who entertain prejudices against things theatrical may meet" to be "entertained and instructed." Out of this meeting, the sanguine critic believed, will come an increased audience for the theater.[66] A few years earlier, a reviewer for the *New York American* had reminded his readers that "there are millions of people in this country who regard theater-going as a sinful attraction." But these "non-theatergoers, having been once tempted inside the playhouse by 'Ben-Hur,'" will "gradually get the habit and become good, enthusiastic supporters of the theater."[67]

These and similar commentators obviously found in *Ben-Hur's* success a hope that the stage might become a greater force for enlightenment and moral uplift—and that it would attract larger theatrical audiences. Yet it is equally clear that many Americans expected more from *Ben-Hur* than moral elevation. A reviewer in 1906 suggested that many of the first-timers among the *Ben-Hur* audience attended only because they expected that this play would "redeem" the stage, at least "for the time being."[68] Broaching a similar but different thought was one of the most frequently circulated *Ben-Hur* press releases: it said that in the healing of the lepers scene, the most "beautiful, spiritual, inspiring and edifying" scene ever produced, "the stage seems to have concentrated itself and all its resources to the service of Christianity." The phrase "consecrated itself" suggests that the stage, having come under the control of God, was now performing his will in the world.[69]

In 1916, the nation's leading evangelist, Billy Sunday, saw *Ben-Hur* in New York City and was deeply affected. As a result, he agreed to endorse and publicly promote the play. The result was a remarkable example of a corporation using the best-selling religious novel of the age and the nation's most celebrated evangelist to advance its own financial goals. The ad in the November 6, 1916, edition of the *New York American* featured a print sermon by Billy Sunday. The fiery evangelist's topic was, as ever, sensational: "There are lepers on Broadway!" With his unerring sense of showmanship, Sunday focused on the play's most spectacular and memorable scenes: the Roman galley, the celebrated chariot race, and the stunning Mount of Olives benediction. In staccato, one-sentence points that replicated a revivalist's sermonic style, Sunday preached lessons that illustrated the dangers of liquor. The lepers of the novel only had "sick bodies," he asserted, whereas the drunken "moral lepers" he had seen in the gutters of Broadway had "sick souls" that had been incurably diseased by drink. And the galley slaves? They were "better off than the whiskey slave today" because the Roman's whip lashed only the body, whereas whiskey "lashes the whole family and gets into the mother's heart." As for the thrilling race, it represented for Sunday "the race of life," which is won by the just, the brave, and the sober.[70]

"Go see 'Ben-Hur,'" Sunday urged. "Ten million humans have read the book." Still, the evangelist hoped that 100 million people could see the play and then "hear a sermon about it." Sunday declared too that he would like "to talk to 50,000 men and women just after they had seen 'Ben-Hur'" because the play's "powerful effects, its galloping horses in the chariot race," its "lepers and its beautiful 'light' that irradiates the world," is like "a plow digging deep into men's thought and stirring their consciences." Having challenged all Americans to see *Ben-Hur*, Sunday then urged the nation's theatrical managers to reform and redeem the U.S. stage. As perhaps the greatest showman of that era, Sunday paid homage to theater's potential. "There is in the stage a marvelous power that goes to waste," he asserted. "I hope that theatrical managers[,] seeing Lew Wallace's 'Ben-Hur' crowded to the roof[,] will realize that people like what is good and true" and will provide it.[71]

This evangelist's call for a redeemed theater amplified Klaw and Erlanger's assertion that, during a performance of *Ben-Hur*, the stage "consecrated itself to the service of Christianity." It is highly unlikely, though, that the Jewish impresarios who produced the play believed that it would "redeem" a stage that, surely, they did not believe needed redemption. As one of the most powerful theatrical companies in the world, Klaw & Erlanger had an enormous investment in the stage as it currently existed in America. The firm produced an extensive array of theatrical attractions, few of which would have drawn scrupulous Christians. If there was ever a ruthless and hard-driving theatrical producer, it was Abe Erlanger, who was called, for good reason, the "Napoleon of the theater."[72]

Klaw & Erlanger's publicity department sold Wallace's play not only as a sermon but also as the most thrilling play ever produced: an entertaining and instructive travelogue, a heartwarming love story, a chilling tale of betrayal and revenge, and a spectacular scenic, musical, and technical nonpareil in theatrical history. *Ben-Hur* was the play that had it all. By seeing it, Americans could have it all, too, according to the publicists' assurances that Bible-lovers did not have to make a choice between their religion and the theater. They could have both. Klaw & Erlanger publicists, and later many clerics and a well-known evangelist, told the nation that, by attending the theater to see *Ben-Hur* they could embrace this aspect of the modern secular world without ceasing to be religious. This mighty play was the first instance in which corporate America used Wallace's *Ben-Hur* to serve its own ends. It would not be the last.

June Mathis's Ben-Hur

A Tale of Corporate Change and the Decline of Women's Influence in Hollywood

THOMAS J. SLATER

On July 15, 1922, June Mathis signed her first contract with Goldwyn Studios. She had been chosen to organize production and write the screenplay for the most anticipated production of the era, *Ben-Hur*. Following the tremendous success of Lew Wallace's novel and the Klaw & Erlanger play, public demand for a film was so high that Abraham Erlanger (having parted ways with Marc Klaw) offered the rights for an unbelievable $1 million. Although no studio could afford this expense at the time, the struggling Goldwyn company made a deal to obtain the work in exchange for $500,000 and concession of final script approval to Erlanger.[1] Mathis at this time was at the pinnacle of her career after having achieved great success with the production of *The Four Horsemen of the Apocalypse* (1921). This blockbuster had brought stardom for the previously unknown Rudolph Valentino, whom she had cast, and director Rex Ingram, who was also Mathis's choice for the film. Now, with the same responsibilities for *Ben-Hur*, Mathis's future in Hollywood seemed unlimited.

Two years later, Mathis's work on *Ben-Hur* ended in disappointment: "After six months of hard work in Rome, Vienna, Berlin, the edge of the desert and other places, I do not feel that the ideals I have had for 'Ben

Many thanks to Barbara Ryan, Milette Shamir, and Kevin Brownlow for their suggestions and assistance.

Hur' ever since I began work on the script two years ago can be realized under [present] production conditions." When Mathis left the production site in Italy in 1924, her script was rejected, her choices for director and lead were replaced, and she was fired by the newly formed Metro-Goldwyn. Rather than leading to new heights of influence, her work on *Ben-Hur* had initiated a career decline. Although she continued working steadily and achieved some success during the remaining years of her life (she died at age forty in 1927), Mathis never again reached a position of such high opportunities as she had in 1922.[2]

The story of Mathis's *Ben-Hur* experience has become a minor part of film history. Kevin Brownlow recognized her efforts in *The Parade's Gone By . . .* (1968), as did André Soares more recently in *Beyond Paradise: The Life of Ramon Novarro* (2010).[3] These projects encompass Mathis's work within the greater story of the production of the first feature-length *Ben-Hur*, which reached the screen under Fred Niblo's direction in 1925. But her experience also casts light on a far more important story: that of the cultural dominance achieved by industrial capitalism by that time.

The success of this system, which provided the basis for our current society, appears now to have been inevitable. But it was not without cost. "The rise of imperial ambitions, the redirection of social conflict, the renewal of ruling-class rule, the incorporation of vitalist impulses— these developments were essential to the making of modern America," observes T. J. Jackson Lears. Still, these things "were not the whole story, and they should not obscure the myriad private struggles to regenerate larger meaning amid the triumphalist inanities of empire." The major winners were White men, at the expense of White women and all African Americans. The African American story is well known: after the Civil War, African Americans made huge gains in obtaining land, jobs, rights, and public office. However, with the rise of Jim Crow legislation, these gains were wiped out. Simultaneously, industrialized technology and urbanization created tremendous opportunities (and, often, the necessity) for other Americans to enter the public sphere in areas where race could still matter but gender was not a factor. One of these areas was the fledgling motion picture industry.[4] Women achieved noteworthy success between 1915 and 1923 as directors and production unit chiefs with many men under their leadership. At Goldwyn in 1922, Mathis was said to have obtained "the most responsible job ever held by a woman" because she was not only taking control of *Ben-Hur*, but also of hiring and assigning directors and giving the go-ahead to various projects.[5]

Sadly, though—and in lockstep with the rest of society—as the motion picture industry "matured," women's opportunities behind the scenes (rather than as actresses) declined drastically. Antonia Lant and Ingrid Periz write that

> following a brief but severe recession in 1921, and in order to keep up with the escalating prices of film production, the film industry was to reorganize itself in the early 1920s, and, among other things, woo Wall Street banking for support. Women filmmakers were incompatible with this newly emerging image of an efficient, big-business Hollywood, particularly in the eyes of New York capital; Wall Streeters would trust their dollars only to other men.[6]

Opposition came from within studios, too, when unions and professional organizations such as the Academy of Motion Picture Arts and Sciences excluded women. As a result, the mid-1920s saw the nearly complete elimination of women directors. By the 1930s, women were also being removed from film history. In 1933, for instance, journalist Adela Rogers St. Johns (who certainly knew better) wrote that only three women had ever directed a film.[7] If even the successful work of directors such as Cleo Madison, Marion Fairfax, Alice Guy Blaché, Nell Shipman, Ruth Stonehouse, Ida May Park, and others could be forgotten, prospects were even worse for the failed effort of a writer/producer like Mathis. Hypocritically, Erich von Stroheim's unfulfilled efforts on *Greed* (1925), which Mathis approved for production at Goldwyn and hoped to produce as von Stroheim envisioned, are remembered in numerous books as the heroic struggle of a visionary artist. Mathis's work on *Ben-Hur*, in contrast, has been almost completely neglected. In fact, the number of her productions and critical successes easily matched those of almost any male director of her era.[8]

Thus, the story of Mathis's work on *Ben-Hur* has great relevance for our understanding of film and social history. Not only does it mark a critical turning point in the career of a major figure in U.S. silent film (who happened to be a woman), it is also representative of women's removal from almost all positions of influence in the motion-picture industry in the mid-1920s and the start of their erasure from film history. What is especially critical to recognize is that women's deletion from cultural memory is also part of a removal of their identities, achievements, and perspectives from silent film's origins. Like many other women in film-making, Mathis worked her way up to a position of tremendous influence through constant effort and boundless creativity. Then she was shunted aside as the industry became highly incorporated. As a result, her immeasurable contributions to the artistic and economic success of U.S. film have gone practically unrecognized.

Mathis's screenplays show consistently insightful adaptations and strong knowledge of editing and cinematography. Her job was not merely to produce a script but to envision the completed film, which she did by gaining technical knowledge that was mainly restricted to men. Mathis's confidence in these realms measures the significance of our discovery that her script for *Ben-Hur* represents a vision less pragmatic, and noticeably more spiritual, than that of the men who were taking control of the industry as she struggled with this massive production.

My consideration of Mathis's work in this essay emphasizes the impossible task she was given, the significance of her failure in relation to women's declining influence in Hollywood in the 1920s, and the spiritual vision within her work. As Lears points out, the early twentieth century witnessed "myriad private struggles to regenerate larger meaning amid the triumphalist inanities of empire."[9] I propose that Mathis's work on *Ben-Hur* is one of those struggles. Furthermore, the fact that her struggle took place on a public stage makes it especially significant because this exposure brought wide attention to the impact of the masculine materialist drive on women who had forged advanced positions in the most important artistic medium of the day. It can be no small matter, from this vantage, that Mathis's work asserted "feminine" spiritual values.

Women's Opportunities in Hollywood

As Wendy Holliday explains in *Hollywood's Modern Women* (1995), the women who came to Hollywood in the early twentieth century practiced a feminism based in modernism rather than in gender politics. Many had, like Mathis, spent years in vaudeville and theatrical touring companies making low pay and living in very rough conditions. When they began their film careers as writers, performers, or directors, they sought primarily to advance their personal fortunes rather than to promote personal philosophies or fight gender battles. Although men overwhelmingly dominated most aspects of the business (with areas such as film processing reserved for women), women were present in enough numbers to be visible. Additionally, those employed for their talents were achieving enough to earn respect. Because much of the film audience was comprised of women, female filmmakers were valued for their ability to reach these ticket-buyers. Director Lois Weber was well known, for instance, for her social themes. But her primary asset was the same as that of Mathis: her films made money. During their years in theater, these women had worked in mixed-gender environments. Now, they did so again, and they expected the situation to improve.[10] They had little motivation for pushing an overt feminist agenda.

However, this pragmatic consideration can be overstated. To probe historically, we must also question what a feminist push for change might have looked like and whether women filmmakers of the silent film era were already achieving as much as was possible at the time. Few realize that in addition to acting, writing, producing, and editing, some women controlled their own production companies, established their own facilities, and even, as with Mary Pickford, co-founded studios.[11] This degree of achievement has surely never been matched by any other group of women in a single industry. Women of this era have been so thoroughly excised from film history, however, that their achievements have never received due recognition. The simple fact is that women like Mathis did not foresee how thoroughly they would be blocked from maintaining their presence in the industry. But maybe they should have, because the signs were present.

Injecting "New Woman" Elements

Karen Ward Mahar has shown that, from cinematography's beginning, this field, "like most other professionalizing fields, appeared gender neutral but in fact restricted membership to men." The American Society of Cinematographers placed high value, for instance, on comradeship among its members and enforced this bonding through gendered exclusivity.[12] Still, women directors, editors, and screenwriters had to become thoroughly knowledgeable about technology. Mathis's *Ben-Hur* script reveals her efforts to stay current about the latest developments in cinematography and how each could be used. For example, in a scene that introduces the Magus Melchior, Mathis instructs,

FADE IN LONG SHOT (TINT FOR NIGHT) A STOCK SHOT OF THE LOFTY HIMALAYAS OR LOCATION SEEN THROUGH GLASS OR BY WILLIAMS PROCESS SHOWING HIMALAYAN MOUNTAINS.

This material reveals Mathis's knowledge of several technical elements (tinting, glass, Williams process) and the resources available (stock shot). The description further reveals screenwriters' obligation to envision the completed film, including how it should be shot, rather than merely creating continuity and dialogue. Instructions as precise as this example from Mathis's script would save time and money by relating how certain scenes could be created in the studio rather than on location. This factor was critical for a production like *Ben-Hur*, which would be filmed overseas. Further references to technology to achieve an effect Mathis envisioned include her note in the scene where the Sanhedrin faces Herod: "(This shot can also be taken with an Akeley camera).")[13] Similarly, in a fade-in of a long shot, she noted: "It might be a very good thing to use the new lens shown us by Gaudio, as this is just about the tone that would enable us to do this in the daylight."[14] This suggestion indicates Mathis's work off the set to keep up with the latest technology.

This degree of professionalism reminds us that Mathis was, like many other women in filmmaking, "new." The term "New Woman" was first applied, Mahar explains, "to women in the middle classes who ventured into the public sphere" as reformers, career women, students, and athletes. Increasingly, these women were seen "enjoy[ing] the new mixed-sex venues of amusement parks, dance halls, and nickelodeons, where they flaunted new styles and new behaviors." Attitudes evinced by New Women in the arts included openness to sexuality that acknowledged, or even vaunted, homosexuality and cross-dressing. Mathis spent fourteen years in vaudeville and theatrical touring companies where both were far more prominent than in the general public. For four of those years she worked with the gay performer Julian Eltinge, who was the most popular female impersonator of the time. As recorded effects of this pre-film experience, Mathis's scripts for Valentino in 1921–22 contained frequent references to sexual identities and behavior. She was especially proud of including the "drag" scene in *The Four Horsemen of the Apocalypse*, which, she remarked, would only be comprehensible in full "to people who really know life."[15]

Ben-Hur provided Mathis with another opportunity to present homosexual desire on screen. She wrote this theme into a scene revised from Wallace's novel in which elite Romans indulged in wild debauchery on the night before the chariot race:

> Just at this point a huge dark-skinned slave, bronzed all over to reflect the light and to make him a thing of beauty, enters, bearing upon his back a white boy, who has been painted silver. He is nude but for a jeweled clout, and wearing a weird headdress, with cymbals in his hands; he is carried to the table clanging the cymbals. The slave places him upon the table where he starts to dance. This relieves the tenseness of the situation. The Romans sink back upon their couches, and start to sip their wine, and look toward the dancer with interest.[16]

To be sure, infusing carnality into the movies was not simply a project of women filmmakers. Niblo's *Ben-Hur*, for instance, included male nudity with a slave chained standing up in the galley with his back to the camera and female nudity with bare-breasted women leading a parade celebrating Ben-Hur's athletic triumphs. Significantly, though, Niblo did not present these figures as the objects of homosexual desire or, indeed, anyone's sexual desires, except perhaps that of filmgoers. They are simply naked and part of the scenery.

Injecting Anti-Modernism

Returning to Mathis's script, her depictions of female characters contrast intriguingly with those of Niblo. One significant figure is Ben-Hur's love interest. Mathis kept Esther the extremely passive figure she is in Wallace's novel and the Klaw & Erlanger play. This decision seems less progressive than Niblo's because in his film, Esther appears early, has more interaction with Ben-Hur and his mother and sister, and goes to them in the valley of lepers to bring them to Jesus for healing. Niblo's Esther is thus a much more interesting character than her creator, or any previous adaptor, had produced. However, Mathis constructed Iras with a great deal more depth than would Niblo. In the novel and Mathis's script, Iras is the daughter of the Magus Balthasar but she rejects his idea of Jesus as the promised savior. As a result, she is solely interested in personal gain and is constantly shifting allegiance between Ben-Hur and Messala to obtain the best situation for herself. At the conclusion of Mathis's script, Ben-Hur, hating Iras for her betrayal, refuses to forgive her or his childhood friend. This characterological decision keeps him layered rather than plaster-saint perfect. Mathis's use of Iras was intended to alert filmgoers to the reason why the admirable, yet still-flawed, Ben-Hur is not present in the final shot; he is not shown to be the agent who reunites his family. In this way, Mathis kept viewers focused on a light that emerges from a depiction of Jesus entering Jerusalem on Palm Sunday.[17]

Mathis's characterization of Iras appears to be a negative depiction of a New Woman: one who has stepped beyond domestic bounds and produced evil as a result. However, Mathis's Iras has motivation. She is self-seeking, but after veering between Ben-Hur and his friend-turned-foe, she ultimately shows "great love for Messala" even though he is crippled and penniless after the chariot race. Coming to Ben-Hur, she begs on Messala's behalf: "He did thee wrong—but deeply did he deplore it! Forgive the past—restore his fortune—save him from poverty!"[18] By contrast, in Niblo's version, Iras is simply evil: a vamp who tries to help Messala destroy Ben-Hur and then disappears. She is not the daughter of Balthasar, and she has no motivation.

Mathis's script thus makes Iras more human and complex (though in a way unlike the Iras that David Mayer sketches in his "wish list" in this volume). Mathis's script also makes Iras more sympathetic. Rather than a depiction of evil to be condemned, Mathis's Iras seeks forgiveness. This aspect of her characterization makes the spiritual light, mentioned above, a source of hope for all. The resolution blends elements of Victorian attitudes with twentieth-century calls for greater honesty about sex and straightforward depictions of the dilemmas faced by women who heeded these calls.

In this regard, Mathis's work exhibits what Lears refers to as "the paradoxically antimodern impulse animating many forms of modernist thought." His point is that although modernization standardized labor and regulated daily routines, "widespread yearning for regeneration— for rebirth that was variously spiritual, moral, and physical—penetrated public life, inspiring movements and policies that formed the foundation for American society in the twentieth century." In the Victorian ideology in which Hollywood's foundational figures were raised, women were considered essentially spiritual in nature and therefore a guiding force for the worldly life that was dominated by men. Mathis agreed with this ideology in an article in *Film Daily*. In "Harmony in Picture Making" (1923) she states that the best movies are the product of a male director and female screenwriter, or a male writer with the sensitivity of a woman.[19] Mathis was known for the kinds of achievements associated with New Women: learning about technology, gaining authority, and building a career in a male-dominated field. This formula worked for her. Collaborations with male studio heads and directors elevated her to a position of great influence. Other women might have felt differently if they longed to direct, but Mathis showed no longing of that kind. "Harmony in Picture Making" clarifies her concurrence with certain gendered ideals of days gone by.

Press reports that describe Mathis's belief in spiritual forces offer additional evidence of her ideology. For example, Mathis wore a "hoodoo" ring that she claimed brought success to her writing. She believed that narratives traveled through the atmosphere, where they could be accessed by writers, and she shared her belief in spiritualism—talking with the afterworld—with another major proponent, Sir Arthur Conan Doyle.[20] The last fact is germane because it reiterates Mathis's belief that although women were distinctively spiritual, this quality was not limited to women: men could possess it too. This indication of potential for transcendence implied that men could steer successfully through the industrial-materialist world and reject violence and money-grubbing by following women's examples.

Missteps in Picture Making

Mathis's beliefs are important to keep in mind when reviewing her peak moment and decline in the film industry. The studio announced her assignment to a top spot on *Ben-Hur* with great fanfare by simultaneously purchasing a $1 million life insurance policy for her. Amping excitement, the press named her the "Million Dollar Girl." Following her tremendous success with Valentino in *The Four Horsemen of the Apocalypse* and *Blood and Sand*, the insurance policy was a promotional ploy that would build excitement for the new *Ben-Hur*. Searches for the director and male lead were also excellent publicity gimmicks. Casting the lead role in *Ben-Hur* was "the 1920s equivalent of the later search for Scarlett O'Hara."[21]

Unfortunately, the primary factor in these selections was keeping costs low. Mathis chose George Walsh to play Judah Ben-Hur because she believed in him and he looked the part. It did not hurt, though, that he was already under contract to Goldwyn and he agreed to a low salary. For director, Goldwyn had talent like von Stroheim, King Vidor, and Victor Sjostrom to choose from. Yet, Charles Brabin received the assignment mainly because he had just produced a successful, low-budget, independent film.[22]

The importance of money in the production of *Ben-Hur* is also evident in Niblo's report from when he took control of the production in 1924. He stated that the cast was colorless, the costumes and wigs shoddy, and the production staff in need of special effects people. Niblo knew he could make these large changes with no worry about costs. He was working for the new Hollywood in which funding no longer came from the studios but from New York banks that could absorb large potential losses—but that also held all power. Niblo reported surprise that Mathis could have made such bad decisions.[23] But she had been working under very different conditions. She purchased cheap costumes from Germany because they were exactly that: cheap. The same criterion apparently influenced the decision to film in Italy where other recent productions had been able to capitalize on low labor costs. The Goldwyn people failed to cope with the fascist labor unions, though, or to build the number of ships they would need for the sea battle scene. The ships they did build were of such poor quality that they were not allowed out to sea. A further sign of cost-cutting was when Goldwyn sent their star to Europe with a second-class ticket.[24] Evidently, saving money on Walsh's fare was considered more important than building hype over his arrival in Italy.

As for Goldwyn's use of talent searches as anticipation builders, another problem was that the payoffs had to bespeak glamour and intrigue but reassure fans that the talent was equal to the project's status. In addition, results of such searches had to have an element of surprise. Because this formula had worked when Mathis chose Valentino for *The Four Horsemen*, she likely believed that a similarly "unconventional" choice for the lead in *Ben-Hur* would bring comparable results when Valentino proved unavailable. Less clear is why she passed over Rex Ingram for director. He would have been a wise choice due to his skillful handling of the massive spectacle of *The Four Horsemen*. Furthermore, Ingram greatly wanted the film; he had even promised the lead in his most recent project at the time (an ancient world picture) the starring role in *Ben-Hur*. Mathis thus had a golden opportunity to gain a prestige director. But she passed Ingram over. Why? Perhaps because she believed he would be too safe a choice and thus kill the intrigue of a search, perhaps because she couldn't afford him, or perhaps because they had had major arguments following their collaborations in 1921 and Mathis wanted a director she believed she could control.[25] Whatever the reason, she surprised everyone by announcing that her director would be Brabin (not a major figure) and her star Walsh (mostly known for work in low-budget Westerns).[26]

These choices thrilled no one, and the press was not willing to give them a chance. After Walsh's selection, for instance, *Photoplay* ran a one-page article featuring pictures of him in costume with a short paragraph in very tiny print that said, "Well, he looks like Ben-Hur anyway." The comment is accurate because Walsh does look virile and handsome in each shot, suggesting that with skilled directing he may have fit the role well. The condescending "anyway" could have been replaced with more supportive material, such as interviews with Walsh, Mathis, and Brabin. One would think that Goldwyn had a publicity department capable of arranging better coverage, or one dedicated to promoting *Ben-Hur*. But the *Photoplay* piece and Walsh's second-class ticket indicate how shabbily he was treated even before he boarded ship for Europe. Worse was to come for Walsh: when Metro-Goldwyn replaced him with Ingram's choice, Ramon Novarro, they did not bother to tell Walsh. He showed up to the set one morning, ready to work, only to learn from Francis X. Bushman, who was cast as Messala, that he no longer had the part.[27] Being dismissed before even having a chance to prove himself was humiliating for Walsh. That this humiliation could have been avoided sketches the new mood in Hollywood.

Conversely, Brabin may have deserved removal. Niblo would report senseless spending, much of it outside Italy, which irritated the Italians with whom the production team had to negotiate. In addition, Brabin apparently did nothing to help the company's morale in Italy. When Mathis arrived to supervise the production for which she had huge responsibility, she was shocked to discover she was not allowed on the set. When the company split between her supporters and Brabin's, no usable footage was produced. Particularly foolish was how Brabin's interdiction wasted two of Mathis's irrefutable gifts: working with actors and spotting production problems. The stars of *The Four Horsemen*, Valentino and Alice Terry, praised her warmly for guiding their performances. When her husband Sylvano Balboni was directing *The Masked Woman* in 1926, a magazine writer noted Mathis's keen perception during a scene in which she spotted an extra trying to do "a stellar walk" in the background. The writer comments, "Not for a second had her eyes left the scene while the cameras were grinding."[28] Brabin, a talented director, may not have wanted such eagle eyes on his set. If so, it is possible that Mathis should have been more aware of his resistance.

These production factors make it somewhat unfair that Mathis's failure to achieve her goals for *Ben-Hur* has never received anywhere near the consideration given von Stroheim's agonies over *Greed*. A major difference, however, is that the surviving film of *Greed* reveals his artistry. Also, the few people who saw his massive complete work had warm praise for it.[29] By comparison, Mathis became a scapegoat for her failed production of *Ben-Hur*. Historians are left with only her script to help them determine whether her plans were worthy of the regrets she expressed about her ideals for the *Ben-Hur* she had envisioned, or whether those regrets were just a face-saving statement for the press. Does the script reveal that her *Ben-Hur* is an unfortunate loss that merits examination? Or, if that asks too much, does Mathis's script suggest that at least some of the women who were nearly written out of film history created distinctive ideas that deserve recovery?

Ben-Hur as a Personal Statement

Ben-Hur seems like it would have been the ideal project for Mathis. It begins with an oppressive militarism that destroys a stable, prosperous household and leaves a fatherless young man seeking male guidance. These were appropriate themes for the post-war era that Mathis addressed in scripts for Valentino. However, in contrast to the lead characters in those films, Judah Ben-Hur already has a strong faith. His challenge is to resist the temptations of violence and materialism. To do so, he needs to find an appropriate father figure. He does this first through Quintus Arrius, the Roman patriarch who provides him with the freedom to search for his own answers, and then through a Nazarene who shows him the path of peace and forgiveness. Significantly, Judah's first meeting with Jesus comes while the former is chained to other slaves as they are driven to serve on the galleys. Jesus provides him with a drink of water that makes a greater impression on him than the gladiatorial training that Arrius will provide.

Interest in home and family in many of Mathis's scripts indicates these topics' centrality to melodramas of the time and also possibly to her own concerns. As Christine Gledhill writes, in melodrama, the overwhelmingly dominant genre of U.S. silent film, "home is where the heart is."[30] It lacks a physical location. So do Mathis characters, who tend to be cut loose from domestic bliss. She may have worked so successfully with this narrative pattern because she had lived it. Although she was always very close to her step-father, step-siblings, grandmother, and mother, she does not seem to have been strongly connected to a sense of home.[31] As a child, she moved from Leadville, Colorado, to a new family in Minneapolis and then to Salt Lake City and San Francisco, where she began her performance career in 1901 at age fourteen. Thus began a long-term transient existence as she shuttled from one town to another while in the theater, and from New York to Los Angeles in her screenwriting career. Mathis's lifelong familiarity with this condition allows us to define it as part of her personal vision.

For the men of Mathis's day, who set the standards for U.S. public opinion and behavior, "home" could be achieved through hard work. Victorian ideology defined men's places as heads of household and controllers of the public spheres of business, labor, and politics. T. J. Jackson Lears explains that men were to provide "a crucial centripetal force against the centrifugal energies of markets and monies." Within the industrial/consumer society, the ideal man was to be "so hardworking . . . that he produced his own success, his own social identity" to become a "paragon of autonomy" and "the apotheosis of solidity and reliability." For women, however, or those men who, as Mathis would say, "possess a woman's sensibility," "the truly regenerated self was a sincere and transparent self, whose outward conduct corresponded perfectly with his inner experience of grace." This definition describes a spiritual identity not associated with the "solid anchors" of hard work, ownership, and autonomy, but rather with compassion and justice, the ability to overcome boundaries, and discovery of identity through diffusion and giving rather than gathering and holding. Lears argues, however, that the "masculine ideals" stated above were deceptive: "Success was a slippery business. Titans of industry, who seemed the apotheosis of solidity and reliability, turned out at crucial moments to be confidence men."[32] In response, melodramas like *Ben-Hur, The Four Horsemen,* and others presented unbelievable spiritual elements, extremely chance occurrences, and incredible coincidences. In doing so, they revealed the instability, cruelty, and corruption of the temporal world.

Further discussion is needed to determine whether Mathis's vision for *Ben-Hur* can be defined as offering a more spiritual message than the message in the film directed by Niblo, written by Carey Wilson, and produced by Irving Thalberg. I have argued that Mathis's oeuvre stresses home and spiritual themes, and that her script for *Ben-Hur* does too. But was her message substantially different from Niblo's?

Mathis's script was written for the film's presentation as a major event in a large urban movie palace. It includes cues for musicians and singers, yet it begins by describing the light of the projector hitting the screen as the curtain opens. It may not be surprising to find that no other script has ever bothered to mention this detail. Why should they? The light coming from the projector should just be taken for granted. Mathis, though, was hoping to make *Ben-Hur* her masterpiece, surpassing not just her previous successes but even all other films. Her reference to the projector's light on screen reveals that she wanted *Ben-Hur* to be what *Birth of a Nation* (1915) and *Intolerance* (1916) were for D. W. Griffith. She was incorporating every element of the performance, even the projector's beam, into her mise-en-scène. By describing the projector's light hitting the screen as the curtains open, she established—even before the story began—the importance of people lifting their heads to receive a new illumination. Immediately afterward, the film proper begins with the Magi looking up, receiving messages from angels, and journeying to Bethlehem. As Mathis's script ends, all characters "turn and kneel as the light, similar to the effect of the Star of Bethlehem, moves towards the camera."[33] This shot was meant to suggest the light moving back toward the projector. Translated, Mathis's message was that the light that can illuminate the world is not just that of Christianity, but of cinema itself. However, it was not a claim that the cinema is equal to Christianity; rather, the message was that cinema is capable of presenting such a great message. Mathis's creative tactic conveys as well that Christ preached a spiritual message of enlightenment that was not tied to possessions or physical locations of home.

By contrast, Niblo's *Ben-Hur* emphasizes Christianity fulfilling physical needs and healing divisions. It does not suggest that people need to lift their gazes or seek enlightenment. As Ruth Scodel explains, "although Jesus's healing is available only to those who 'believe', it is not clear what this belief entails beyond the belief that Jesus can, in fact, heal. The Christian message is entirely concerned with peace and love." Jesus is presented as a supreme provider of compassion, not as a savior. This message is admirable as proclamation of a path of peace. But, as Scodel comments, "nowhere does the film refer to atonement or to sin, and nowhere does it hint at an afterlife."[34] Rather than Christ preparing a place for the saved in paradise, as the Gospel of Matthew reports, Niblo's film ends with Judah, reunited with his mother and sister, telling them that Christ "is not dead. He will live forever in the hearts of men." Instead of imploring viewers to follow the light, therefore, this *Ben-Hur* reassures them that Christ accomplished his mission and they only need to remember him.

Ben-Hur's family reunion in Niblo's final shot surely pleased many filmgoers. But it provides a much higher degree of closure than that of Mathis's ending. It also confuses Niblo's message. During the last half of the film, Ben-Hur raises an army to rise against Rome. He awaits indication from Jesus that this is what he should do. He even wears armor, carries a sword, and calls out to the Nazarene as he bears his cross toward Calvary. Then, though, Ben-Hur hears Jesus's voice in his mind, saying that his kingdom is not of this world, and battle is averted. This quelling of strife becomes Jesus's main achievement in Niblo's film. But it is overshadowed by Ben-Hur's return home. The net effect is that Christ's peace becomes more of an absence of war rather than an internal spiritual peace. As Ben-Hur looks out from his balcony in the closing shot, he can see empty crosses in the distance. But with no resurrection (or indication of sin that had to be redeemed), what the crosses signify is not clear. How and why should Jesus's example be followed?

Mathis's script, by contrast, ends with Jesus's triumphal entry into Jerusalem on Palm Sunday. Traditionally, he was never presented physically in stage versions of *Ben-Hur*. Instead, he was represented by a beam of light. Mathis planned to continue this tradition. In her final scene, the light would begin on screen in the midst of the crowds surrounding Jesus and then grow to cover the screen and move out over the audience. Her script concludes: "joyous music swells and the picture ends."[35] This ending is more open than the one in Niblo's version. Like his version, it does not preach the contents of Jesus's message. As a commercial narrative, Mathis's *Ben-Hur* would have faced a similar requirement of remaining amenable to varied interpretations. Still, rather than emphasize the comfortable idea of having all issues resolved with the hero's return, Mathis focused on spiritual triumph that individuals must pursue on their own. The promise of opportunity for spiritual growth is open to all who seek it. That this opportunity receives a greater emphasis in her script than in

Niblo's film intimates that Ben-Hur's return home, and Jesus's living on in the hearts of men, were worth all the latter's suffering.

The achievement of getting this film on the screen was eventually realized through superior financial resources and production facilities, plus tough guidance.[36] These factors produced an admirable film that achieved strong commercial success against long odds. Niblo's *Ben-Hur* may well have been more popular than the version Mathis could have produced. It certainly represented what could be achieved by deeper financial resources and a more strictly organized production process. However, these factors are not the only ones worth studying. By analyzing Mathis's forgotten script, we can rediscover some of the incredible talent of New Women in the silent film industry. We can also honor some of the spiritual values their projects offer.

Getting Judas Right

The 1925 *Ben-Hur* as Jesus Film and Biblical Epic

RICHARD WALSH

Fred Niblo's 1925 *Ben-Hur: A Tale of the Christ* was the first feature-length film version in an already strong tradition of reiterations of Lew Wallace's well-known novel.[1] As the title of both novel and film indicate, the *Ben-Hur* tradition offers two parallel stories: (1) the story of Judah Ben-Hur's tragic fall and restoration, and (2) the Gospel story of Jesus Christ. The Jesus story provides background for the foreground story about Judah.

Although it does not focus on Jesus, the film does contain enough of the story of Jesus to be considered a "Jesus film" (see table 1). The first section of this essay is a comparison of Niblo's use of fragments of the Jesus story to contemporaneous Jesus films' representation of that same story. Clearly, Niblo depicts Jesus more minimally and elliptically than most of these other films. Niblo's Jesus often reaches into the cinematic frame or appears as an ethereal light. This portrayal of a sacred "other" transcending the material world (represented by the cinematic frame) coheres with Wallace's famous reluctance to have an actor depict Christ. It also matches Klaw & Erlanger's earlier use of limelight to represent Christ.[2]

Instead of Jesus, the film focuses on Judah's story. Although it may not be immediately obvious, Judah and Judas are English versions of the same Hebrew name. Unlike the typical portrayal of Judas in Jesus films, however, Niblo's film "gets Judas right." The 1925 film's Judah/Judas learns the spiritual nature of Jesus's kingdom/message. Niblo achieves this empathetic portrayal by situating Judah as the hero of a Christian/Roman epic, rather than as a character in a Jesus film. The second section of this essay is a comparison of Niblo's film to such epics. The turn to this genre and consequent depiction of Judah as a spokesperson for a rather vague, modern religion of love and forgiveness allow Niblo's film to avoid the Christian supersessionism that bedevils Jesus films and is so much a feature of Wallace's far more evangelistic novel.[3]

The portrayal of Jesus in the 1925 film still does, however, suggest a quite orthodox Christ. Furthermore, the film's "parallel stories" approach invites viewers to notice similarities between Jesus Christ and Judah Ben-Hur. The final section of this essay examines parallels between Judah's Via Dolorosa and that of Jesus to suggest that the film replays the Gospel as Judah's story and Christ-figures Judah. Here again, viewers may sense a lingering Christian supersessionism. By moving through a discussion of this film's use of three different cinematic genres—Jesus films, Christian/Roman epics, and Christ-figure films—I contend instead that the film ultimately "gets Judas right" for a modern audience.[4]

Ben-Hur as Jesus Film

Like other versions of the Ben-Hur story, the 1925 film bookends Judah's story with Jesus's infancy and the Crucifixion.[5] This selection is not surprising because, in Niblo's day, church pageants dramatizing the infancy and Passion were popular elements of Christian holiday celebrations. Passion plays in particular have had a long performance history. The most famous of such plays is that of Oberammergau, the performance of which began in the seventeenth century and continues today at ten-year intervals. A film version purporting to record the Oberammergau play was shown in the United States in 1898.[6]

Although Passion plays and early Jesus films center on Jesus's tragic time in Jerusalem—beginning with the triumphal entry or the arrest and continuing through the Crucifixion (and resurrection)—they also include "front matter" such as Jewish Bible tableaux or incidents from the infancy and ministry of Jesus. For example, Léar's *Passion du Christ* (1897) includes twelve scenes: (1) the birth of Christ, (2) Jesus at the synagogue, (3) Jesus blessing the little children, (4) the resurrection of a widow's son, (5) the triumphal entry, (6) the Last Supper, (7) the agony in Gethsemane and Judas's betrayal, (8) Jesus before Pilate (the second time) and his condemnation,

(9) Via Dolorosa, (10) the Crucifixion, (11) the descent from the cross, and (12) the resurrection.[7] Slightly later films have similar scenes, but they expand their pre-Passion materials and are therefore often titled "lives of Jesus Christ." The Passion remains so important in these films, however, that it often still garners special mention. Such films include Ferdinand Zecca and Lucien Nonquet's *La Vie et Passion de Notre Seigneur Jésus Christ* (1902–1905, 1907), Alice Guy's *La Vie de Christ* (1906), and Sidney Olcott's *From the Manger to the Cross* (1912).[8]

These films add more miracles to the Jesus story and more women and children to Léar's scenes. Alice Guy makes women and children particularly prominent in *La Vie de Christ*. Despite containing little Jesus material, D. W. Griffith's *Intolerance* (1916) also emphasizes women and children in its pre-Passion material with scenes depicting the wedding at Cana, the woman taken in adultery, and Jesus among the children. This feminization reflects lingering Victorian attitudes toward religion, which are even more evident in Wallace's novel.[9] Although well outside the Victorian era, the 1925 *Ben-Hur* continues this focus on women not only in its concentration on the plight of Judah's mother and sister, but also in the two pre-Passion Jesus scenes it depicts: a discussion among women of Jesus's parables and his kingdom at the Pool of Siloam, during which a woman remembers Jesus's Sermon (19), and the scene of the woman taken in adultery (31).[10] Of the Jesus films mentioned above, only Griffith's *Intolerance* includes the woman taken in adultery (although this scene is common in the Passion play tradition and in subsequent Jesus films). None make reference to Jesus's parables.

These cinematic dramatizations surround the Passion with miracle stories, the most important (and common) of which are the infancy and the resurrection. Niblo's *Ben-Hur* devotes more time to the infancy than does either the play or the 1959 film. The star that marks the cave is suitably prominent (although it is even more so in the 1959 film). The family is holy and the Virgin Mary is awe-inspiring; people respond to her as they do to the sacred in biblical epics. The sacred is reflected in their awed, transfigured faces, as it is in Ben-Hur's face when he first encounters Jesus at Nazareth's well (11). The difference is that the audience also sees the holy Mary. The mere sight of Mary's face calms an angry mother

TABLE 1. Jesus Segments in *Ben-Hur*

Segment	Novel	Play	1925 Film	1959 Film
Infancy	Wise men gather	Wise men gather		Census
	Holy family to Bethlehem		Holy family to Bethlehem	
	David's cave			
			Shepherds and wise men	Shepherds and wise men
		Star (prologue)	Star	Star
	Birth and shepherds		Shepherds to David's cave	
	Wise men and Herod			
	Wise men to child		Wise men with gifts (2–4)	Wise men to manger (2)
	Star over Bethlehem (1)			
Child			Rumors of messianic child (8)	Joseph: Jesus does his father's work (4)
				Romans talk about messiah and carpenter who does magic and speaks of God within (6)
	Jesus gives cup of water to Judah (2:VII)		Jesus gives cup of water to Judah (11)	Jesus gives cup of water to Judah (18)

TABLE 1. **Jesus Segments in** *Ben-Hur* (continued)

Segment	Novel	Play	1925 Film	1959 Film
Reports and memory	Judah remembers cup (3:VI, 7:V, 8:IX–X)	Judah remembers cup (6:1)	Women talk of parables (19)	Judah remembers cup (22, 53, 58)
	Balthasar and spiritual kingdom (4:XV–XVII, 7:III)	Balthasar remembers child (3:1, 4:1)	Balthasar remembers child (30)	Balthasar remembers child (29, 31, 53)
	Simonides and earthly kingdom (5:VIII, 16)	Light of the world (4:1)		Esther reports rabbi who speaks of forgiveness, loving enemy (34, 55, 56)
				Sermon on the Mount (53)
Ministry	John the Baptist (7:I, 5)			
	Judah reports miracles (8:II)	Judah (6:1) and Amrah (6:2) report miracles	Sermon (19)	
			Stoning of adulteress (31)	
	"Triumph" (8:IV)		Triumph (31)	

TABLE 1. Jesus Segments in *Ben-Hur* (continued)

Segment	Novel	Play	1925 Film	1959 Film
Hur family healed	"Triumph" (8:IV)	"Triumph" (6:2–6:3)	Via Dolorosa (37)	During crucifixion (60)
Passion			Last Supper (33)	
	Betrayal, arrest, ear, flight		Report of arrest (34)	
	"Whom seek ye?"			
	Judah as naked young man (8:VIII)			
	Report of hand washing and blood curse		Before Pilate	Hand washing
			Report of healings and resurrections (35)	
	Via Dolorosa (8:IX)		Via Dolorosa	Via Dolorosa
			Miracles	Whipping
			Kingdom not of this world (36–37)	Another carries cross (57)
				Judah offers water (58)

TABLE 1. **Jesus Segments in *Ben-Hur* (continued)**

Segment	Novel	Play	1925 Film	1959 Film
	Crucifixion		Crucifixion	Crucifixion
	Jesus's sayings		Father forgive (37)	Balthasar: For our sins
	I am resurrection and life			Thieves (59)
	Darkness		Darkness, quake, storm (38)	Darkness, storm, quake
	Judah takes sponge to Jesus (8:X)			Family healed (60)
Aftermath	Antioch church		Balthasar: forgiveness and love	Judah reports "Father forgive"
	Catacomb church (8:X)		Judah: live forever in hearts (38)	Shepherd before cross (61)

Note: The information in this table is based on the following sources: Lew Wallace, *Ben-Hur: A Tale of the Christ* (New York: Harper, 1901); William Young, "Ben-Hur," in *Playing out the Empire: Ben-Hur and Other Toga Plays and Films, 1883–1908. A Critical Anthology,* ed. David Mayer (Oxford: Oxford Univ. Press, 1994), 189–290; Fred Niblo, *Ben-Hur: A Tale of the Christ* (MGM, 1925); William Wyler, *Ben-Hur* (MGM, 1959). Parenthetical references are to the novel's book and chapters, the play's acts and scenes, and the films' DVD chapters (Warner Home Video DVDs).

in Jerusalem (2) and beguiles a churlish Bethlehem innkeeper into finding the family a cave in which to sleep (3). In the nativity scene, which is in Technicolor, Mary has a nimbus. All worship her and the baby she holds.[11]

Given Niblo's choice of these opening scenes for *Ben-Hur*, the resurrection's absence from the film is notable.[12] Niblo opted instead to conclude with Ben-Hur's assertion of Jesus's lasting spiritual (or psychological) influence. This choice bespeaks a more theologically liberal or even secular cultural portrayal of Jesus than that of other early films and in Wallace's evangelistic novel.

The 1925 *Ben-Hur* does, however, have its share of miracle scenes. After hearing about Jesus's healings and resurrections, Esther, Ben-Hur's love interest, collects Ben-Hur's mother and sister from the Valley of the Lepers and brings them to Jesus to be healed. The women find him on the Via Dolorosa where Jesus resurrects a dead baby (36) and restores the Hur women to health (37). The healing of lepers is quite rare in Jesus films. Of those mentioned thus far in this essay, only Olcott's *From the Manger to the Cross* contains such a scene.[13] The lepers' healing (as Milette Shamir notes earlier in this volume) is the climax of Niblo's *Ben-Hur*. However, this scene does detract from Jesus's suffering on the Via Dolorosa and at the cross. The focus is instead on his Passion as a miracle for others.[14] The final scene foregrounds the "resurrected" Hur family (38), not Jesus's cross (in the background) or the resurrection (not shown). Thus, the film's arc moves from one holy family (2–4) to another (36–38). That this scene is in Technicolor, like many of the Jesus scenes, further emphasizes the Hur family's holiness.[15] Given this finale, the Jesus story does not bookend the Hur family story. Instead, the Jesus story introduces a different holy family story and provides the miraculous vehicle that restores the Hurs' tragically destroyed family.

Jesus's healing of the Hur women connects Niblo's twinned Jesus and Hur stories. Other intersections include descriptions of the people's hopes for a messiah or deliverer and suggestions that Jesus might be that figure (1, 8, 11, 19, 30) as well as the wise Balthasar's recollections of the messianic child he once saw (30). Although Judah's recollections of the cup of water Jesus gave him on his march to the galleys provides cohesion for the 1959 film,[16] the 1925 film does not use the incident in this repetitive manner. Instead the scene in the 1925 film introduces the (nearly) adult Jesus and implies Christ's divinity. Jesus's provision of water overwhelms the Roman soldiers who have denied Judah water, leaves Judah with the awed face of one who has seen the sacred, and responds to Judah's question, "is there no God left in Israel?" (11). Along with the healing of the Hur women, this scene is Niblo's major addition to the Gospel Jesus story. These additions serve to "Judahize" the Jesus story.

Niblo's version of this Nazareth scene also demonstrates his film's allusive portrayal of Jesus. The star and the holy Virgin Mary, not the Christ child, dominate the earlier nativity material (although the star does have a cross-like shape) (3). In the Nazareth well scene, euphemistic intertitles refer to Jesus as the carpenter's son and son of Mary, and he appears elliptically as a hand on a saw, as the hand that offers the cup of water to Judah, and as the hand that soothes Judah by touching his head. His foot is also visible near the prone Ben-Hur as Judah looks up to divine the source of this refreshing water.

Later in the film, women talk about a "strange man" by the Pool of Siloam (19). One woman describes what she has heard Jesus say, and the audience sees a tableau of the Sermon on the Mount and Jesus's gesturing hand as he calls the heavy-laden to him (from Matt. 11:28, not the Sermon on the Mount). After Ben-Hur's victory in the chariot race, Jesus's hand appears at the frame's edge as he intervenes to stop the stoning of the adulteress (John 8:2–11) (31). An intertitle quotes Jesus's authoritative saying, "he that is without sin among you; let him first cast a stone at her" (John 8:7). The crowd disperses and the hand withdraws as the woman, bathed in an ethereal light (cf. John 8:12), worships. Similarly, when Jesus enters Jerusalem in triumph, the camera shows him from afar on a black donkey and then focuses instead on a woman who places her cloak before him and worships as he passes (31).

Jesus next appears in a scene that resembles a photographic tableau of Da Vinci's *Last Supper* painting (the scene is introduced by an intertitle quoting Matt. 26:20) (33). The tableau differs from Da Vinci's famous painting, however, in that Judas appears on the audience's side of the long rectangular table—a positioning common in other paintings of this scene.[17] This placement hides Jesus from view, except for an eerie blue glow, which may allude to Klaw & Erlanger's famous representation of Jesus by limelight. Instead of eucharistic words, an intertitle offers Jesus's love command (John 13:34a) before the visuals return to prayerful disciples and a long shot of the Da Vinci table.

At the Roman trial (Matt. 27:2), Niblo has soldiers obscure Jesus from view as he stands before Pilate (35). A beam of heavenly light illumines the space where he presumably stands. As the trial continues, reports of miracles prompt Esther to race to find the leprous Hur women. Meanwhile, Pilate hands Jesus over to "the mob" (cf. Mark 15:15). The cross he carries largely prevents viewers from seeing Jesus, who glows, transfigured, on the Via Dolorosa thereafter (36). As previously, the camera focuses on those who see Jesus, not on Jesus himself. When Judah offers to unleash the legions to fight for him, Jesus says, "my Kingdom is not of this world. Put up thy sword, for the Son of man is not come to destroy men's lives, but to save them." The film cites no source for this quotation, presumably because it merges John 18:36; Luke 9:56; and John 18:11. Next, Jesus's hand moves away from Judah, who stands transfixed. His hand hovers gently to resurrect a woman's child and to dramatically transform the Hur women (37). After a shot of his bloody footprints, an intertitle refers to the soldier's division of his clothing (Luke 23:34b) before showing the holy women and soldiers at the foot of the cross. Another intertitle returns to the same verse to quote Jesus's words: "Father, forgive them; for they know not what they do" (Luke 23:34a). Darkness and earthquake follow, but the visuals focus on the collapse of the Roman praetorium and Balthasar's report of Jesus's message of love and forgiveness, which stops the rebel legions from marching on Jerusalem (38). The legions pray, and the restored Hur family rejoices in the final scene, with Golgotha's crosses in the far background.

The allusive depiction of Jesus stems, in part, from agreements made in deference to Wallace's well-known hesitancy to portray Christ. These agreements enabled the studio to obtain the film rights to the story.[18] The resulting portrayal of Jesus is a classic example of the cinematic depiction of the sacred through symbolic transcendence, a means that mimetically represents the sacred "other" that transcends the material world or cinematic frame.[19] That Jesus literally reaches into the film's cinematic frame time after time strongly asserts that Jesus is not at home in the picture, but is rather a stranger from afar who temporarily enters the film. The ethereal, transfigured glow in which his hand (or clothing) often appears only adds to this transcendent effect. Furthermore, although this depiction may suggest docetic or gnostic views to theologically sophisticated Christians, it is the Jesus film tradition's favored way of presenting its implicitly orthodox, divine, or Johannine Jesus.[20] Not incidentally, this allusive, symbolic portrayal also allows non-Christian or secular viewers to interpret the film according to their own ideologies.[21]

Such transcendent portrayals make the Jesuses of Jesus films into icons, rather than characters, or into the vacuous, sacred centers around which more interesting stories revolve. These other stories are about characters who come into contact with this mysterious figure and whose lives are then ethically defined by their positive (conversion) or negative (degradation) responses to him.[22] Christian/Roman biblical epics like *Ben-Hur* foreground these other stories and characters and thus portray Jesus even more minimally than Jesus films. In both genres, Jesus is a talisman evoking and symbolizing the sacred. He is a symbol of non-violent conquest. In the 1925 film, he is that which calls the Hurs and the audience to forgiveness and love of the enemy and that which makes possible the Hur family reunion.[23]

Getting Judas Right: Love Conquers Vengeance in the Christian/Roman Epic

For modern audiences, the most interesting character in the Jesus story is often Judas, perhaps because of the enigma the various Gospel versions of Judas present and because Judas, like moderns, is the insider-turned-outsider vis-à-vis the Jesus story.[24] The Gospel Judas is determined (by oracle), scapegoated, and demonized.[25] Modern portrayals of Judas are more sympathetic, but they seldom evoke empathy. Film, in particular, typically depicts Judas as the excluded "other": the person whom modern humans do not want to be, although they may have some suspicion that they resemble Judas.[26]

In fact, the overall history of the portrayal of Judas is so negative that Kim Paffenroth ends his book by describing the way he wishes Judas's story had gone. In Paffenroth's empathetic fiction, Judas is a "regular guy" who winds up embroiled with authorities who "cover up" Jesus's resurrection and pay Judas to keep his knowledge of it quiet. In return, Judas asks that the authorities circulate a rumor that he committed suicide so he can retire to a quiet family life in the country. Paffenroth summarizes, "it's just a story of a guy who makes a mistake but still gets forgiven, and then goes on to get the money and the girl."[27]

This synopsis could represent the story of any number of cinematic characters. It certainly recaps *Ben-Hur*, making one wonder if the choice of the name "Judah" for the film's hero was incidental. Although the character's name stems from the novel and befits a prince of Jerusalem, viewers should not overlook the fact that Judah and Judas are, in effect, the same name. More precisely, Judas is the Hellenized form of the Hebraic Judah.[28] Given this Judah/Judas connection, *Ben-Hur* deserves to be seen as the film that "gets Judas right" by offering an empathetic, modern account of Judah/Judas.

Although a Gospel Judas does appear in the film—alienated on the wrong side of the Last Supper table—Judah Ben-Hur incarnates (part of) the pattern traced by many, if not most, cinematic Judases. For the English-speaking world, Thomas De Quincey first popularized this version of Judas. The De Quincey Judas sees Jesus as the messiah who can restore Israel's political kingdom (or freedom). When Jesus fails to establish this kingdom quickly enough for Judas, Judas betrays Jesus to force him to liberate Israel. Although this account portrays Judas's motivation somewhat sympathetically, De Quincey further asserts that Judas's spiritual blindness led him to mistake the nature of Jesus's kingdom. In short, (Christian) theology or spirituality is simply beyond the human (and Jewish) Judas.[29]

Some version of this Judas (or an otherwise politically motivated Judas) dominates Jesus films.[30] This Judas is most central, however, to Nicholas Ray's *King of Kings* (1961).[31] An opening voiceover (by Orson Welles) details Rome's long oppression of the Jews and claims that they survived through their hope for a messiah. Although the film includes obligatory nativity material, its action effectively begins with Barabbas and his lieutenant Judas harassing Pilate's military escort as Pilate arrives to govern the Jews. The film pairs this epic battle with Jesus's baptism. Attracted to

Jesus's charisma, Judas is torn between the messiah of war (Barabbas) and the messiah of peace (Jesus). Manipulating Judas, Barabbas stages a revolt as Jesus arrives in triumph and preaches in the temple. When the Romans crush the revolt and arrest Barabbas, a devastated Judas betrays Jesus to force him to defeat Rome and save Judas's imprisoned friends. Instead, the betrayal initiates Jesus's Passion.

Parallels with the 1925 *Ben-Hur* are striking. It also opens with repeated observations about Rome's oppression of the Jews and Jewish hopes for a deliverer (1–2, 5, 8) and with a nativity (2–4, 9–10) before turning to its primary story of the Hurs' demise. Ben-Hur's family tragedy motivates Judah to prepare for the militant king to come (10–11, 30–37). Although Niblo's Judah/Judas does not choose between messianic claimants, he does choose ultimately between messianic ideas: a messiah of war/vengeance and one of peace/love (19, 36). One might see Judah Ben-Hur, then, as the earliest example of the De Quincey Judas in U.S. film.[32]

However, unlike the Judases of De Quincey, *King of Kings*, and the cinematic tradition in general, Niblo's Judah/Judas ultimately follows Jesus "correctly." In the dramatic scene on the Via Dolorosa, he offers himself and his legions to Jesus for the war of independence, only to have Jesus stupefy him by his touch and with his words of a kingdom not of this world. Miraculously converted (from vengeance/nationalism to love), Judah drops his (Roman) sword (36) and embraces his restored family (37). Underlining this decision, the only words spoken by Jesus from the cross in Niblo's *Ben-Hur* are: "Father, forgive them; they know not what they do." Balthasar stops the revolutionary legions with similar words so that the rebels kneel, pray, and worship.[33] Furthermore, Judah's (and the film's) last words are that Jesus "will live forever in the hearts of men." As with Paffenroth's fictional Judas story, this Judah story ends happily, with family and wealth.

The 1925 film "gets Judas right" largely because its hero is the protagonist of a Christian/Roman epic and not a minor character in a Jesus film. Typically, Christian supersessionism—the notion that Christianity replaces an obsolete Judaism—is less of an issue in the Christian/Roman epic than it is in Jesus films. The Gospel Passion story and the sermons in Acts make Judas (the Jew) and the Jewish religious authorities into villains who are primarily culpable for the innocent Jesus's death. At the same time, the Gospel and Acts minimize Roman involvement in the Crucifixion and in later Christian suffering. By contrast, Christian/Roman epics feature villainous Romans, and Jews virtually "disappear" from the story. The dramatic difference between Acts' Jewish villains and the Christian/ Roman epics' Roman villains is quite noteworthy.

Ben-Hur deviates from the typical Christian/Roman epic pattern because it has a Jewish hero and is set during Jesus's life and Passion, rather than in Neronian Rome.[34] The return to the Gospel setting and flirtation with the De Quincey Judas reintroduce potential elements of Christian supersessionism.[35] The De Quincey Judas certainly involves supersessionism if one identifies hopes of an earthly kingdom (and/ or *lex talionis*) with Judaism and a spiritual kingdom (and/or love) with Christianity.[36] Wallace's novel does so too, although it also extols the lasting cultural and theological contributions of Judaism's ethical monotheism. Furthermore, in distinction from the films, the novel meticulously reports the "conversion" of Judah, Esther, and other Jews to Christianity and the Hurs' subsequent financial support of Christian communities in Antioch and Rome. The 1959 film demonstrates far less supersessionism because its Judah remains a practicing Jew at the film's end (he lovingly touches the mezuzah as he enters his family home after the Crucifixion).[37] Because this Judah already stands for non-violent religion in early discussions with Messala (8, 10), one might say that his "conversion" is simply his restoration to non-violent Judaism after a brief flirtation with Roman vengeance (55).

What, then, of the 1925 film? Should audiences read Judah's "conversion" from violence to love on the Via Dolorosa as a conversion from Judaism to Christianity? Judas does give up his skullcap early on in the film. Despite this action and his militant Jewish nationalism, which recalls the De Quincey Judas, Niblo's Judah converts from Roman military violence to a Jewish Jesus's forgiveness and love, rather than from Judaism to Christianity.[38] In this film, Jesus and Judah are Jewish not only because of ethnic or religious markers but because they are the primary examples of all those oppressed by Rome. Thus, the film has no Jewish trial of Jesus. It concentrates on Jesus's appearance before Pilate and the Roman official's deliverance of Jesus to the mob (of mixed nationality). Roman soldiers whip Jesus along the Via Dolorosa and gamble at his cross. Then, the Crucifixion earthquake topples the Roman praetorium (John 18:23), not the Jewish temple. In short, the film's ethical polarities situate oppressive Rome against the Jews and the oppressed, who are represented in particular by the Hur family and Jesus.[39]

The dichotomies of the Christian/Roman epic typically oppose Rome and Christianity, so Niblo's *Ben-Hur* essentially equates Jews and Christians. Given the film's predominantly Christian audience, such an equation might be tantamount to supersession, or simply a rather vague depiction of religion. In fact, if the religion advocated by the 1925 film is Christian, it is an incredibly bland, non-creedal form that emphasizes love and forgiveness of enemies. Such a religion is not necessarily in conflict with modern secular values or with liberal forms of Judaism.[40] Thus, what Judah converts to is a form of religion palatable to a 1925 U.S. audience.[41] That religion may be nominally Christian, but its essential components are religious tolerance (or respect for freedom of religion); acquiescence to, if not support of, the status quo; and intense individualism.[42] The religion of *Ben-Hur*'s Jesus is not really Jewish or Christian but a modern or liberal commitment to love and forgiveness or, more accurately, a commitment on the part of the individual to leave religion out of social and political matters. Accordingly, Judah concludes the film by saying that Jesus "will live forever in the hearts of men." In sum, Judah converts primarily from an inappropriately "political" religion to an appropriately "spiritual" one, or to a religion that is a matter of the individual's free subjectivity.[43]

The 1925 *Ben-Hur* avoids supersessionism, then, to the extent that it endorses this modern apolitical religion and/or to the extent that it follows the patterns of Christian/Roman epics, rather than those of Jesus films. Unlike Jesus films, these epics revel in violence (e.g., *Ben-Hur*'s galley slave scenes, the sea battle, and the chariot race). However, their concentration on the hero's (or heroine's) conversion from the Roman values of violence, militarism, and oppressive empire (as well as debauchery on many occasions) to the Jewish, Christian, or modern U.S. values of love/ forgiveness, peace, and freedom (of the individual) rejects the violence in which the epic lives. In Victorian terms, this transition is also a turn from the masculine, public world to the private, feminine world. Typically, this move involves the Roman male hero's nominal conversion to the Christianity of his romantic interest, but in *Ben-Hur* it is primarily the turn from vengeance/revolt to the restoration of the family. *Omnia vincit amor*, but the love is primarily romantic and familial, not Jewish or Christian.[44]

Judah Ben-Hur as Christ Figure

The feminization of Judah Ben-Hur brings his story into harmony with the Jesus story it parallels. The overall format of a twinned story invites comparisons between protagonists. In *Ben-Hur*, the stories are initially rather far apart, despite their common setting and intersections, because Judah's story follows a trajectory of violent vengeance and revolt whereas Jesus's story is one of love and forgiveness. The scene in which women discuss different messianic conceptions at the Pool of Siloam illustrates the twinned stories' distance from one another (19).[45] When Judah drops his sword on the Via Dolorosa, however, the stories finally mesh. Does that mean that Judah becomes a Christ figure?[46]

The 1959 film offers an elaborate sequence of references to the cup of water that Jesus gives to Judah on his way to the galleys (18, 22, 53, 58, 59). The film uses this water motif to connect the twinned stories and to parallel the two characters.[47] Instead of the cup of water, the 1925 film uses the Via Dolorosa motif to create parallels. Thus, Judah has his own Via Dolorosa. He too is an innocent condemned without appropriate trial, and he is marched, not to Golgotha, but across the "way of death" to the galleys (11). When the condemned, including Judah, fall in the road, the Romans whip them back to their feet or leave them for dead. Appropriately, the journey is through Nazareth and leads to the first meeting between Jesus and Judah. As if intentionally underlining the similarity between this road and Jesus's Via Dolorosa, the film ends Judah's road in a slave galley, which includes a crucified slave (a slave on an upright, cruciform whipping block) (12). Later, during Jesus's Via Dolorosa, Judah watches Jesus fall, be whipped, and continue to his cross as Judah once went to his death (36). Judah senses the parallels, for he drops his sword and joins Jesus in accepting their joint (Roman) fate.[48] Ironically, this joint submission fulfills Messala's prophetic words: "To be a Roman is to rule the world! To be a

Jew is to crawl in the dirt!" It does not, however, fulfill Messala's ethical corollary: "Forget you are a Jew!" (8). On the Via Dolorosa, Jesus and Judah both become Jews "in the dirt," united in their oppression by Rome.

Given the cultural weight of the Gospel, this parallelism also makes both Judah and Jesus into suffering Christs.[49] For example, Judah arrives at his second Via Dolorosa after forsaking Roman glory (an implicit temptation narrative) and after foregoing love (from Esther) for familial duty (30). Although the rejection of love for duty is a common heroic trope, stretching back in biblical epics to the heroine of Griffith's *Judith of Bethuliah* (1914), it may also unite Judah with Jesus's dutiful choice of suffering in the Gospel's Gethsemane account (e.g., Matt. 26:36–46). If so, the scene with Esther becomes Judah's Gethsemane. Interpreted this way, Niblo's film replays the Gospel Jesus story as Judah's story instead of Jesus's story, particularly because the film does not include Jesus's own Gethsemane experience.[50]

If Judah is, in some sense, a Christ figure, does this once again imply the supersessionism that the Christian/Roman epic patterns in *Ben-Hur* largely mitigate or avoid? An analogy may illustrate the complications. What happens with the Jewish messiah in *Ben-Hur* is similar to what happens in the quest for the historical Jesus. For Albert Schweitzer, this search begins with Samuel Reimarus. Reimarus contended that the historical Jesus was a Jew trying to establish a political kingdom and that the more spiritual notions of the Christ and his kingdom were developed by Jesus's disciples only after his Crucifixion.[51] According to Reimarus, the subsequent Christian church wrote Christ over the Jewish Jesus. As Schweitzer's work illustrates, later Jesus historians ignored Reimarus's arguments to "find" a liberal Jesus in history "behind" the Gospel (and spiritual) Christ. It is hard to see this modern discovery as a revitalization of an ancient Jewish Jesus, whether that Jesus was political or not.[52] Instead, the discovery writes a modern, cultural Christ over Jesus (and over the neoplatonic, creedal Christ as well). Because the teachings of the liberal (Jesus) Christ that these historians found were of peace, love, and brotherhood (sic), the trajectory of historical Jesus scholarship is remarkably like the story arc in the 1925 *Ben-Hur*: from political to spiritual king and from Jewish Judah/Jesus (and from creedal Christ) to modern, liberal

Christ(s). Whether this similar story line bespeaks primarily Christian supersessionism or the construction of modern U.S. identities (admittedly with a dash of a rather vague Christianity) may ultimately depend on the perspectives viewers bring to this film and the choices each analyst makes among the various suggestive, yet conflicting, generic categories on which this contribution to the *Ben-Hur* tradition draws.

Take Up the White Man's Burden

Race and Resistance to *Ben-Hur*

BARBARA RYAN

As World War II looms, a Scottish knight treks through Arctic wilds to rescue a New Yorker and the backwoodsman who has led him astray. This story sounds like a far cry from *Ben-Hur* in any of the formats in which it has thrilled tens of millions. Recently, though, analysts have begun to find evidence of the *"Ben-Hur* tradition" where it has lain previously unsuspected. The premise of this sort of inquiry serves here too: the ubiquity—for decades—of Lew Wallace's tale, the Klaw & Erlanger show, Fred Niblo's 1925 film, and/or some amalgam of two or more adaptations. This essay does not offer irrefutable evidence of John Buchan's opinion of *Ben-Hur* or its influence on his novel, *Sick Heart River* (1941).[1] But it does prod thought about how tricky it could be for Christians to resist the quest-saga, featuring Jesus, which some fans deemed near sacred. I show how *Sick Heart River* resists *Ben-Hur*, but I also show how this tale, written by a Church of Scotland elder, hints at a reservation that Geza Vermes has probed: some Christians have trouble seeing Jesus as Jewish.[2] Cotter-pinning this inquiry is a character in *Sick Heart* who is described in ways that evoke Judaism or, more precisely, certain Christians' stereotypes of Jews. This character is an American backwoodsman and autodidact. Buchan named him—wait for it—Lew.

This overview sounds quite unlike the oeuvre of a Scot who was, and is, best known for spy thrillers like *The Thirty-Nine Steps* (1915). Indeed, *Sick Heart* is unique in Buchan's voluminous output. This posthumous tale is his most somber. It is also his only proselytizing publication, in a career that includes fiction, non-fiction, journalism, poetry, biography, and more. Affection is evident in the sorrow with which a fan dubbed *Sick Heart* "the last Buchan." Admiring, though, is the blogger who, knowing that Buchan dictated *Sick Heart* from his deathbed, described this tale as "a dying man's last conversations with God."[3] She prioritized, as I do, Buchan's devout faith. Only some of his readers shared it. But nearly all had, like Buchan, grown up with *Ben-Hur*. His U.S. readers likely played the Ben-Hur board game, read about the Ben-Hur paddle-wheeler, or quaffed Ben-Hur coffee. Throughout the modernizing world, though, by the time Buchan started dictating his last tale, many of his fans had enjoyed the 1925 film version of *Ben-Hur*. Many, too, had enjoyed the film's re-release, with sound, in 1936.

Back in 1925, some people had disliked the decision to cast a Mexican heartthrob as Ben-Hur. Better accepted was the decision to let an actor, Claude Payton, play Jesus. The filming of Payton from the back bears no blaring relation to the way in which Buchan crafted *Sick Heart*. Yet by omitting Payton from the credits, Niblo finessed a fraught issue: Jesus's race. Facets of *Sick Heart* show finesse too. Loud and clear, however, is the pure-dee whiteness of a Scottish knight who dies so that others may live. Amplifying Sir Edward Leithen's whiteness is the mixed-race heritage of the misguider who urges him to live at others' expense. This pairing maps onto Satan tempting Jesus in the wilderness—an interesting point inasmuch as these false and true guides meet in an unmapped Arctic valley. However, Lew Frizel is not evil; rather, his good qualities are stunted by clannish pharisaism that Buchan ties to vengefulness, self-seeking, and a "halfling" grasp of God's ways.[4] As Sir Edward achieves a firmer grasp on these ways, he exhibits compassion for sufferers he had despised when his quest began. These extensions of the false/true guide clash hint at a supersessionist conceptualization of the inferiority of Jew-Lew to Christian-Leithen. They may not be cause to recall Vermes's attention to some people's balk at Jesus's Jewishness. However, that balk is alluded to by Buchan's decision to make his true guide pure white and his false guide half-white even though *Sick Heart*'s plot gains nothing from these fillips.

Scholars such as Shawn Kelley, Jeffrey S. Siker, and Ella Shohat have studied historical interest in Jesus's race. Pictorially, Jefferson J. A.

5. Ben-Hur coffee on sale in Los Angeles in the 1930s. From the Mott/Merge Photograph Collection of the California History Room, California State Library, Sacramento, California.

Gatrall reminds analysts that "[i]n becoming historical, Jesus . . . acquired race" as nineteenth-century romancers "tested the sacral possibilities of the historical Jesus precisely to the extent that they made his unfamiliar figure appear real."[5] Born in 1875, but publishing nothing until much later, Buchan is not usually considered a nineteenth-century romancer. A twentieth-century fan was right nonetheless to dub Buchan "the last Victorian" due to his values.[6] Some may assume that the last Victorian was a *Ben-Hur* fan. Knowing, though, that "Victorian" signifies as variably as "Christian," I gather hints that the last book by the last Victorian preached against Niblo's *Ben-Hur* and, if not against Wallace's tale, at least against immature admiration for it. This does not sound like a racial matter. But *Sick Heart* "whitens" the character who most resembles the historical actor whom Wallace made Greco-Jewish and whose race Niblo finessed. A key consideration in this register is that Buchan did not rest content by making his hero a Scot. In addition, he showed how this knight of the realm masters a misguider of mixed-race descent: a métis.

It is not clear if Buchan had pondered Ernst Renan's claim that Aryanness can be inborn but may be attained by mastering threats to Christianity whose intrusions on this "modern" faith mark sub-whiteness. Still, even if he knew nothing of this nineteenth-century claim, the memoir he dictated along with *Sick Heart* defends the credo Rudyard Kipling designated "the white man's burden."[7] This credo's Christian girding points to how overtly Sir Edward grows from contempt for aboriginal Americans to self-sacrifice on their behalf. This plot development does not cue *Ben-Hur*; it cues Jesus. That cue dovetails, however, with a characterological decision that does cue *Ben-Hur*: the misguiding métis's name.

This hint is minute. But it is recurrent *and* alliterative in that Lew stands in relation to Leithen as Judah Ben-Hur stands to Jesus Ben-Joseph. Why would a Christian try to guide seekers away from *Ben-Hur*? Not for literary reasons but from duty to God: to shepherd seekers to Jesus. Because many Christians feel that *Ben-Hur* does this effectively, a ground-clearing question is, where did Buchan see sheep going astray? Part of the answer lies in his decision to make Lew half-Scot, half-Cree. There is nothing shy about *Sick Heart*'s defense of the white man's burden. To the contrary, this quest-saga promotes the knot of race and religion that tangles higher melanin count with the pre-Christian belief that "burden" proponents denigrate as primitive. Something very like this knot informed Wallace's decision to make his Jesus character whiter than Fagin or Shylock. Six decades later, Buchan made his self-sacrificer whiter still and blared this choice by giving Sir Edward a leadership rival who is half-white only. Does this choice indicate that Buchan had heard the rumor about Wallace's mixed-race heritage? No documentation records this. However, *Sick Heart*'s "whitening" of its self-sacrificing savior does echo a notion that an Anglo-German advanced in 1899: Jesus's body held "not a drop of real Jewish blood."[8]

Seen from this angle, the Lew/Leithen "foil" pattern signals Jew/non-Jew. The Jew figure, Lew Frizel, is clannishly pharisaical, self-seeking, and, though not vengeful himself, impelled toward the Sick Heart River Valley "as if vengeance followed him" (115). The New Yorker who follows him ends up lamed and abandoned. From these ills, Sir Edward rescues the financier rather easily. He finds it quite hard, however, to undo the spell Lew has cast over the New Yorker's imagination. It reduces him to a state of staring dependency. None of this recalls *Ben-Hur* except the name Lew. Yet Sir Edward ponders at one point that the name "Frizel" is a derivation of "Walsh." This is not quite "Wallace," but it is close enough to be indicative. The indication gains vigor from the realization that Sir Edward's pondering about names has no plot value. Some may feel, moreover, that the name "Frizel" sounds Jewish. Certainly some Jews have taken this Scottish surname.

Was Buchan innovative in seeing how *Ben-Hur* could lead seekers astray? No, because concern about this tale's vengefulness was expressed in some early reviews. Was he original, then, in making racial considerations important? No, considering the remarks of an 1890s fan who praised Wallace's protagonist at the expense of Jews in general. The *Ben-Hur* fan added, gratuitously, that few Jews recognize Jesus as Lord because they are made of such vile clay. How this claim refracts Jesus's Judaism, he did not say. Other detractors hinted at racial hierarchies obliquely by denouncing Ben-Hur's vengefulness.[9] This sampling of prior reception sketches what Buchan had to manage if he hoped to resist *Ben-Hur* without disparaging its fans or casting explicit aspersions on Jews. Making his road stonier is the fact that while he wrote, he was serving as governor general of Canada.

These considerations add up to a strong cause to mute resistance to a tale that many loved. Strong too, however, was the eschatology of Buchan's agenda. Antic in contrast is the slap Buster Keaton gave *Ben-Hur* in the film *Three Ages* (1923). Maria Wyke's discussion of this spoof pioneers recovery of tacit references to *Ben-Hur*. I push this sort of inquiry further by discerning resistance where it has lain unsuspected: in the last tale by the last Victorian. When it comes to *Ben-Hur*, my findings are more speculative than those Wyke develops because she could draw on visual cues (e.g., togas and chariots).[10] Rock solid, though, is *Sick Heart*'s "white man's burden" homily.

This aspect of Buchan's last book is not muted. Rather, quite openly and even pleadingly, Lew tempts Leithen by urging him to put his own survival above that of an ailing First Nation group. Lew's heart is good in the sense that he thinks the group unworthy of this sacrifice; he is trying, that is, to protect his friend who is indeed a good man. However, that the group is not Cree makes Lew's scorn for them clannish. Worse though, for Buchan, is the American's assertion that "we white folk"—meaning, people like himself and Sir Edward—stand above natives (189). That such pharisaism is base, in Buchan's view, is signaled by the knight's private certainty that the métis overreaches: he is part-white, yes, but part not.

Is the decision to name the false guide "Lew" the sole evidence of *Sick Heart*'s resistance to *Ben-Hur*? No, because Buchan is known to have re-read childhood favorites as he lay dying. No, with more force, because Sir Edward's first visit in Canada is to a verdant meadow he remembers from his young manhood. On his return decades later, he is shocked to find the vale horribly polluted. The villain is a factory called "Glaubstein's." Readers could, and can, think this name German. But if they investigate this authorial decision, they learn that "Glaube" means faith. The intimation that a faith that offered no bread (only a stone) was polluting beauty can be interpreted as reproof of Nazism. In an American setting, though, the reference to happy youthful memories and dismay about venality, as well as the name "Glaubstein," whispers worry that Hollywood had corrupted a youthful treasure. Buchan would have been no happier, I infer, with the June Mathis script that Thomas J. Slater finds spiritual but not Christian. But with Buchan being unaware of that short-stopped script, his target in *Sick Heart* lay somewhere between what Richard Walsh calls Niblo's "bland, non-creedal Christianity" and Wallace's gift for glistening images that may lead seekers astray.[11]

◆ ◆ ◆

Now, plot. Sir Edward, learning that he will die soon due to lung damage suffered in World War I, travels to Canada. His goal is selfish: he wants to evade friends' helpless compassion. Wishing at this point only to show courage, he agrees to find a lost New Yorker. Soon though, Lew Frizel becomes a major part of Leithen's mission as he realizes that the financier has been led astray by the métis, who is more seeker than guide. As the knight turns seeker to find the lost men with Lew's brother Johnny, he learns the reason for the search: Lew quests for a remote river valley that has caught hold of his religious imagination. Despite pain and fatigue, the Scot steels himself to waken the métis from his fantasy. After long, painful trekking, the true and false guides meet in the Sick Heart cleft. There, the whiter man takes charge with leadership ability not shown by the rough-hewn Lew, effete financier, or "bullet head" Johnny (108). None of this can be inferred from commentary that after "Sir Edward Leithen gives up his languishing political career," he "heads for the Arctic to rescue a New York banker, and dies in the attempt."[12] This account is unfair. The Scot does die, true, but only after he has saved fellow seekers, natives imperiled by superstition, and his own soul. Discerning this, a wise priest explains that Sir Edward's last days are happy and blessed because "he knew that he would die; but he knew also that he would live" (318, cf. 314 in Latin).

Commentators who accept Buchan's donnée perceive how Sir Edward's trek gives him a chance to explore "private, humble, suffering truths with Christ-like significance." In agreement was a reviewer who judged *Sick Heart* "as good a sermon to lift the downhearted as has ever been given in the form of a novel."[13] Ignored, however, is Buchan's decision to make Sir Edward's "foil" half-white. Where does the American go wrong? Buchan would have admired Lew for seeking God. The snag is that this "strong child of Nature" seeks without benefit of minister or doctrine (195). A near-fatal result is that Lew casts aside the financier who trusts and follows him. Though bedeviled as if by vengefulness, Lew is wrong to pull a soul-sick quester with him and then abandon the man selfishly. He admits this wrongdoing when he asks Sir Edward to take charge of the pilgrimage. Still, Buchan urges readers to forgive the seeker who is lost himself as he quests for a showy yet barren river valley that he romances as a "New Jerusalem with all my sins washed away" (181).

If you are familiar with Buchan's best sellers, these thoughts are startling: allegory was not his métier. Nor do his other tales issue jeremiads against willingness to follow blind guides. Bracing this approach to *Sick*

Heart is the realization that nothing could stop fans from enjoying *Ben-Hur*, in any format, in any way they liked rather than as Buchan thought right. This realization trains a spotlight on aspects of *Sick Heart* that urge readers to leave behind (with childish things) thrills as low as those of a chariot race, emotion as soul-sickening as vengeance, and scene-painting as gorgeous as the sort Wallace, Klaw & Erlanger, and Niblo offered. Niblo's reliance on the Klaw & Erlanger show, in converse with perceptions of Jews' prominence in Hollywood, makes it germane that Buchan has been accused of anti-Semitism. The accusation is plausible: some references to Jews in his publications, if brief, are ugly. The usual defense is his name on a Nazi list of enemies due to his support for Zionism.[14] Yet to be reckoned, however, is *Sick Heart*'s concern about Hollywood's capacity to lead seekers astray. Ruth Scodel has written about "the Jewish question" that arose when Hollywood filmed Wallace's Bible-extender.[15] Remembering Renan's explication of Aryanization, it becomes clear how *Sick Heart* confronted Jewish Hollywood: by attacking its clamor. The implied opposite is the godliness of a still, small voice (1 Kings 19).

◆   ◆   ◆

To track all of this, it helps to know that Buchan, born a commoner in lowlands Scotland, rose in public service until he was made a baron as a prelude to serving the Crown in Canada. Sir Edward is also a lowlands Scot, born a commoner, who earns a title for services to the Crown. No wonder readers agree that Leithen is the Buchan character who most closely resembles his creator. Buchan's portfolio was thicker than Leithen's, however, because he combined civil service with successful careers in publishing and as a best-selling author. In the last two capacities, at least, he would have been aware of *Ben-Hur* in its varied formats. Earlier, though, as a lad raised in Scotland's adamantine Free Kirk, he had surely enjoyed Wallace's book considering his love of tales like that of Robert Louis Stevenson and the praise for Wallace's work in Presbyterian print.[16] A boy's affection for the first *Ben-Hur*—not Jews' adaptations—is thus a likely factor in *Sick Heart*'s resistance. However, as an adult, Buchan would have calculated additional considerations. In the mix, for instance, may have been "smart set" mockery at the re-release of Niblo's film. Pictorializing such mockery is a *New Yorker* cover from 1936 that lampoons the chariot race.[17]

As I discuss later in this essay, Buchan also crafted a re-visioning of the chariot race. But lampoon was not an option due to his concern for lost sheep. Judging by how quietly *Sick Heart* resists, he was open to any good that *Ben-Hur* might do, in any format, among all who found it "a builder of spiritual muscle."[18] Indicative in this regard is how Johnny defends his brother: the New Yorker "was bound to hang on to Lew or get lost and perish" (140). Therefore, Lew has something to offer. That he needs, all the same, to be kept under firm control is implied by the Aryanization in Sir Edward's ability to master this misguider. This achievement accrues a geopolitical twirl from *Sick Heart*'s arraignment of a New Englander who diagnoses a U.S. propensity for noisy godlessness but does nothing about it. His lack of care for the demos leaves Sir Edward the only character white enough (refer to the saying of his day, "be a white man") to lead a polity that, my reading implies, Buchan did not limit to a First Nation tribe. Rather, in its quiet way, *Sick Heart* was his bid to save America's soul.

Sick Heart's arraignment of the New Englander should be contextualized by realizing that the U.S. Department of the Treasury paid tribute to Wallace in 1942.[19] Buchan did not live to see this aspect of the British-U.S. war effort. Still, this publication's esteem for Wallace explicates the care that Canada's governor general would have taken not to blast one of America's, and the world's, favorite tales. Therefore, analysts will ponder not only that Sir Edward starred in earlier Buchan stories of a psychic-spiritual nature, but also that Buchan's sole allegorical tale is also the only one in which he gave Leithen an alliterative "foil." That the bookish, feeble Leithen proves the true guide and savior signals adherence to a Victorian quality: manliness.

This quality, understood as Christianized elevation of (mere) masculinity, dovetails with the white man's burden. This burden means different things to different white men; a gauge of Buchan's sense of it is found in Susannah Heschel's study of Nazis' openness about how "genocide of the Jews represented a Christian expurgation and a cleansing." When she adds that "longing for a virgin theological territory" was thought to justify "eliminating the savage for the sake of civilization," Sir Edward's self-sacrifice for a First Nation group reconfigures as a "God-and-Country"

Briton's rebuke to Hitler's deployment of Aryanist thought.[20] For Buchan, Aryanization does not lead to genocide; quite the contrary, it shepherds flocks who are unable to care for themselves. Therefore, Aryanists may espouse Zionism. They may do so, however, in the spirit of wishing Jews well but preferring them to be kept at a distance from the British Commonwealth.

Here again is Victorian-era thinking. Long before Victoria rose to power, though, an Old Testament scourge expressed concern for flocks that need care. As the King James team translated Jeremiah's concern, he grieved for hearts that are sickened by sin (e.g., Jer. 3:18, 9:14, 18:12). No help was offered these hearts, from Buchan's perspective, by clerics like one who took a bold stand in 1889. "A man may learn what the healing of a leper meant by reading the New Testament," this Presbyterian minister advised, yet "get a more vivid idea by reading 'Ben Hur.'" When that happens, he added, he would hold that "'Ben Hur' has done him the most good."[21] Buchan may not have seen this advice because it was published in the United States when he was only fourteen years old. If he did see it, he might have been shocked by so arrant a break from orthodoxy by a spokesman for a denomination noted for rock-ribbed adherence to scripture (Buchan's denomination, as it happens). Either way, though, he had a shock waiting for him when he came to live in North America in 1935.

Part of that shock might have concerned clerical opinions of *Ben-Hur*. But another, which is surer, concerned literary critics. Buchan found men of letters to be as derelict in their duties as the minister. He knew that *Ben-Hur*'s huge sales seemed such powerful proof to litterateurs of the crowd run amok that in 1901 a Briton smirked: "the presence of 'Ben Hur' in a list of 'the best books' suggests a grave doubt whether the list-makers knew what a good book is."[22] In the context of a tale that romances the Bible, this is supple wordplay. The snag was that it could leave *Ben-Hur* fans believing that literary authorities were godless. Confirming this belief in 1905 was an article in the *Bookman* that mockingly stated, "one cannot always be fifteen years old and retain that age's impression of the lasting greatness of *Ben Hur*." The *New York Times* riposted in 1915: "It is snobbery to deny greatness to . . . 'Ben Hur.'"[23] How, amidst this hammer and tongs, could a Scottish Christian shepherd American seekers who enjoyed this quest-saga in any format? It would be prudent to do so quietly, but it could be Christ-like to forego ridicule to offer, instead, manly leadership that is graced by loving kindness.

A sign of loving kindness in *Sick Heart* is Buchan's decision to make Lew Frizel's grasp of God's ways weak because, unlike Sir Edward (and Buchan), the American is self-educated. Buchan likely knew that Wallace, raised in Indiana while it was a frontier state, was self-taught. Still, if Buchan did not know Wallace's background, he could have inferred self-education by re-reading *Ben-Hur* as an adult. He would not have denied what fans chorused: Wallace had worked hard to "gen up" research for his Holy Land tale. Buchan would have agreed nonetheless, as an adult if not before, with all who found *Ben-Hur* marred by untutored study ("cram").[24] *Sick Heart*'s depiction of a guide named Lew intimates belief that Wallace was sincere and that his intentions were good. Buchan made it less damning, for example, than forgivably errant that the métis urges the New Yorker toward the barren Sick Heart in the vain dream that it is "a land flowing with milk and honey, and angels to pass the time of day!" (200). Besides, Lew comes close to dying of starvation on his overly independent quest. Buchan's lesson is that the métis's halfling yearning to know God's plan is good in itself but is rendered perilous by the educational deprivations of backwoods life.

Backing up this analysis is the fact that Johnny does not exculpate his brother but does defend him: "you can't just blame Lew" (140). I infer Buchan's implied contention that regardless of the format in which one engages *Ben-Hur*, it can be understood in a right way or a wrong one. The right way, for Christians, is homiletic: receptors are supposed to realize that Judah wallows in vengeful feelings until Jesus saves him. Buchan may not have judged the results as first-class literature, but he would have thought this reading of *Ben-Hur* in line with the Bible's teachings. The snag is that some fans heroized the charioteer while he quested vengefully rather than when he kneeled to the Christ. Bespeaking this error is a man who reportedly cried out as the chariots raced in the Klaw & Erlanger show, "Beat him, Benny!" Making such cries more likely was the glow cast around Wallace. Print from the 1880s and 1890s kept it lambent by heroizing the "Gallant Soldier and Author of 'Ben-Hur.'"[25] Klaw & Erlanger's publicity team cast the glow further, Hollywood cast it in klieg lights, and the 1936 re-release of Niblo's film revived it. Any maleficent effect could be spurned by Christians who were instructed doctrinally. Speaking for this cohort was a fan who told Wallace that reading all of his other books, but particularly *Ben-Hur*, made her "a wiser, better, and more useful woman than [she] otherwise would have been." However, with other fans cheering on a vengeful Jew, Christians as rock-ribbed as Buchan had cause to worry that the glow around Wallace gained luster from Niblo's decision to cast Ramon Novarro in the starring role.[26] Exacerbating this worry would have been products as sexy as the Ben-Hur embroidered blouse, as stimulating as Ben-Hur whiskey, and as speedy as the Ben-Hur racing bicycle.

But how did Buchan satisfy thrill-seeking readers? He crafted critique that is somber and quiet because critique as comic and blaring as "smart set" snickers had not served the cause he thought God's. At the same time, he used cues as aural as alliteration and the name "Lew." Buchan probably did not know that Wallace bolstered his book's success by reading from it on lecture tours (because no tour left North America). I discern metaphor, therefore, in *Sick Heart*'s insistence on the warmth and beauty of Lew Frizel's voice (179, 195, and 287). The métis's use of his alluring voice to try to dissuade Sir Edward from a righteous act could make this metaphor recall Odysseus's temptation when sirens called out, enticingly. Buchan esteemed the classics. More germane, though, to *Sick Heart*'s preaching than a Greek quester is recognition that Leithen starts his quest as clannish, and nearly as pharisaical, as Lew. This discussion reveals that the thrills that Buchan planned for his readers were profound and moral rather than sensationalized in the manner of a chariot race relished only for its derring-do rather than, for instance, its depiction of a freed man triumphing over his enslaver.

To track Sir Edward's growth, recall a point raised earlier in this essay: at first, he feels no interest in, or responsibility for, First Nation people. That he decides, eventually, to die so that they may live measures his superiority to the halfling, who elevates himself above the natives on dubious grounds. Racializing the knight's growth in Christian comprehension are authorial decisions like these:

- where Ben-Hur consults Semites—his mother, Balthasar, Ilderim—Sir Edward ponders ancient England's Alfred and Rome's Vespasian;
- where *Ben-Hur* portrays a thrilling scene of ruthless male-male agon, *Sick Heart* portrays Leithen saving Lew from the Sick Heart; and
- where *Ben-Hur* moves thereafter to the subplot in which a vengeful Jew trains and arms fighting Jews, *Sick Heart* has a Scot rise above a métis (whom he has mastered) by sacrificing himself in God's service for a First Nation group.

These bullet points sketch a racialized project. To investigate it further, I return to *Sick Heart* to look for additional plot parallels and revisions.

◆   ◆   ◆

Like Ben-Hur, Sir Edward first consults wise, yet non-Christian, elders. Alfred and Vespasian do not steer him wrong; they are white according to Buchan's scale of values. Only when the Scot moves from these guides to the Psalms, though, does he grasp God's mercy. The Psalms are a Jewish source, but they are also beloved by Christians. They step Sir Edward toward the Jew whom so many, be they Jews or Christians, have trouble seeing as Jewish. This strand of *Sick Heart*'s plot is familiar; a quester finds his way to Jesus. Therefore, this strand is all Buchan needed to espouse the white man's burden by having a Scottish knight sacrifice himself for First Nation people. However, he complicated this homily considerably by introducing one in which the knight masters a métis whose crude grasp of the Bible's teachings makes him a pollutant of their beauties.

That Lew does not quest as successfully makes him Sir Edward's inferior. It is reprehensible that he leads the New Yorker astray, but it is worse that he argues against rescuing a First Nation group who are poised to die due to their superstitious beliefs. One reason this later act is worse is because more people would suffer. Another reason is that Lew needed to be saved, by Leithen, from the Sick Heart. Once in that steep, ice-walled cleft, the métis realizes it is death's bourne: "there's no life here" (182). Sir Edward rescues him from this slough of despond, despite his own physical pain and weakness, with alpine skills that turn the American's knees to jelly.[27] The scene is described tautly, yet it refuses male competition or ego. In this anti-chariot race, readers were meant to see that the whiter man helps the less white one, whom he could have abandoned if all that mattered was personal salvation.[28]

Already in *Sick Heart*, the ease of forging on alone has been rebuked by Lew's willingness to abandon the New Yorker to slow death. Later, this false, yet not evil, guide explains why he let visions allure him selfishly: he sought too easy an evasion of man's fallen nature. "There was times when my sins fair bowed me down," Lew tells Leithen. "Then I got the notion of this Sick Heart as the kind of place where there is no more trouble, a bit of the Garden of Eden that God had kept private for them as could find it" (186). Rough syntax reflects limited education. But it also alerts readers to the crudity of yearnings that bracket Jesus. However, the backwoodsman is no fool: he realizes once he enters the Sick Heart that its allure is "the temptation of the Devil and not the promise of God" (187). Leithen agrees: the Sick Heart is a trap for living men. Still, he realizes that its austere beauty has a message for anyone who expects omniscience's ways to thrill the senses as, for example, Hollywood does for profit. The result is that whereas the métis hates the valley, the "pure" Scot hears its rock-ribbed homily: eschew clannish pharisaism to show humility before God by serving his creatures even at Jesus's cost of self-sacrifice.

This homily girds Sir Edward's decision to die in service to First Nation people who have fallen prey to malaise. Lew is not wrong to worry that this ministry will sap Leithen's strength just as his lungs have begun to heal in the chill Arctic air. Sir Edward, though, being whiter, grasps the Crucifixion's meaning more truly. When he sends Lew to fight Hitler, he shifts the métis from the role of guide to a position fitted to his strengths: Lew will be led by better men. Readers were (and are) to infer that the masterful though mild Scot guides men of "Britannic identity" to their rightful task: the manly service of bearing arms for the Crown.[29] Service of this kind is no death sentence; some men return from war. To any who read Buchan's memoir, though, the impact of World War I on many of his university friendships murmurs the possibility that Lew will never misguide again.

These coded messages take a bit of digging. It is significant that at the start of Sir Edward's quest, he figures out what the New Yorker's U.S.

friends haven't: spiritual malaise sent the financier to Arctic Canada in search of redemption. The reason that these brilliant and caring men have not realized this about a friend they have known for years, whom Sir Edward has never met, is that he is suffering from his own spiritual malaise (though he does not know it yet). Later, the Scot shows more manliness than a New Englander who diagnoses U.S. social ills without trying to cure them. He sighs that his "mighty noisy country" has fallen prey to "bogus deities" (83). "I'm saying nothing against my country," he tells Sir Edward; "I know it's the greatest on earth. But, my God! I hate the mood it has fallen into." Impelling the mood, he opines, is the split of church from state: "We haven't got any kind of common creed. All we ask is that a thing should be colourful and confident and noisy. Our national industry is really the movies. We're one big movie show" (83). Relating this diagnosis to Niblo's *Ben-Hur* is this character's equation of the big movie show with effeminate "wops"—meaning heartthrobs like Novarro. With diagnosis being all this character offers, though, readers are urged to realize that whiteness alone does not mark a leader. Rather, mastering a misguider in the British manner is the true test.

Leaving this white (although not Aryan) character in his wake, Sir Edward quests on. The further he and Johnny trek into the wild, the less they encounter color, confidence, or noise. The knight is tasked hard: "He who had once had the stride of a mountaineer now teetered like an affected woman" (169). Hampering too are guides who can lead him only so far. Early on, the words of Alfred and Vespasian stiffen the knight's determination to persevere as he learns of Lew's obsession with a gorgeous river valley. However, neither helps him master the métis misguider. For this feat, Sir Edward needs to ponder the Psalms first and then Jesus's teachings about God's compassion for all creatures. Having done so, he masters Lew. This feat recalls Renan's idea that Aryanization may be inborn but can be achieved by mastering a threat to Christianity. Buchan's hero is thus white at the start of *Sick Heart* but Aryan as well by its close. Then and only then does he replicate the act that brings Ben-Hur to his knees: Jesus's willing self-sacrifice so that others may live.

What is it that gives Sir Edward greater access to God's plan for mankind than Lew manages? Buchan teaches, most clearly, that the distinction lies in doctrinal training. His widow would reveal, too, that *Sick Heart*'s working title was "Pride's Purge."[30] This makes sense because pride in physical prowess stunts Leithen and Lew: both bow at first to this bogus deity. Eventually the whiter man spurns this false god as bodily frailty purges him of pride and he accepts the chastening. This acceptance wakens the Scot, who has lived decently but not been conventionally religious. Only then does he minister to other pilgrims. As Sir Edward comes to glory in this burden, he chooses to sacrifice his regained vigor—despite Lew's pleas—to serve natives. Point taken: Lew would have led the knight astray as he had led the New Yorker to unforgiving fastnesses and abandoned him there. Sir Edward grasps this due to Calvinist home-training: he was taught that God's word is unyielding. Just as significantly, he grasps this concept because he is "Britannic" with a completeness not shared by his fellow questers. "Compared to his companions," a pivotal passage explains, "Leithen suddenly saw himself founded solidly like an oak. He was drawing life from deep sources," whereas the New Yorker has lapsed from Catholicism and the Frizels live like "grassy filaments which swayed in the wind, but might any day be pinched out of existence" (267, 266).

This remark can be construed as a glance at the "wandering Jew." But even if it isn't, with this direct authorial instruction, readers were advised to find one man able to guide the pilgrims from death in the wild: the one who understands God's ways most fully. This man is also the one who is whitest but, additionally, Aryan. Emblematizing this distinction is the resolve with which the frail Scot earns respect from the "splendid" métis who knows better than he how to survive an Arctic winter (195). Putting mastery into words, Leithen explains to Lew, just before he sends the backwoodsman off to fight Hitler: "*There is a river the streams whereof shall make glad the city of God.* That's what you've always been looking for" (288). This is no blast at *Ben-Hur*. In fact, this shepherding suggests enough fondness for Lew Frizel, and by extension Wallace, to hint that Buchan thought *Ben-Hur* a good children's book, yet still a book that should be outgrown to avoid ensnarement in a halfling miscomprehension of God's plan. An implication of this view is that he judged Niblo's version more pernicious.

Why not say so, then, in 1925? I tie this decision to three factors. One is incontrovertible: Buchan came to live in North America just before *Ben-Hur* was re-released with sound. The second is speculative: Buchan chose to re-read childhood favorites as he lay dying, and this list may have included *Ben-Hur*. The third factor is speculative too but better evidenced: *Sick Heart*'s use of quiet aural cues implies an attempt to imitate not Jeremiah but rather the still, small voice that is threatened by Lew's warm and beautiful voice of misguidance. This voice is all but drowned out by Hollywood's noise, particularly—as the date of *Sick Heart* implies and the New Englander's diagnosis confirms—as film added sound. Still, cinema could be a force for good, even with sound effects; Buchan had no objection to a "talkie" being made of *The Thirty-Nine Steps*. Acknowledging this potential are hints in *Sick Heart* of Buchan's hope that his last, and atypically personal, quest-saga would be filmed. For instance, many passages in *Sick Heart* describe nighttime scenes in the Arctic that rely on a palette of black to silver, with white snow all around. Especially suggestive, however, is the restricted palette Buchan used to describe the Sick Heart Valley.

Here is what Sir Edward is told of the Sick Heart early on: "It's a fancy place that old timers dream about," Johnny tells him; Lew had spotted it "from the top of a mountain, and it sort of laid a charm on him" (91–92). As Johnny follows his brother's trail to this remote yet alluring place, Sir Edward enters a world that is new to him. Buchan narrates his fight to march on through white snow against a grey sky, and of his weariness at night, with only the star-dotted black sky overhead and hundreds of miles of winter-stripped trees circling their small fire. Then, at last, the valley lies before him. "Leithen found himself staring breathlessly not up, but down—down into a chasm nearly a mile wide and two thousand feet deep. . . . It seemed to him that he was looking at the most marvelous spectacle ever vouchsafed to a man. The elements were commonplace—stone and wood, water and earth—but so had been the pigments of a Raphael. The celestial Demiurge had combined them into a masterpiece" (159–60). Compared to Buchan's best-told tales, this scene-painting is tepid. That may be because his strength was failing, but it may also reflect deliberative use of a restricted palette. Readers learn: "There was little colour in the scene. Nearly all was subfusc, monochrome, and yet so exquisite was the modeling that there was nothing bleak about it; the impression was rather of a chaste, docile luxuriance . . . [s]tripped and blanched" (160–61).

Buchan's repeated use of the words "sudden" or "suddenly" implies that he wanted to induce awestruck silence in his readers. The word appears in a description of a flash of insight that distinguishes Sir Edward from his fellow questers: he "suddenly saw himself founded solidly like an oak." Then, Buchan uses this word again to describe the knight's advent on the Sick Heart, from above, so that its chilly contours lie before him with the drama of revelation (or skilled film editing). In addition, Buchan uses "sudden" to relate that Sir Edward (but not the false guide, Lew) learns to prize the Sick Heart as a place so sublime that it needs "no bird-wing or bird-song, no ripple of fish, no beast in the thicket." Rather, this valley's austerities have so little to do with color, confidence, and noise that this remote spot evokes "a silence . . . of the world as God first created it, before He permitted the coarse welter of life" (184). One can almost see a cinematic "dissolve." Buchan is urging seekers to turn to nature for God-crafted sensory delights, rather than fall prey to celluloid's bogus deities. This homily had, and has, meaning beyond *Ben-Hur*. When set against that favorite, though, *Sick Heart* more explicitly preaches against flashy, or feel-good, substitutes for Calvinist rigor.

It would not be odd for a lifelong Christian to have wondered, as he lay dying, how cinema could serve his faith better than it had been served by a visually stimulating tale of the Christ that, some held, glorified vengefulness. In particular, Buchan may have striven to outdo a film version of the tale that reduces Jesus's teaching to a decision not to wage war, to which Metro-Goldwyn-Mayer added sound effects that made it even harder to hear the still, small voice. It would be as reasonable, however, for a proponent of the white man's burden to reflect on Hollywood's decision to bring *Ben-Hur* to a huge audience with for-profit motives that made it expedient to finesse Jesus's race. No student of Aryanization would have missed this maneuver. To rebut it, Buchan "modernized" *Ben-Hur* by relegating to the past all who fail to follow Christ (i.e., bullet heads and halflings, superstitious First Nation peoples, and Jews). Although this Renan-like intervention is muted, it evinces unease about Jesus being a Jew.

It is valuable to recover resistance to *Ben-Hur* from certain Christians after this tale had been declared a Christian classic. At the same time, amplification of *Sick Heart*'s murmurs recaptures concern about the celluloid destiny of a major British ally as Hitler gained strength. The false prophets Buchan discerned in proponents of totalitarian rule were as worrisome as bogus deities from this vantage. Real men, *Sick Heart* taught allegorically, lead seekers away from dazzling yet barren visions. Therefore, an implication of this essay is that *Ben-Hur* was not just current but, for some receptors, pressing, for far longer than is apparent from most American literature syllabi, histories of reading, and studies of Christianity. In these respects, this essay blazes new research avenues regarding *Ben-Hur* in any and all formats. The value of pursuing one or more of these avenues lies in what this quest-saga has meant to all who have folded it into their conceptualizations of race, Christianity, burdens, manliness, and/or the United States—for good or ill.

The Erotics of the Galley Slave

Male Desire and Christian Sacrifice in the 1959 Film Version of *Ben-Hur*

INA RAE HARK

The Metro-Goldwyn-Mayer film version of *Ben-Hur* that was released in 1959 begins with several sequences depicting people in motion. Joseph and Mary travel to a crowded Bethlehem to report to the tax assessor, and the trip results in Jesus's birth in a manger. A star that shines over the manger guides three kings there. After this prologue, the scene shifts to the Roman Messala's return to Judea. He travels through Galilee to assume command of a garrison that enforces the nation's imperial occupation. Messala's route takes him by the village of Nazareth wherein Jesus traverses the hills, neglecting his carpenter's work to do the business of his father, the God whom Jesus's fellow Jews worship. Next appears the film's protagonist, Judah Ben-Hur, along with many others.

Of all of these characters, only Jesus incarnates the Holy Spirit. After being crucified, he will rise from the dead to offer salvation to humankind. Jesus is the answer to the conflict this film articulates early via Messala: why do Jews worship a disembodied spirit when they could ally themselves with a human yet divine Roman emperor who offers worldly dominion? The incarnate son of the Hebrew God will prove "marketable" to gentiles who have trouble wrapping their heads around an invisible deity concerning whom Jewish law forbids even representation in graven images. Yet before this son dies as a lamb, even the Hebrew God is recorded, in the Old Testament, urging his followers to violence against unbelievers.

Quite differently, the son whose embodiment proves amenable to pagans demands an ethos of compassion, peace, and forgiveness that is new to both Roman and Jewish dispensations. The cinematic issue is this: as an incarnate God made celluloid flesh, *Ben-Hur*'s Jesus raises questions about divinity, gender, sexuality, and the male body that the 1959 film thematically foregrounds while simultaneously making efforts to disavow.

Eroticism and the Martyred Body

In a poem subtitled "After the Proclamation in Rome of the Christian Faith" (1866), Algernon Swinburne's speaker laments the exhaustion of the Greco-Roman worship of lusty gods and goddesses through rituals that mirrored their sensuality. He grieves for its replacement by an ascetic Christianity: "Thou hast conquered, O pale Galilean; the world has grown grey from thy breath."[1] Georges Bataille, a foundational theorist of the role that eroticism plays in religious practices, also sees in Christianity a decided break from the devotional forms that had preceded it. Whereas pre-Christian religions allowed for a delimited space to accommodate the transgressive erotic desire and violent impulses that worshippers' devotion may generate, Christianity reframed faith's intersections with eros and thanatos as sin that must be separate and "other" from sanctioned religious practice. "At the pagan stage," Bataille writes, because "religion was based on transgression,"

> the impure aspects were no less divine than the opposite ones. The realm
> of sacred things is composed of the pure and of the impure. Christianity
> rejected impurity. It rejected guilt without which sacredness is impos-
> sible since only the violation of a taboo can open the way to it.

The concept of religious sacrifice becomes a nexus of the difference between pagan and Christian theologies. An integral part of many pre-Christian faiths, religious sacrifice is also central to Christianity: Jesus dies to redeem the sins of humankind. His death on the cross parallels the function of the scapegoat in biblical Jewish practice. The scapegoat was an actual animal upon which the priest, following completion of Day of Atonement observances, symbolically transferred the sins of the community to expel them by driving the animal into the wilderness. More often, though, religious sacrifice involves the ritual killing of an animal or even a human. (Abraham does not regard God's commandment to sacrifice his son Isaac as an unheard-of perversion.) Unlike sacrificial practices among the ancient Hebrews and their pagan neighbors, however, Jesus's sacrificial death is not part of a ritual conducted by his followers. As Bataille notes, "in Christian sacrifice the faithful are not made responsible for desiring the sacrifice. They only contribute to the Crucifixion by their sins and their failures."[2]

Here is the rub, though: doctrinal difference cannot banish transgressive desires out of existence simply by proscribing them. The "leavings of racks and rods!" and "ghastly glories of saints, dead limbs of gibbeted Gods!" that Swinburne disparages in Christian iconography can have their own subversive appeal to eros.[3] Even more problematic, this appeal can activate desires believed deviant in religious contexts (and often outside of them): homoeroticism and sadomasochism. Such deviancy is especially fraught in the case of visual representations of the Crucifixion and echoes of it (i.e., saints' martyrdoms). In 1959, William Wyler managed this transgressive desire by deflecting it from the body of Jesus (played by Claude Heater) onto that of Judah Ben-Hur (played by Charlton Heston). In the process, this film asks obliquely whether male desire and Christ's teachings can properly coexist.

It seems counterintuitive for the maimed body of a sacrificial victim to arouse erotic desire. But Bataille makes a compelling (if phallocentric, heteronormative, and disquieting) case by comparing the body of such a victim to that of a woman experiencing phallic penetration by a man:

> The lover strips the beloved of her identity no less than the blood-stained priest his human or animal victim. The woman in the hands of her assailant is despoiled of her being. With her modesty she loses the firm barrier that once separated her from others and made her impenetrable. She is brusquely laid open to the violence of the sexual urges set loose in the organs of reproduction; she is laid open to the impersonal violence that overwhelms her from without.

Richard Rambuss finds such a metaphorical parallel throughout seventeenth-century devotional verse that depicts the Christian worshipper's representations of Jesus as beloved: "The fulcrum of interest in these poems, indeed the trigger for their devotional profusions, is not merely the exhibition made of Christ's body, but the spectacularization of it as a body that is penetrable and penetrated."[4] He also points out a semantic connection to erotic desire in the term used to describe the torturous series of punishments the Romans inflicted on that body: the Passion.

Such arguments seem in line with Andrea Dworkin's assertion that patriarchy views heterosexuality as requiring the violent domination of women. They diverge from Dworkin's claim in that they generalize even further to assert that all phallic penetration carries the seed of such violence. It is not surprising that Bataille (who devotes several chapters to Marquis de Sade's writings) sees "normal" erotic desire as part of a continuum that a few carry to the deviant extreme of erotic satisfaction only through torture or murder. Still, even if Bataille's theories look too extreme when broadly applied, evidence can be adduced for the representation of a gibbeted God, or saint martyred by racks and rods, to evoke erotic desire. One need look no further than Saint Sebastian, who was often painted during the Renaissance as a beautiful and voluptuous youth. His iconic martyrdom—he was bound to a stake and pierced by arrows—has become a resonant image of homoerotic sensuality. In a review of seven artworks by Guido Reni that portray Sebastian's martyrdom, Charles Darwent asserts that Sebastian is "an enduring, homo-erotic icon" before adding, tongue in cheek: "Sebastian's appeal to gay men seems obvious. He was young, male, apparently unmarried and martyred by the establishment. Unlike, say, St Augustine of Hippo, he also looks good in a loincloth and tied to a tree." Such flippancy obscures just how central images of Sebastian have been as the "symbol of choice," as Richard A. Kaye remarks, "[f]or writers of aestheticist leanings who . . . sought a coded means of denoting homosexual desire."[5]

To be sure, Christ's crucified body has never been so openly hailed as an icon of gay devotion. Vivid, all the same, is its potential to induce such a blasphemous erotic response. Rambuss cites the main character in Antonia Bird's controversial film *Priest* (1994); he confesses that praying to the crucifix on his wall to try to repress his homosexual desires has precisely the opposite effect: "I turn to him for help. I see a naked man, utterly desirable. I turn to him for help, and he just makes it worse."[6] No wonder,

6. Anonymous, after Guido Reni (1575–1642), *The Martyrdom of St. Sebastian*, n.d. Oil on canvas. Reprinted with permission of the Boston Athenæum.

then, that Jesus on the cross rouses anxiety in mainstream filmmakers who want to inspire the faithful rather than shock—or arouse—them.[7]

Deflecting Christ's Eroticism in *Ben-Hur*

Several factors render representations of Jesus tricky in mainstream Hollywood films. The most obvious factor concerns the evolution of

Christian iconography. *Ben-Hur* scholars have mounted varied arguments about Lew Wallace's decision to describe Jesus's face (see, e.g., Jefferson J. A. Gatrall's essay in this volume). When the issue is, instead, the realities of death by crucifixion, it is most salient that during the Renaissance the erotic potential of crucifixes, and of depictions of grisly martyrdoms, was neutralized by these images' ubiquity in the visual arts. The same is true now in societies that are majority Catholic. In the United States, however, most of the Christian population is Protestant, and churches typically display crosses rather than crucifixes. Veneration of saints is less central, moreover, and a communion wafer stands in for the body of Christ in a symbolic way only. Films that depict the Crucifixion do not find among people raised in this milieu an audience whose sensibilities have been dulled by frequent exposure to such scenes, or by religious practice that foregrounds martyrs' bodies.

Another factor that complicates filmed representations of the Crucifixion is found in psychoanalytic film theorists' attention to the implications of a body being put on display. In her foundational essay "Visual Pleasure and Narrative Cinema," Laura Mulvey posits that mainstream filmmakers align the camera with the point of view of a male character as a relay for the spectator's subjectivity. The resultant "male gaze" tends to render women as "spectacularized," turned into a fetish that is valuable only for being looked at, and deprived of agency.[8] This theory spurred analysis of the possibility, and implications, of a "female gaze" when filmmakers spectacularize a male body.[9] Kaja Silverman's *Male Subjectivity at the Margins*—the cover of which sports an image of St. Sebastian—builds on the work of Jacques Lacan and Michel Foucault to examine various artistic depictions of masculinity displaced from its assumed position of superior phallic subjectivity. Whether or not such subjectivities are "feminized," they cohere around the principle of "saying 'no' to power."[10] This principle is key to what Wallace did, and Wyler after him, in their portrayals of Jesus.

As for other cinematic depictions of masculinity, ancient world epics rank first among genres that characteristically display men scantily clad, offered up to the spectatorial gaze, and subject to torture: Rambuss's penetrated and penetrable bodies. Steve Neale uses several examples from these epics in his response to Mulvey, "Masculinity as Spectacle."[11] The eroticism, and especially homoeroticism, of such films has been discussed widely in the literature but also in popular culture. For example, who can forget the avuncular but pedophilic pilot in the spoof *Airplane!* (1980), who leers at a prepubescent boy and asks, "Joey, do you like movies about gladiators?"[12] In Wyler's *Ben-Hur*, Heston's tall, broad-shouldered, and generally large physique has often provided a starting point for talking about "The Body in the Blockbuster," as Steven Cohan titles the chapter on the Ten Commandments in his study of 1950s film masculinity, *Masked Men*.[13]

One last obstacle confronts Hollywood filmmakers (and, of course, directors of stage or television productions) who seek to portray Jesus: a mere human must impersonate the son of God. Wallace resisted dramatization of his "tale of the Christ" because he considered such a performance blasphemous. The theatrical version he authorized solved this problem by using "a shaft of blue light" to portray God's son made flesh.[14] Three decades later, Cecil B. DeMille compelled performers in *The King of Kings* (1927) to abstain from off-set activities such as dancing, drinking, or gambling that some devout people think irreligious. Additionally, the actor who played Jesus was whisked to and from the studio in a car with darkened windows; he also wore a black hood over his head when he was not filming. Since then a number of actors have tackled the role of Jesus without taking similar precautions; these include Jeffrey Hunter in Nicholas Ray's *King of Kings* (1961), Max von Sydow in George Stevens's *The Greatest Story Ever Told* (1965), Robert Powell in Franco Zeffirelli's *Jesus of Nazareth* (1977), Willem Dafoe in Martin Scorsese's *The Last Temptation of Christ* (1988), and Jim Caviezel in Mel Gibson's *The Passion of the Christ* (2004). There is, however, an alternative. If a film's protagonist is a man who comes to believe in Jesus as the Messiah and interacts with the Nazarene during his last days on Earth, filmmakers may show the Prince of Peace only elliptically or from a distance.

This is the technique Wyler chose. He often filmed his Jesus character from behind and never shows his face. Equally significant, audiences never hear Jesus's voice, nor do they have access to his subjectivity. When encountering Jesus in Wyler's *Ben-Hur*, therefore, the audience gazes not at the son of God but rather at other characters' reactions to him. Repeated close-ups of Heston's expressive facial reactions reveal Jesus's beatific effect on the film's protagonist. Yet Wyler makes good use of minor characters too. For instance, when a Roman guard charges up to prevent Jesus from giving Ben-Hur water, the guard freezes once Jesus (his back to the camera) confronts him. Looking confused, the guard then backs off.

In addition to this method of portraying Jesus, Wyler provides a way into the savior's subjectivity at a safe distance for avoiding blasphemy. He does this via Judah Ben-Hur's narrative, which in many instances parallels Jesus's narrative even though the divine-human distinction dictates that Jesus must die for humankind's sins while Judah must live to experience this redemption and pass it on to others. The latter, the victim of unjust arrest and persecution by Romans, spends years rowing in a galley (a prolonged Passion). After a symbolic death when the galley sinks, Judah is "resurrected" as Young Arrius. He is present, later, to offer succor to Jesus on his way to Calvary, just as Jesus gave Ben-Hur water as he marched to the galleys. Forging this connection more tightly, the Magus Balthasar (played by Finlay Currie) at first mistakes Judah Ben-Hur for the adult the Holy Child grew into. This mistake is predicted by the title of Wallace's novel: *Ben-Hur: A Tale of the Christ* constructs an apposition that grammatically equates Judah with Jesus. Yet in truth, this title would make better rhetorical sense if it were *Jesus the Nazarene: A Tale of the Christ*.

As co-author on the *Ben-Hur* 1959 film script, Gore Vidal helped minimize the possibility of generating a homoerotic charge by repressing Christ's corporeal presence. However, true to Wallace's odd title, Wyler's film brings back this possibility by making Judah a metonym for Jesus. This approach is even more intriguing because Vidal reported that a gay subtext for the film was intentional. Vidal maintained that the rupture between childhood friends that brings about so much profound suffering results from Messala's desire for Judah. His desire may linger from a teenaged affair, but Judah has moved on regardless. His refusal of Messala's advances motivates the latter's vendetta against him and his family, though the overt cause is the Jew's refusal to sell out his people's interests by collaborating with Roman oppressors.[15]

Even if Vidal had never said a word about this subtext, it would be hard to miss. Gordon Thomas observes: "There's an undeniable emotional bond between [Messala and Ben-Hur]—it's right up there on the screen—and there's no reason why this should not have been Vidal's idea, but the gay vibe relies more on Wyler's direction than the writing. The dialogue in the reunion scene could have been played a number of ways, but the game is up the minute that Boyd, running his eyes over Heston's strapping form, giggles like a schoolgirl."[16] Many commentators have pointed, also, to Freudian implications in the spear-throwing contest in which Messala and Ben-Hur plant their lances millimeters apart at the place where two crossbeams meet. Although their boyhood mantra was "down Eros, up Mars," Messala's manner suggests his hope of raising Eros's lance instead; note, for example, how frequently he manages to put his hand on Judah's arm. After the spear toss, when Judah makes clear that Judea does not reciprocate the Roman Empire's "fondness" for its people, Messala's reply seems to conflate his feelings with Rome's, and Judah's with Judea's: "Is there anything so sad as unrequited love?" All the while, the film establishes that Messala's attraction to Judah is not an aberration; rather, despite dalliances, Messala is consistent overall in his homosexual preference. Gary Devore confirms this by noting, "after his quarrel with Ben-Hur, Messala finds a new male companion. This new friend, named Drusus in the credits, stands mutely by his side, protecting Messala from physical attack. He is even there at Messala's messy death, cradling his head like a melodrama heroine."[17]

This bond is on display visually. But Wyler's *Ben-Hur* goes beyond this case of subtextual thwarted homosexual passion to use erotic attraction between men less literally. Several other men in the film "desire" Judah in some way, seeking to have him under their sway to fulfill a goal or supply a need. Even if we are not supposed to see these men wanting Ben-Hur as a sexual partner, symbolic gestures toward a non-heteronormative interpretation of these relationships pop up consistently. Vidal, himself gay, probably did not plan on having such a subtext become shorthand for all that is not Christian in the film. Yet that is essentially what happened. Even if this desire circulates between and among men, however, it is not primarily homoerotics the film portrays as perverse. Rather, the film targets the tendency of male desire to fuel erotics of power and domination among men. Contrasting Judah's final acceptance of Jesus as his savior to his other relationships with men demonstrates the varieties of desire that Judah must cast off in the narrative.

In the novel, Wallace makes clear that Judah and many of his fellow Jews initially follow the Nazarene because they believe Jesus will give them earthly power to defeat the Roman oppressors. As several contributors to this volume have pointed out, only when Judah witnesses the Passion does he understand that Christ brings his believers salvation that has nothing to do with political dominion and spiritual peace that bears no relation to redress of their earthly wrongs. "The arc of Wallace's story—and the message dovetailed within it—demands that God's law, given solely to the Jews, be completed by God's love, arriving first in the form of the Messiah and then radiating throughout the world as Christianity," Gordon Thomas explains. He goes on to assert that the novel genders these forces by having "the thoroughly male Judah impulsively taking up arms only to encounter a womanish Man of Peace arriving just in time to disarm him. So much for the insurgency, a bad idea, apparently, caused by too much testosterone."[18]

In Wyler's film, Messala presents the most extreme portrait of the destructive erotics of mastery. His childhood dream was to command the Roman garrison in Judea. He cannot fathom why Ben-Hur would revere the unseen, heavenly spirit that is the Hebrew God when he could ally himself with a divine emperor who wields "real power on Earth." Ego drives Messala's worldview: his boyhood comrade can be "either for me or against me." Messala's desire for Ben-Hur appears genuine, but when the latter refuses to deliver Judean insurgents into the tribune's grasp, Messala is happy to use Ben-Hur to pursue his ambition in another way. By condemning an innocent family known to be his old friends, Messala brandishes his loyalty to Rome. The formerly moderate patriot becomes fixated on revenge. "May God grant me vengeance," Ben-Hur tells Messala before he is hauled off to the galleys. "I pray you will live till I return." That the Hebrew God sanctioned vengeance is one of Wallace's briefs against him. This speech shows that God's vengeance will not satisfy Ben-Hur. He wants Messala to live long enough to meet his fate at the hands of his friend-turned-victim. The desirous tribune fails to seduce the Jew into becoming his and Rome's lover. But he manages quite well to turn Ben-Hur into a vengeful hater of both.

The other men in Ben-Hur's life suggest alternatives to Messala's erotics of power. They also hint at how male desire can be redeemed. Their lessons are incomplete, however, until the Jew has wreaked his desired revenge (only to realize it is hollow). The first glimpse of an alternative comes during Ben-Hur's forced march to the galleys. Denied water when the prisoners stop in Nazareth, he appears close to succumbing to despair. Yet he does not abandon faith; instead, he implores: "God, help me!" Right on cue, accompanied by the choir music that is his theme, a man of the village leaves his carpentry work to bring water to the parched slave. This scene emphasizes Jesus's hands, which are large and masculine. They touch Judah, though, with maternal tenderness, washing his face and stroking his hair as well as helping him slake his thirst. Here the film establishes the elements needed for salvation: willingness to succor others in whom one has no personal investment; repudiation of subjugating masculinity (which drains out of the guard, too, when he looks Jesus in the face); and a symbolic transfer of water that becomes the film's central organizing metaphor.

The next sequence shifts to three years later, on a Roman galley. While inspecting the slaves who power his ship, Quintus Arrius singles out one known only by his bench number, 41. When the Roman strikes this slave with his whip, unprovoked, he notes approvingly that 41 has the spirit to fight back but the good sense not to give into the impulse and risk death. Amazed that 41 has survived years in the galleys, Arrius shrewdly diagnoses the source of his longevity: "Your eyes are full of hate, 41. That's good. Hate keeps a man alive. It gives him strength."

These galley scenes provide a site to represent the sadomasochistic trappings of the ancient world epic: whips, chains, and leather. But they isolate these things from the film's elliptical portrayal of Christ's suffering at Roman hands. Ironically transformed from the clean-shaven, close-cropped, richly attired Ben-Hur of the rest of the diegesis, 41, with his loincloth, beard, and longer hair, resembles the Jesus who gets nailed to the cross (if Jesus had been an action star). Furthermore, the animating hatred that Arrius discerns is anything but Christian. Still enmeshed in violent masculinity and a corporeal vision of rescue, Judah attracts in Arrius another Roman admirer.

The erotic subtext between these characters is even more pronounced than that of Ben-Hur and Messala. The key scene occurs when Arrius stages a drill devised to gauge how well the rowers will perform in battle. He gives orders to a crew member who uses large mallets to beat the rhythm of the oar strokes and accelerate the tempo in stages that culminate in the suggestively named "ramming speed." Close-ups of Arrius observing his men alternate with those of Ben-Hur maintaining eye contact with him while managing to keep his oar upright (many around him drop their oars). The metaphoric parallel to male climax and release could not be more obvious.

With this successful performance during the drill, Ben-Hur qualifies for Arrius's special regard. The Roman summons the slave to his quarters during his next rest rotation, but then forgets having done so. Startled, therefore, when Ben-Hur enters his bedchamber, Arrius awakens to the rower's hard body clad only in a skimpy loincloth. The erotic subtext is again strong as Arrius marvels that 41 did not take advantage of the situation to kill him and therefore offers to train Ben-Hur as one of the stable of gladiators and charioteers he keeps in Rome to enter into competitions. In the novel, Judah is quite calculating in trying to curry Arrius's favor, making suggestions about how to maximize the galley slaves' rowing efficiency and pleading his innocence at every opportunity. When the ship sinks in battle, his first thought is to make sure Arrius survives, lest he lose his ticket to freedom and revenge. In the film, though, Ben-Hur asks only his God for assistance and declines Arrius's offer, even when Arrius reminds him that he will either row until he dies or go down with the ship, chained to his oar, in the event that an enemy prevails.

Here we see repetition of homoerotic desire as a trope in which the Roman commander/Jewish subservient dynamic seen in Messala's relationship with Judah grows more pronounced because Arrius is literally Ben-Hur's master. The vital difference is that Arrius is a better man than Messala. He does not glory in power. Instead, he devotes himself to duty and honor to assuage a deep despair. Rather than claim that Rome's divine emperor trumps the Hebrew God (as Messala had), Arrius counsels that both his gods and 41's "God of my fathers" are mere fantasies: human existence is meaningless. As incredulous as he is that 41 can maintain belief in the Hebrew God after all that has happened to him, Arrius's nihilism manages to touch the angry Ben-Hur. A glimmer of Jesus's compassion back in Nazareth is seen when Judah asks Arrius, with some sympathy, about what made the Roman lose his own faith. The answer—Arrius's loss of his only son—explicates the Roman's later decision to adopt Ben-Hur and offer him a new identity: "Young Arrius."

This and other subsequent events show that Arrius does not repeat the Roman patriarchal ideology that girds Messala's reaction to a rebuff from a colonial subject. He acts instead, as Ben-Hur does too, in ways that show Jesus's qualities. Ben-Hur recalls the Nazarene when Arrius orders that he be unchained during a sea battle. "Once before a man helped me. I didn't know why then," Ben-Hur says in response to his bench mate's inquiry about this puzzling gesture. When their galley is overtaken and begins to sink, Ben-Hur first helps unchain his fellow slaves and then fights his way onto the deck, reaching it just in time to prevent a pirate from killing Arrius. He then gets his benefactor onto a life raft provided by floating wreckage *and* prevents him from committing suicide (several times). When it turns out that the apparent Roman rout was in fact a great victory, Arrius rouses enough to entertain the possibility of a divine presence, even if he expresses this possibility with urbane irony: "In his eagerness to save you, your God has also saved the Roman fleet."

Ben-Hur's rescue of Arrius can be thought of as self-interested, but his prevention of Arrius's suicide shows compassion. One of Arrius's telling gestures after they are rescued is Jesus-like: he passes the ladle of water offered to him to Ben-Hur so that he may drink first, completing the parallel to Jesus at the well. Both men have thus adhered to Christ's principles; the selfless gestures of each allow the other to preserve his counterpart's physical existence.

Nevertheless, Judah's soul is still in peril. Arrius's magnanimity in freeing him from servitude and adopting him as his heir serves only to facilitate his return to Judea to exact vengeance upon Messala—now less for his own wrongs than for the disappearance of his sister and widowed mother. By winning the chariot race, Young Arrius becomes, according to the new Judean governor, Pontius Pilate, "the people's one true god." Adorned with a laurel wreath rather than a crown of thorns, Judah Ben-Hur offers visual mockery of the actual one true God whom Pilate will condemn to death mere days later. Ben-Hur's defeat of Messala would mark an appropriate conclusion were this a tale of a noble Roman or a secular hero of an historical adventure narrative. This being instead a "tale of the Christ," the race finds its victor much closer in spirit to Messala, as the good Esther pointedly reminds him, than to Jesus (or even Quintus Arrius).[19]

In keeping with the way in which victory in the race renders Judah an inverse redeemer, the fatal injuries that Messala suffers in the race subvert Jesus's death, ironically. The tasteful and elliptical presentation of the Crucifixion later on in the film contrasts notably with the graphic (for 1959) depiction of Messala's broken body as he lies in restraints, unwilling to begin surgery to amputate his crushed legs until he has once more confronted his foe. Here is Bataille's erotic sacrificial victim—except that the ritual is a perverse self-immolation on the altar of domination and revenge. Jesus's unselfish compassion, as well as that of Arrius, has been weakening Judah's conviction of the righteousness of his quest for vengeance. He prays before the race for God to forgive him for seeking vengeance. Afterward, Messala's injuries give him so much pause that, when he arrives at the operating room, he puts aside his laurel crown and rejects Messala's assumption that he has come to gloat over his enemy's fall: "I see no enemy." Messala, however, still does see an enemy. He has one last ember, too, with which to stoke the fire of vengeance in his former friend: the information that Judah's mother and sister are still alive but banished to the Valley of the Lepers. His dying words are not of the "Father, forgive them" type but of a rivalry even death cannot end. There is "enough of a man left here for you to hate," he croaks. "It goes on, Judah, the race is not over." Another encounter with Jesus, at the point of his final sacrifice, is needed to combat the influence on Ben-Hur of this antithesis to everything the savior represents.

Fathers and Sons

Near the end of his novel, Wallace writes that from the day the Nazarene died, "the most sacred names possible of utterance by men were
always coupled worshipfully together, GOD THE FATHER AND CHRIST
THE SON" (8:X). Although he depicts Judah Ben-Hur's faith in the Hebrew
God as praiseworthy, he does not find it sufficient. God the father must
always be coupled with Christ the son. In streamlining the narrative, the
1959 film renders this injunction schematically through the choices available to its protagonist. Shall he assimilate and subordinate the God of his
fathers to the emperor of Rome (becoming like his erstwhile brother Messala)? Or shall he remain a steadfast Jew and violently oppose Rome or,
alternatively, complete his faith by accepting the brotherhood of Christ's
salvation and live in peace?

The novel's title stresses its protagonist's filialness: his Hebrew surname marks him as a son ("Ben") of the house of Hur. In the film though,
oddly enough, Judah's father has no presence; none of his survivors so
much as mentions him. We assume that he is dead because Judah refers
to inheriting a legacy: the slave Simonides. In the novel Arrius had known
the elder Hur, having enjoyed a close cross-cultural friendship with him
that never curdled like the relationship between Judah and Messala. This
friendship is the primary reason Arrius believes in Judah's innocence when
he meets him on the galley. The film eliminates this connection between
the protagonist's biological and adoptive fathers. Instead, it provides a
series of father substitutes who represent the different paths the son might
take. Arrius wishes Judah to adopt the nobler aspects of the Roman worldview by becoming a replacement for his dead heir. Simonides, tortured by
the Romans at the time of Judah's arrest, emerges as a passionate advocate
of a Jewish uprising against the oppressor; according to his daughter, he
is "burned up" with hatred. Balthasar, seeking the grown Messiah, sees
something of him reflected in Judah. Sheik Ilderim, chafing at the condescending racism the Romans display toward colonial subjects, sees Judah's
victory in the chariot race as a vindication for Jew and Arab alike.

These fathers obsessively seek to repair or regain something they have
lost: a child, freedom, a savior, ethnic pride, etc. Each believes that Judah,

the avatar of sonhood, should become their instrument in doing so.[20] As a result, none guides him away from the obsessive dynamic of his vengeful conflict with Messala. If their manipulations lack the skewed eroticism the film strongly implies between the boyhood friends who were once so much "like brothers," certain textual moments gloss the older men's desires as departures from heteronormativity.

Earlier in this essay I discussed the homoerotic subtext between Arrius and Judah on the galley. Traces of this subtext persist as Arrius frees and adopts Judah.[21] As for the father substitute of Simonides, torture has left him paralyzed and most likely impotent. Balthasar's motives are the purest, but the sinister air with which he leans over a sleeping Ben-Hur at the oasis, supposedly to study the Jew's face, has the young man springing up and reaching for his dagger as if he anticipated assault. Finally, Sheik Ilderim travels with six wives, yet when he summons those dearest to his heart into his tent for a nocturnal embrace, they are his four magnificent Arabian horses: "children" that no wife has borne him. Additionally, as Melani McAlister observes, Ilderim "plays the central role usually reserved for women" when he cheers Judah on during the chariot race that Judah's wife-to-be does not attend.[22]

Esther and Ben-Hur's mother and sister are the only women to whom the film grants agency and voice. We never see any of the men who interact with Ben-Hur display romantic affection toward a woman in the film. Judah and Esther are the only heterosexual couple who converse. Most characters' spouses are unaccounted for; for instance, Ilderim's wives remain off-screen. It is, however, the women in Ben-Hur's life who convince him to heed Christ's message. Esther, believing in the "young rabbi," convinces Judah to take his mother and sister to seek healing from Jesus. The miraculous return of their sound bodies sets up Judah's epiphany: recognition of the man who gave him water and his attempt to return the kindness during Jesus's painful journey to Calvary. A witness at the Crucifixion, Judah feels "his words take the sword from my hand." Meanwhile, the rainstorm that ensues washes the leprosy from Miriam and Tirzah's bodies, emblematizing what Christ's sacrifice will do for the sins of all humankind.

In brief, as the film presents masculine desire, it is incompatible with salvation. It seeks to dominate and manipulate its objects in the service of personal obsession or violent ideological competition. In the film, Jesus is not overtly "womanly" in the ways he is in the novel. But his virtues are female ones and he causes men who believe in him to drop their swords. (Contrast his teachings with Ilderim's non-Christian appraisal of Balthasar's pacifistic philosophy: "Balthasar is a good man but until all men are like him, we must keep our swords bright."[23]) It is fitting that the last shot we see of Judah Ben-Hur finds him surrounded by mother, sister, and bride-to-be, with no other men in sight (prefiguring the risen Christ's encounter with the three Marys.) Could Wallace, despite his patriarchal pronouncement of the linked authority of divine father and son, intentionally or subconsciously have chosen his protagonist's surname to mark him as most importantly a son of *Her*, of a mother? Opinions about this may differ. Surely, though, Wyler, Vidal, and other members of the 1959 film's creative team point us to this conclusion. If, as happens in the novel's coda, Judah and Esther eventually have children—transitioning him from son-brother-lover to the fraught position of father—the film suggests that all will be well only if every one of his children is a daughter.

◆   ◆   ◆

Bataille's analogy of the religious sacrificial victim to a woman having heterosexual intercourse encapsulates the three ways that *Ben-Hur*'s representation of Jesus's death on the cross might trouble the traditional Christian believer. It potentially eroticizes the spectacle, feminizes the savior, and arouses homoerotic desire in a male spectator. Wyler's elliptical depiction of Jesus deflects these issues onto his metonymic avatar: Judah Ben-Hur becomes an erotic spectacle and attracts the desiring gazes of other men in the film. In the end, however, this eroticism is not primarily about sexuality or gender identification *per se*; it is about power. In accepting Jesus as his savior, Judah Ben-Hur says "no" to power in the way Silverman specifies all marginalized masculinities must. Doing so positions him as a man relating only to women. But where Wyler leaves Ben-Hur may not be where the audience does. Otherwise we would have to acknowledge that a non-phallic and non-violent masculinity, whether religious or secular, becomes impossible whenever two or more men are gathered together.

Challenging a Default Ben-Hur

A Wish List

DAVID MAYER

Since the publication of *Ben-Hur* as a novel in 1880, there have been approximately eleven dramatized versions: six live stage and "arena" productions, four motion pictures, and one animated film. The very first of these live productions to be authorized by Lew Wallace was an amateur production of tableaux vivants in 1892, performed by female school children who made up the vocal choruses and provided choreographed interludes.[1] The children were abetted by a troupe of local businessmen portraying Roman soldiers and a dozen or so other adults, few of whom are likely to have had prior stage experience, who were miming the novel's named roles. This first sanctioned attempt to dramatize *Ben-Hur* was unique not only for being performed by amateurs but also because it staged every episode contained in Wallace's book.

By contrast, subsequent dramatizations are all abridgments of the novel that, by and large, observe a distinctly similar (and now default) narrative with preordained set-piece scenes. People who have encountered *Ben-Hur* through viewing William Wyler's 1959 film (the most ubiquitous source, certain to be repeated several times annually on U.S. and British television) know only this default narrative. The obligatory episodes are principally scenes of action rather than scenes depicting psychological intimacy. Because of these commonly accessible adaptations, this sequence of scenes is now altogether familiar and predictable: the fracture of the boyhood friendship between Judah and Messala, the accidentally dropped roof tile that leads to arrest and dispersal of the Hur family, Judah's imprisonment on a Roman galley, the sea battle and Judah's rescue of Quintus Arrius, the moment Judah becomes Arrius's heir, his reunion with Simonides, including Esther's liberation from slavery, Judah's desert encounter with Sheikh Ilderim, the wager, and the chariot race that ends with Messala's defeat (and his death shortly thereafter). Also familiar are the rescue of Judah's sister and widowed mother from the lepers, his confession of love for Esther, his witnessing of Jesus's agonized progression to Golgotha, the Crucifixion, and the concurrent healing of the Hur women. Since Wallace gave permission for William S. Young's 1899 stage adaptation, leading to the many touring stage productions copyrighted and controlled by Marc Klaw and Abraham Erlanger, this default narrative has rarely been challenged.

My purpose in this essay is not to condemn or criticize any of these adaptations. I recognize that each offered its audiences some experience of the novel whilst making visible—and sometimes audible—actions and characters that the novel could relate only in words. Each adaptation offered a vision of the first-century Roman and biblical worlds. Each, albeit in the disguise of period fiction, addressed social, political, and cultural issues that were immediately contemporary with the live or film version and were tacitly understood by those audiences. In addition, each adaptation presumably satisfied its audience that Judah had achieved both temporal justice and spiritual growth.

Based on my experience as a theater and film historian who has worked with nineteenth-century "toga" literature and dramas, I intend to demonstrate that there are elided, unused, and misunderstood elements within the novel that, if brought into subsequent *Ben-Hur* adaptations, would refresh the narrative and offer new approaches to a remarkable tale. In short, my essay is a wish list for future productions—ones with emendations to a long-established default sequence. It will require boldness to realize such a wish list, but the adaptor who returns to the novel will find the necessary ingredients in hand. To demonstrate, I will discuss dramatists' or directors' decisions that have shown the limits of the adaptor's understanding of the novel or reflected reluctance to confront sexual behavior that the novel makes evident.

In this essay I discuss the considerable attention that Wallace pays to the acquisition, possession, use, and power of money. In effect, he wrote a late-nineteenth-century capitalist manifesto or, at the very least, an acting-out of the decisions that a wise and generous man, comfortable with his wealth and prepared to use it for good purposes, can make— and the good that his riches can effect. Wallace's plot stresses how wise entrepreneurial risk-taking (venture capitalism) can result in huge profits. Recovery of this facet of his book brings to the foreground Simonides and Malluch, the capitalist heroes (the CEO and the CEO's gopher). They manage the Hur Trust, enrich it ceaselessly, and put its riches beyond imperial interference. A non-default *Ben-Hur* can highlight these men of business, perhaps to some slighting of Judah's role.

Another challenge to the default is the role that the anachronistic Zealots' revolt of AD 63–66 plays in the narrative.[2] I show how this Jewish intifada and Judah's reluctant role as a terrorist leader can be harnessed to modern adaptations. I also consider the episode in the Palace of Ildernee. This episode, wholly absent from the default *Ben-Hur*, finds Messala and Iras conspiring to murder Judah to avenge Messala's humiliating defeat in the chariot race. Judah's death, they imagine, will nullify the crippling debt that Messala and his Roman associates owe to the victorious Sheikh Ilderim and Judah.

Finally in this essay, I review Iras's complex role in *Ben-Hur*. Although obviously linked to the Messala plot, she is the means by which sexual temptation is introduced and by which it runs, a vivid scarlet thread, from mid-novel to the last chapter (in which a now-raddled Iras calls on the very domestic Hur family [8:XI]). A gift to any dramatist, Iras is nonetheless the most misunderstood character in *Ben-Hur*. She is also the most marginalized in dramatizations and, perhaps, the most ambiguous—if not the most critical—character in Wallace's tale. She has been altogether banished from some dramatized versions, permitted a token appearance in others, and in one version (the worst of all) replaced by a Greek prostitute who graphically beds Judah and, *faut de mieux*, deserts him for Messala.[3]

Iras must be understood in the context of nineteenth-century melodrama: a pervasive narrative genre that gave form to the Victorian novel as much as to stage pieces. She must also be understood in the context of Wallace's brief examination of feminism, "how the beautiful came to earth" (7:IV), and her parable of Ne-Ne-Hofra (5:III). Comparison of Iras to the three Jewish women—Esther, Tirzah, and Judah's nameless mother—is also important. The confidence with which Iras deploys her sexual allure ties her characterization to the episode in the Syrian Grove of Daphne (4:V-VI). If Wallace had depicted the grove as it was understood by the ancient world (*Daphnici mores*, meaning a resort for easy, no-questions-asked sex), licentiousness would be more obvious. Instead, the same author who created the tempting Iras chose to transmute the historical Daphne into something almost benign and anachronistically American.

◆   ◆   ◆

If Wallace's novel relies on an overriding thematic element—other than the Jewish charioteer's pursuit of revenge as it gives way to the moral and spiritual growth he achieves by encountering Jesus—that thematic element is the acquisition and possession of wealth that extrapolates, at times, into the immunity from hardship that money grants. That wealth "matters" in *Ben-Hur* is indicated by the fortune made by Judah's deceased father. Under Simonides's management, the already massive sum of 673 gold talents is parlayed into wealth so vast that it makes Judah the wealthiest man in the Roman Empire and biblical world. His fortune exceeds King Solomon's annual income of 666 talents.[4] Wallace's characters refer repeatedly to weights of gold and silver talents and to coinage of the Mediterranean world: the shekel, denarius, sesterce, and drachm. Judah is one such character. But we never witness him conducting business or dealing in property except, significantly, when he frees Esther from slavery. Rather, Judah's business is done for him by Esther's father, Simonides. Simonides trades from his Antioch warehouse and builds a fleet of vessels, whilst Malluch does the day-to-day legwork, and Judah merely receives the ancient world's equivalent of monthly bank statements. Only once does Judah refer to the vastness of his wealth. Facing down a blackmail attempt by Iras, Judah honors Simonides's fealty by referencing a steward who was unfaithful to the emperor at the time, Tiberius:

Tell [Messala] that when the Lord Sejanus comes to despoil me he will find nothing; for the inheritance I had from [Quintus Arrius], including the villa, has been sold, and the money from the sale is out of reach, afloat in the marts of the world as bills of exchange; and the caravans with which Simonides plies his commerce with such princely profits are covered by imperial safeguards. (7:VI)

The point of this taunt is that Simonides is no usurper or cheat. As readers learn chiefly through exposition, he is a faithful steward who suffers for his fidelity when Romans (under Sejanus), determined to seize the Hur estate, subject him to body-breaking torture. Simonides resists, though, and survives to rebuild the Hur family wealth. At the end of his trial of endurance and loyalty he is sought out by Judah. Faithful to his trust, Simonides tests the young man. Only when certain of Judah's identity does he render to the younger man's possession the financial accounts—and his beloved daughter. Like Esther, Simonides is a slave. But he will become Judah's father-in-law as well as one of Judah's successive surrogate "fathers": Quintus Arrius, Ilderim, and, ultimately, Jesus.[5]

Converted to primitive, pre-papal Christianity, Simonides survives to a comfortable old age and becomes a benign, crippled grandfather. However, if directorial attention is justly given to Judah's massive wealth, more attention must be paid to those who have enriched him. The challenge for a dramatist is how to foreground the daily activities of business and businessmen. Unlike a stage play, where such activity would require a full scene and dialogue, a film can depict Simonides and Malluch supervising the loading of vessels and dispatching laden caravans, receiving the profits from successful voyages, and sequestering the accumulated talents. A film can similarly show these custodians of the Hur wealth instructing a naïve young Judah in ways of trade and commerce. The issue is, as noted, that Wallace celebrates acquired wealth and describes a hero who knows how to spend wisely and, most important, generously.

Some may feel that it detracts from *Ben-Hur*'s action narrative to turn Simonides and Malluch into heroes of commerce. Judah's wealth is, however, the premise for two neglected, full-throttle episodes from the novel.

The first takes place at the Palace of Ildernee; the second concerns Judah's leadership role in a Zealot revolt.

The Palace of Ildernee episode starts when Judah, his victory race won, receives a message, purportedly from Iras, inviting him to a nighttime assignation. Expecting a sexual or a romantic encounter, Judah accepts the invitation. Travelling alone and unarmed, he enters the darkened palace only to discover that the door is locked behind him. Awaiting him are two contract assassins: skilled gladiator-Cesti who have killed in the arena.[6] This episode illuminates Iras's duplicity. She has appeared to be a loyal, supportive girlfriend. For instance, she claimed that she would wear Judah's colors in the chariot race. Until this moment, there has been no indication that she and Messala were allies and no hint that she has become his mistress. Nor is there any point in the narrative where, in retrospect, we may connect the villainous pair. Now, however, in the Palace of Ildernee, the possibility of a deadly conspiracy arises to the reader, if not yet to Judah's mind, but is pushed aside by the urgency of Judah's situation: he must immediately extricate himself from deadly peril. Judah's solution is twofold: first, he fights with fists and wrestlers' tricks to defeat and kill the lesser of the hitmen; and second, he uses his winnings from Messala and his Roman backers to bribe the other would-be assassin to pass off the corpse of the dead hitman as a murdered Judah. This ploy frustrates Messala's plotting.

This scene is rich with intrigue, danger, deadly physical combat, the revelation of Iras's guile, and Judah's answer to it with a strategy of his own. Yet it has never appeared in a *Ben-Hur* dramatization (apart from that first pantomime in 1892). Why? The answer, if there is one, may lie in the cinema adaptors' decisions to have Messala fatally injured in the arena and to terminate the "Judah seeks vengeance against Messala" plot either with the Jew's grim satisfaction at the Roman's death or with Judah anticipating his conversion to Christianity by forgiving his dying enemy. With either ending to the Messala plot, Iras is expunged from the narrative. Before the films were made, though, Klaw & Erlanger's massive six-act stage adaptation kept Messala crippled, but alive and impoverished (as well as offstage). This gambit let audiences witness Iras acting as Messala's agent when she attempts blackmail. Aware of Judah's leading role in raising a rebel army, she implicates him in plotting and leading an armed revolt against Roman rule—unless he foregoes his winnings and pays blackmail money. This part of the script confirms her duplicity and hitherto covert alliance with Messala.[7] But it also implies interest in the Zealot subplot that the twentieth-century films omitted.

In the second full-throttle action sequence in the novel, Judah participates in the Zealots' revolt against the Roman occupation. The Zealots' revolt, a Jewish uprising against the Roman occupation of the Holy Land, is one of Wallace's few anachronisms. Although he specified no explicit time frame for his novel, we may assume (because the action falls chiefly between the birth of Christ early in the first century AD and the reign of Sejanus that ended in AD 31) that, apart from the coda, which is set "about five years after the crucifixion" (8:XI), all events are contemporary with that period. The Jewish revolt, however, happened approximately twenty-five years later than this final scene and was not in the least influenced, let alone ended, by nascent Christianity. Nevertheless, the revolt and the expectations of a Jewish savior fit with Wallace's overall narrative.

With his sister and widowed mother still not found, and because he is disheartened and dismayed at the continuing Roman dominance in Jerusalem, Judah (influenced by the prophetic visions of the Magus Balthasar) begins to seek the coming Messiah. This deliverer, he expects, will not be the pacific, weeping Jesus but a warrior king whose cause he will join. He devotes much of his wealth, therefore, to raising, training, and equipping a guerrilla army three legions in strength. Eighteen thousand trained and armed men is no inconsequential nor inexpensive military force. However, once Jesus offers a very different means to a kingdom not of this earth, Judah's legions are simply abandoned and dropped from the narrative. We don't know what happens to those men; they are left to fend for themselves.

The most recent television version of *Ben-Hur* treats the Jewish revolt not as a future uprising but as an ongoing terrorist problem, with sporadic moments of armed resistance against the occupying Roman army. It is a growing rebellion that Judah must disavow and, in repudiating rebellion, kill one of the guerilla leaders. So, although this segment of Wallace's novel can be (and has been) overlooked, today's circumstances have made it one of the more contemporary and adaptable in terms understandable to modern audiences.

Finally, there is Iras herself. Her presence in the novel, as much as her absence (or curtailed role) in some dramatized versions, raises questions. So does her brilliance, in contrast to Esther's dutiful submissiveness. It is easy to understand why Judah's head is turned by Iras's charm, wit, and overt sex appeal; it is harder to understand and to dramatize why he chooses Esther over the Egyptian. But these are questions that *Ben-Hur*'s adaptors have elected to ignore by omitting Iras from stage and film versions. Iras and her function in the narrative have been deeply misunderstood—or intentionally overlooked—by dramatic adaptors. For the sake of what might have been construed as "decency" in a tale of the Christ (i.e., concealing Iras's sexually predatory nature), this fascinating character has been deliberately pushed aside. Whereas numerous earlier and contemporary Victorian dramas brought sexually predatory women on stage, Klaw and Erlanger's decision to downplay Iras may reflect concern that the onstage presence of a temptress and a sexually susceptible protagonist, in a drama in which Jesus plays a part, was too much of a risk at the box office.

Yet, as depicted in Wallace's novel, Iras is a remarkable figure. This is particularly apparent in contrast to Judah's mother and sister—rich privileged women who live for their son/brother but appear to have little identity and scant roundness as characters. Esther's character is more developed. But whereas Esther is beautiful, obedient, and calm, Iras is glamorous, sexy, independent, and highly intelligent. Where Esther knows that her place is within the Hur household, and accepts a submissive role, Iras appears and flirts in public. Knowing the protocols that limit female behavior, she subverts them. She wears cosmetics, and Esther does not. She is musical, and Esther is not. She is wryly funny, and Esther is dour. She speaks in metaphor and parable, and Esther does neither. She eavesdrops on men's conversations and uses her gathered intelligence in adversarial fashion and for her own ends. She is audacious, feisty, cynical, ironic, humorous, sarcastic, iconoclastic, dangerous, and, ultimately, murderous. These traits—most of all her sexy glamour, cynicism, sarcasm, irony, and sense of humor—instantly identify her as the character Victorian melodrama audiences and readers knew as the "adventuress."

The very term "adventuress" references the role's questing and disruptive part in destabilizing otherwise tranquil and settled relationships.

7. Iras in the Klaw & Erlanger theater production. From the Player's edition of *Ben-Hur* (1901).

This term began to appear in novels and stage melodrama in the latter half of the nineteenth century. Mrs. Henry Wood's *East Lynne* (1861) was one of these novels, and Mary Elizabeth Braddon's *Lady Audley's Secret* (1862) was another. Both proved wildly popular with U.S. readers. Catching this trend, Louisa May Alcott published *Behind a Mask* (1866) under a pseudonym and released *A Modern Mephistopheles* (1877) anonymously so that she would not endanger her reputation as a children's author. The most popular and successful of all Victorian "toga plays," Wilson Barrett's *The Sign of the Cross* (1895), was another melodrama that ends with the hero's last-minute conversion to Christianity. It depicted the upright Roman hero who was pursued by two predatory females, both scheming and manipulative, and both rejected for a virtuous Christian heroine.

Interest in the adventuress took hold partly in response to French "woman-with-a-past" plays and novels of the 1850s and partly in reaction to women's increasing calls for social, economic, and political rights.[8] Although sometimes unattached to any man, the adventuress is often paired with the villain; their sexual alliance is implied but not made explicit. The adventuress may attempt to seduce, defraud, mislead, or otherwise place obstacles in the paths of the narrative's innocent or virtuous characters. Iras behaves entirely in accordance with this crucial role. Why, then, when the role is so central to the functioning of melodrama (and a dramatized *Ben-Hur* in all other particulars is a melodrama), should one of the more interesting of all nineteenth-century adventuresses be marginalized or excised in stage and film adaptations of the novel? That is, unless her sexualized subversiveness has been considered inappropriate to a narrative that also contains Jesus? This is my conjecture, not proven fact. It is an unanswered question that mounts a reproach to the dramatists and screenwriters who have addressed *Ben-Hur*.

Iras is so little known to people who know *Ben-Hur* only through the 1959 film version that some background information is necessary. She is not immediately attached to Messala and, as an Egyptian, she is connected neither to Jewish nor Roman interests. However, as the daughter of the Magus Balthasar, she is directly linked to Christian biblical mythology. It is one of the lesser tragedies of the novel that Balthasar loses his daughter when other parent and child relationships—Judah and his mother, Esther and Simonides—are shown to flourish. Wallace's *Ben-Hur* is about fathers (temporal and spiritual) and sons. But it is also about fathers and daughters and about brothers and sisters (that Messala is initially likened a brother to Tirzah makes his acts of imprisoning her and concealing her whereabouts even more heinous). Perhaps Iras's alienation from her father, who is so central to the New Testament narrative, is one of the reasons that she disappears from stage and film adaptations. However, I lean more toward the opinion that her overpowering sexuality and overt sexual alliance with Messala have frightened off successive adaptors.

Despite the known success of the Fort Lee studios' emphasis on "vamp" films, which costumed Theda Bara in revealing oriental dress, and that of the 1920s Hollywood studios, which exploited Louise Brooks and Clara Bow's reputed earthy promiscuity, Fred Niblo's 1925 *Ben-Hur* allowed Iras the merest walk-on part, whilst Wyler's 1959 adaptation eliminated her altogether.[9] With the women's healing and Judah's conversion still to be dramatized, both directors found it far easier to kill off Messala and to elide the episodes in which Judah is lured to the Palace of Ildernee and Judah confronts Iras.

When considering how Iras's overpowering sexuality may have frightened away adaptors, it is important to examine her character's first appearance in the narrative. Iras first appears at the Castalian Fountain, a sibylline site on the approach to the Grove of Daphne. In this chapter, Judah's strength and presence of mind turn Messala's speeding chariot aside, preventing it from crashing into the camel-borne howdah carrying Iras and Balthasar. Wallace brings the three principal characters face to face in this scene, revealing Iras's surface beauty, her instant appeal to Messala, and her flirtatious nature. This is also the moment in which Judah realizes that the means of revenge against Messala are within reach.

Iras, now introduced, is thus linked to the licentious atmosphere of Daphne, a reputed oasis of sexual indulgence. But Daphne, as depicted in the novel, fails to live up to its proverbial ancient reputation as a rural resort for easy promiscuous sex and indolence. Wallace describes a young couple sleeping in a postcoital stupor and an eager female beckoning from the shrubbery as the only evidence that Daphne imperils Judah's innocence. The Klaw & Erlanger production somewhat raised the ante when it turned act 3, scene 3 ("The Fountain of Castalia THE REVELS OF DAPHNE IN THE SPIDER'S WEB") into a dance by the site's alleged temple prostitutes, the "Devadasi."[10] However, any potential for theatrical eroticism was smothered in mass spectacle as ranks of ballet girls waving floral garlands filled the stage. As described by Wallace, the Grove of Daphne, a woodland retreat embellished with a temple and the promise of a lurking deity, resembles an American pastime that arose from the "Great Awakening" religious revival of the 1840s. Wallace's Daphne is similar to rural Chautauqua encampments, which were rustic summer vacation sites for thousands of American families who took their spring wagons, cook stoves, provisions, and tents to the camps to hear preaching, attend lectures on ethics and morality, and enjoy harmless entertainment. Even Wallace, we may infer, trod warily around depictions of frank sexual pleasure.

Wallace was neither the first nor the last author to bring an adventuress to a sad end. In the novel's final episode, we learn that Iras, tired of living with a broken and impoverished Messala, has murdered him. Readers sense that she has meted the justice the Roman deserves. The exact circumstances of Iras's act are left to the reader's imagination. Wallace hints that she then takes her own life by deliberately drowning in the Bay of Misenum, which is not far from the villa where Judah, Esther, and their children live.[11] Both of these incidents can be translated into film and are potentially dramatic, if sordid, episodes in which actions merge with inner emotion. Both deaths bring closure to the narrative of Judah's quest for revenge and justice. Yet perhaps because these deaths distract from the drama of the Hur family's conversion to Christianity, neither has appeared on film.

Sadly for fans of the novel, the default dramatizations are likely to remain in productions of *Ben-Hur*. When Sidney Olcott and Kalem Studios filmed *Ben-Hur* for the first time in 1907, they could safely gamble on a production that abridged William Young's three-hour drama to "six tableaux" running for a mere fifteen minutes each. Early twentieth-century cinema audiences, who were already familiar with the major contours of the novel and stage play, demanded no more than representations of the key scenes and the briefest of narratives.[12] There were no scenes of Judah acquiring and using his vast wealth, no Iras, and no episodes of sexual temptation. Nothing has changed in this regard. On the evidence of so many adaptations, with the likelihood that others will follow in time, the now-ingrained default narrative may resist change. But change can happen. My wish is that a future adaptor will turn to the novel to recognize what additional or alternative materials lay at his or her disposal. It is still a possibility—however remote—that we may experience justice done to the intricacies of Lew Wallace's imaginative novel.

Coda

A Timeline of Ben-Hur Companies, Brands, and Products

JON SOLOMON

The popular success of Lew Wallace's novel inspired a number of commercial ventures. Some of the earliest of these admired the novel's moral tone, many used the vivid chariot race as a trademark, and others relied on its ubiquitous popularity to associate their business with victory and being "the best." For these and other reasons, the name "Ben-Hur," with or without the hyphen, became a veritable brand name. Subsequently, because intellectual copyright and trademark laws in the 1880s did not permit the name or chariot imagery to be officially trademarked, individual Ben-Hur companies, brands, and products proliferated for decades. Some of these were extremely successful. Ben Hur Construction was founded in 1909 and still operates in four cities. Ben-Hur Coffee was one of the dominant brands of coffee, tea, and spices on the West Coast from 1903 until the mid-1950s. The Tribe of Ben-Hur, a charitable fraternal organization inspired by the novel's protagonist, who "exemplified all that is true of brotherly love, relief and truth," was personally authorized by Wallace (he also designed their Roman galley logo).[1] The Tribe of Ben-Hur became one of the largest insurance companies in the Midwest. Several Ben-Hur shrines, most notably the one in Austin, Texas, established in the late nineteenth century, are still active. Ben Hur Perfume is still being marketed as a vintage product.

Established early, unprotected by trademark, and popular everywhere, the name "Ben-Hur" was used for many of the retail items available

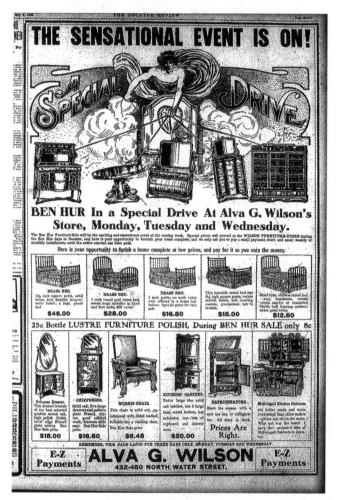

8. Capitalizing on the success of the *Ben-Hur* play, a furniture store in Illinois ran this advertisement in the *Decatur Review* in 1909. Reprinted with kind permission of the *Decatur Herald & Review*; courtesy of the Abraham Lincoln Presidential Library and Museum.

in turn-of-the-century stores, including bicycles, tools, beverages, clubs, fresh and canned foods, razors, shoes, games, toys, clocks, watches, military equipment, and freezers, not to mention nearly twenty musical compositions published as sheet music. The name also spread across many different industries, including gold, silver, and coal mining as well as petroleum exploration, drilling, and refining. Additionally, this name was applied to dozens of ships and trains, amusement park rides, automobiles, and more than ten race and show horses, prize dogs and farm animals, new plant hybrids, famous people (e.g., Ben Hur Lampman, Oregon's poet laureate), and even towns. A search for "Ben-Hur" in Google Maps will also bring up streets, drives, and avenues in twelve states. No phenomenon in the popular arts has had this kind of pervasive impact, especially considering that these companies and products were almost all the result of grassroots popularity rather than strategic corporate programs.

I have compiled the following timeline from a variety of online resources and printed catalogs. A number of items were advertised for sale on eBay and other online auction sites. Many of those items were of unknown provenance, so additional research was necessary to determine dates and locations. Even so, pertinent information about some companies, brands, or products is still elusive, and research is ongoing. There is no claim to completeness here. Previously identified products can appear on one of the online sites at any time and then disappear shortly thereafter. Also, it is important to note that the release of the 1959 Metro-Goldwyn-Mayer film produced many tie-ins legally licensed at the time. I did not attempt to include more than a handful of these tie-ins here. However, the timeline does reflect the unparalleled impact of Wallace's novel in so many areas of commerce and its endurance over so many decades.

TABLE 2. Chronology of Ben-Hur Items

Item	Company	Source	Date	City	State/Country
Ben Hur Cigars	Gustav Moebs	Ephemera: labels; John William Leonard, *The Industries of Detroit: Historical, Descriptive, and Statistical* (Detroit, MI: J. M. Elstner, 1887), 131	1886–c. 1910	Detroit	MI
Steam-powered sternwheeler	J. B. Sheppard	*Southwestern Reporter* 30 (1895): 832–33; *Merchant Vessels of the United States* (Washington, DC: Government Printing Office, 1894), 276	1887	Wheeling	WV
Ben Hur Flour	New Lindell Mills	Ephemera: letterhead	1888	Fort Collins	CO
Paddle-wheeler	Eugene W. Thompson	*The Waterways Journal* 71 (April 20, 1957): 10	1889	Portland	ME
Fence	Page Woven Wire-Fence	*Ben-Hur* used for chromolithographed ad; company founded 1883	c. 1890	Adrian	MI
Ben Hur Bicycle	Central Cycle Manufacturing	http://www.thewheelmen.org/sections/bicyclebrands/showresults.asp?which page=2&pagesize=50&alphachar=B	1891–98	Indianapolis	IN
Ben Hur Bicycle	Luburg Manufacturing	http://www.thewheelmer.org/sections/bicyclebrands/showresults.asp?which page=2&pagesize=50&alphachar=B	1892	Philadelphia	PA

TABLE 2. Chronology of Ben-Hur Items (continued)

Item	Company	Source	Date	City	State/Country
Rescue boat	...	*Boston Sunday Globe*, April 13, 1893, 27	1893	Boston	MA
Bicycle wrench	Whitman & Barnes Manufacturing	http://www.datamp.org/patents/search /advance.php?pn=452518&id=25415&set =1	c. 1893	Chicago	IL
Supreme Tribe of Ben-Hur	Supreme Tribe of Ben-Hur	http://nationalheritagemuseum.type pad.com/library_and_archives/supreme -tribe-of-ben-hur/	1894	Crawfordsville	IN
Paddle-wheeler	...	http://www.tshaonline.org/handbook /online/articles/hda03; http://www .austinpostcard.com/gdam.html	1895–1900	Austin	TX
Ben Hur Bitters	...	R. Barlett Saalfrank and Carlyn Ring, *For Bitters Only* (Wellesley Hills, MA: The Pl Press, 1980), 78	c. 1895	...	...
Ben Hur Rye	...	Private collection: promotional glass	c. 1895	...	...
Ben Hur Athletic Association of Brooklyn	Ben Hur Athletic Association of Brooklyn	*Brooklyn Daily Eagle Almanac*, 1899, 105	1897	Brooklyn	NY
Ben Hur Flour	Colorado Milling & Elevator	http://www.trademarkia.com/benhur -71556319.html	1897	...	CO

TABLE 2. Chronology of Ben-Hur Items (continued)

Item	Company	Source	Date	City	State/Country
Ben Hur and Trade Dollar Mines	Republic Mines, Northport Smelting & Refining	http://nwda-db.wsulibs.wsu.edu/find aid/ark:/80444/xv29075	1897–1941	Republic	WA
Ben Hur Prospect	Ben Hur Mining	Ephemera: stock certificate	1898	. . .	NM
Ben Hur Tomatoes	Baumann's (sold by)	*Janesville Daily Gazette*, January 10, 1899, 2	1899	Janesville	WI
Ben-Hur Baking Powder	Packed by The Geiger-Tinney, Indianapolis wholesale coffee and spices	In the possession of the author	c. 1900	Mahomet	IL
Straight razor	Shumate Razor	http://www.uniclectica.com/misc /manuf.html; Austin, TX 1900–1904	1900–1932	St. Louis	MO
Ben Hur Sewing Machine	Van Camp Hardware and Iron	Ephemera: Van Camp advertising envelope	1901	Indianapolis	IN
Mine	Ben Hur Mining and Milling	Denver Public Library; Library of Congress; mining certificate	1901	Leadville	CO

TABLE 2. Chronology of Ben-Hur Items (continued)

Item	Company	Source	Date	City	State/Country
Mine	Ben Hur Copper Mining Company	*Wall Street Journal*, January 8, 1902, 6	1902	Cripple Creek	CO
Theater curtain painting	Metropolitan Theatre, Indianapolis	*St. Paul Dispatch*, March 28, 1902	1902	St. Paul	MN
Ben Hur Flour	Royal Milling	*Saturday Evening Post*, August 1, 1903	1902–15	Minneapolis	MN
Ben Hur Perfume	Andrew Jergens	Ninth annual meeting, Manufacturing Perfumers Association of the United States (1903)	1903	Cincinnati	OH
Ben Hur Coffee and Spices	Joannes Brothers	http://www.you-are-here.com/down town/ben_hur.html	1903–53	Los Angeles	CA
Mine	Ben Hur and Cleopatra Mine	USGS survey no. 26 (1904)	1904	N. Black Hills	SD
Shoes	John J. Schulten	Ephemera: letterhead	1904–13	Louisville	KY
Boat	…	*Tacoma Daily News*, September 4, 1905, 1	1905	Detroit	MI
Mine tunnels	Boston Consolidated	*Mineral Industry* 14 (1905): 137	1905	Bingham	UT
Claim	Grass Roots Gold Developing & Mining	Ephemera: prospectus	1906	Denver	CO

TABLE 2. Chronology of Ben-Hur Items (continued)

Item	Company	Source	Date	City	State/Country
Gasoline motors	Ben Hur Motor	*Automobile Trade Journal*, 11 (1906): 196	1906	Chicago	IL
Barkley's Ben Hur Baking Powder	Thomas J. Barkley	Ephemera: can label	1907	San Francisco	CA
Ben Hur Race (amusement park ride)	W. F. Mangels, Carousell Works	*Billboard* 20 (1908)	1907	New York	NY
Ben Hur Racer	Ben Hur Racing	Ephemera: postcards	1907	Ocean Park	CA
Lew Wallace and Chariot Race postcard	Scofield Pierson	Ephemera: postcard	1907	Indianapolis	IN
Ben Hur and Ben Hur Fraction	Ben Hur Mining	http://nwda-db.wsulibs.wsu.edu/find aid/ark:/80444/xv03425	1907–40	Saltese	MT
Ben Hur Harness and Whips	Geo. Worthington	Ephemera: booklet	1908	Cleveland	OH
Electric sign	Wonderland Building	*Life*, November 13, 1944, 3	1908	Detroit	MI
Slot machine	Caille	http://gameroomantiques.com/Caille SlotModels.htm	1908	Detroit	MI
Ben Hur Construction Company	Ben Hur Construction	http://www.benhurconstruction.com	1909	St. Louis	MO

TABLE 2. **Chronology of Ben-Hur Items** (continued)

Item	Company	Source	Date	City	State/Country
Ben Hur Good Strong Blanket (buggy blanket)	George Worthington	http://ech.case.edu/cgi/article.pl?id=GWC	1909	Cleveland	OH
Ben Hur Interurban Line	Indianapolis, Crawfordsville & Western Traction	Electric Railway Historical Society Bulletin no. 34 (1911)	1909	Indianapolis	IN
Ben Hur Shoe Polish	Ben Hur Manufacturers	Ephemera: advertisement	1909	Portland	OR
Ben Hur Special (train)	. . .	Ephemera: postcards	1909	Castle Rock	WA
Ben-Hur Whiskey (glass)	Rhomberg Distilling	Glass	1910	East Dubuque	IL
Ben Hur Oranges	Redlands Cooperative Fruit Association	*Catalog of Copyright Entries: Musical Compositions* (Washington, DC: U.S. Government Printing Office, 1953), 317	c. 1910–c. 1940	Redlands	CA
Ben Hur Apartment	100th Street and Broadway, NY	*New York Times*, September 23, 1911, 17	1911	New York	NY
Ben Hur Bazaar	McNicol Manufacturing	Ephemera: china plate calendar	1911	St. Louis	MO

TABLE 2. Chronology of Ben-Hur Items (continued)

Item	Company	Source	Date	City	State/Country
Ben Hur Chariot Race paper game	Emil Voellmy (designer)	Ephemera: magazine page of unknown origin	1911	...	...
Paddle-wheeler	...	http://www-personal.ksu.edu /~rcadams/bh_steamboat.jpg	1911	Stillwater	MN
Ben Hur Prospect (gold and silver mine)	F. C. Schrader	http://mineralresourcema?.com/detail /1004526l	1912	Elko	NV
Ben Hur Steel Racing Car	Perry Mason (sold by)	*Youth's Companion*, October 24, 1912, 592	1912–13	Boston	MA
Kaplan's Ben-Hur (department store)	Dave and Bessie Kaplan	Bill Schadewald, "Business Survivors Have Special Staying Power," *Houston Business Journal*, August 12, 2001, http:// www.bizjournals.com/houston/stories /2001/08/13/editorial1.html.	1913–2006	Houston	TX
Ben Hur Fly Reel	William Talbot	A. J. Campbell, *Classic and Antique Fly-Fishing Tackle: A Guide for Collectors and Anglers* (New York: Lyons & Burford, 1997), 186–87	1914	Kansas City	MO
Ben-Hur White Bleaching Soap	Peet Bros.	http://www.trademarkia.com/benhur -71078505.html	1914	Kansas City	MO

TABLE 2. Chronology of Ben-Hur Items (continued)

Item	Company	Source	Date	City	State/Country
Ben-Hur Genuine Black Band Splint: "The Big Blocky Coal"	Meister Coal Mining	*West Virginia Annual Report of the Department of Mines* (1930), 28–29	c. 1915	Bridgeport	OH
Automobile	Ben Hur Motor	Beverly Rae Kimes and Henry Austin Clark Jr., *Standard Catalog of American Cars, 1805–942* (Iola, WI: Krause, 1885), 111	1916	Cleveland	OH
Ben Hur General Purpose Dry Cell Battery No. 6	Burgess Battery	Ephemera: label	1916	…	IL
Ben Hur Racing Association	Speedway Park Association	*Motor Age,* April 13, 1916, 17	1916	Chicago	IL
Magnetic steel straight razor	M. L. Brandt Manufacturing	http://www.uniclectica.com/misc /manuf.html	1916–21	New York	NY Germany
Mine	Ben Hur Divide Extension Mining	http://archive.org/stream/mines registersuc14newyuoft/mines registersuc14newyuoft_djvu.txt	1919	Tonopah	NV

TABLE 2. Chronology of Ben-Hur Items (continued)

Item	Company	Source	Date	City	State/Country
Ben Hur China	Fraunfelter China	http://genforum.genealogy.com/fraunfelter/messages/62.html	1923–39	Zanesville	OH
Ben Hur Apartments	Ben Hur Apartments	400 Hyde Street, San Francisco	1926	San Francisco	CA
Ben Hur Perfume	Andrew Jergens	Ephemera: Carmel Myers blotter, 1925 MGM film	1926	Cincinnati	OH
Ben-Hur Brand Pure Ceylon Tea	Tin maker: Thos Davidson Manufacturing	http://www.onlink.net/~johnell/	Before 1927	...	Canada
Ben Hur Café	Wulfano and Humberto Ruiz (owners)	*Oakland Tribune*, December 15, 1927, 5	1927	Tijuana	Mexico
Clock	Westclox	*Printer's Ink* (1927), 138	1927	LaSalle	IL
Ben Hur "B" Radio Battery No. 281	Burgess Battery	Label	1929	...	IL
Ben Hur Perfume	Andrew Jergens	Montgomery Ward catalog	1929	...	...
Tools	Van Camp (sold by)	Ephemera: unprovenienced magazine ad	1930s	Indianapolis	IN
Ben-Hur Wheat Flour	General Mills	http://www.trademarkia.com/benhur-71312181.html	1931	Minneapolis	MN

TABLE 2. **Chronology of Ben-Hur Items (continued)**

Item	Company	Source	Date	City	State/Country
Quadro Backgammon	Ben-Hur Products	Ephemera: Behr & Hirtenstein	1931	New York	NY
Straight razor	Solingen—Friedrich Herkenrath	Paul Vanderwood, *Juan Soldado* (Chapel Hill, NC: Duke Univ. Press, 2004), 104	1932	Solingen	Germany
Alarm clock	Westclox, Model S2G	http://wkinsler.com/clocks/index.html	1933	…	Canada
Pinball	Pace Manufacturing	http://www.arcade-museum.com/game_detail.php?game_id=11154	1933	Chicago	IL
Bakelite cocktail menus	…	Matthew L. Burkholz, *The Bakelite Collection* (Atglen, PA: Schiffer, 1997), 74–79	c. 1933	New York	NY
Ben Hur Perfume	Andrew Jergens	Sears catalog	1934	Chicago	IL
Honeywell controller	Honeywell	Ephemera: Ben-Hur advertisement	1934	Minneapolis	MN
Ben Hur Ark	R. J. Lakin	http://www.fairground-heritage.org.uk/newsite/learn/people-lakins.html	c. 1935	London	UK
Ben Hur Superior Aviation Ethyl Gasoline	Urich	Ephemera: decal	c. 1935	Los Angeles	CA

TABLE 2. Chronology of Ben-Hur Items (continued)

Item	Company	Source	Date	City	State/ Country
Ben-Hur Coffee Pavilion	Ben-Hur Products	San Diego Pan American Expo, http://www.sandiegohistory.org/amero/notes-1936new.htm	1936	San Diego	CA
Ben Hur Wire Fence	Mid-States Steel & Wire	*Hardware Age* (1936), 138: 601	1936	Crawfordsville	IN
Watch	Bulova	http://mybulova.com	1936	Woodside	NY
Ben Hur Tent	Hettrick Manufacturing	Canvas and Metal Products by Hettrick (1940)	1940	Toledo	OH
Club Sportivo Ben Hur	Club Sportivo Ben Hur	http://www.clubbenhur.com.ar	1940	Rafaela	Argentina
Ben Hur Jeep (1-ton cargo G-518 trailer)	Ben Hur Manufacturing	http://www.earlycj5.com/forums/show thread.php?74865-The-Sears-David -Bradley-Trailer	1941–45	Milwaukee	WI
Ben Hur Advance Tooth Powder	Ben Hur Laboratories	American Dental Association, *Accepted Dental Remedies* (1944), 98; https://www.pinterest.com/pin/501236633505112118/	1944	Los Angeles	CA
Ben-Hur Ford ad (references Wonderland building sign)	Ford Motor	*Life*, November 13, 1944, 3	1944	Detroit	MI

TABLE 2. **Chronology of Ben-Hur Items (continued)**

Item	Company	Source	Date	City	State/Country
Ben-Hur Coffee float	Ben-Hur Products	Pasadena Tournament of Roses, 1946	1946	Pasadena	CA
Ben-Hur Jiffy Camper	Ben Hur Manufacturing	http://www.earlycj5.com/forums /showthreac.php?74865-The-Sears -David-Bradley-Trailer	1947	Milwaukee	WI
Ben Hur Salmon	Oceanic Sales	http://www.labelman.com; eBay	1947	Seattle	WA
Ben Hur Freezer	Ben Hur Manufacturing	http://www.earlycj5.com/forums /showthread.php?74865-The-Sears -David-Bradley-Trailer	1947–61	Milwaukee	WI
Streamline curler, barrettes, pins, etc.	Ben-Hur Hair Products	*Chain Store Age,* June 1947, 13	1947–64	New York	NY
Flour	Colorado Milling & Elevator	http://www.trademarkia.com/benhur -71556319.html	1948	Denver	CO
Freight train (painting only)	Monon	Howard Fogg painting, http://www .railmode.com/cards/117.html	1948	Monon	IN
Sanforized ad	Sanforized trademark	*Life,* March 21, 1949, 5	1949	...	...
Ben Hur Camporee	Boy Scouts of America	Ephemera: patch with date; "East District"	1950	...	...

TABLE 2. Chronology of Ben-Hur Items (continued)

Item	Company	Source	Date	City	State/Country
Ben Hur Refining Company	…	*Los Angeles Times*, May 30, 1949, 11	1950	Grant City	NM
Comic book	Famous Authors Illustrated, Seaboard Publishing	Famous Authors Illustrated #11	1951	New York	NY
Gold Comet truck (Benny racing as a chariot)	Reo Motors	*Life*, June 30, 1952, 5	1952	Lansing	MI
Ben Hur Home	Ben Hur Home (elder care)	http://www.benhurhome.com	1956	Crawfordsville	IN
Ben Hur Entrecote Steak	Cunard Line, RMS Queen Mary	Ephemera: menu	1957	…	…
Comic book	Classics Illustrated no. 147	http://www.amazon.com	1958	New York	NY
Board game	Bell Games	MGM tie-in	1959	London	UK
Cabover Ben Hur 11—Hal Kelly Hydroplane	Clark Craft	http://www.clarkcraft.com	1959	Tonawanda	NY
Comic book	Dell no. 1052	http://www.amazon.com	1959	New York	NY

TABLE 2. Chronology of Ben-Hur Items (continued)

Item	Company	Source	Date	City	State/Country
Picture cards	MGM	MGM tie-in	1959	...	...
Ben-Hur Sword, Scabbard, and Shield Set	Marx	Sears catalog	1960	New York	NY
Marx Ben-Hur Playset	Marx	#4701, series 5000; #4696, series 2000 (Sears)	1960	New York	NY
Marx Ben-Hur Playset	Plastimarx	eBay	1960	...	Mexico
Mechanical Ben-Hur Trotter	AHI Toys, no. 6410	eBay	1960	...	Japan
Play figures	J. T. C. Unicorn (made in Hong Kong)	eBay	1960	Hong Kong	UK
Ben Hur Bicycle	Monark	http://thecabe.com/vbulletin/show thread.php?5728-Ben-hur-Imperator	c. 1960	Chicago	IL
Ben Hur Catsup	Winona Preserving	Ephemera: laɔel	c. 1960	Winona	Canada
Ben Hur Flicker Ring	...	eBay	c. 1960	...	...
Iron toy chariot	Mill	eBay	c. 1960	...	UK

TABLE 2. Chronology of Ben-Hur Items (continued)

Item	Company	Source	Date	City	State/Country
Bra (woman riding chariot)	Maidenform	*Life,* September 8, 1961, 10	1961	…	…
Mine	…	Oklahoma Geological Survey Bulletin 91 (1963): 16	1963	Okmulgee City	OK
Ben Hur Wheat	…	http://www.washingtoncrop.com/documents/Archives-Wheat/Benhur.pdf	1964	Knox City	IN
Car dealership	Ben Hur Ford (owners, Bob Bennis & Hy Hurwitz)	…	1965	Sioux Falls	SD
Hot rod	…	Ephemera: 1967 Annual Fresno Autorama Custom Car program	1967	Fresno	CA
Wristwatch	Caravelle (Bulova)	*Life,* June 2, 1967, 29	1967	New York	NY
Ben Hur Chameleon Sunglasses	Ben Hur	eBay	1970s	…	France
Le Ben-Hur (pinball machine)	Staal Society	http://www.arcade-museum.com/game_detail.php?game_id=12758	1977	…	France
Ben-Hur Soda	Ben Hur Beverages	http://www.ca-yd.com/textfile/bottles/WANTLIST.HTM	c. 1980	Wallingford	CT

TABLE 2. **Chronology of Ben-Hur Items** (continued)

Item	Company	Source	Date	City	State/Country
Ben Hur Quadriga—toy	Airgam Boys	Private collection	1983	…	Spain
Collector plate	Ghent Collection	"American Classics," 1 of 8, e.g., Huck Finn, Moby Dick, etc.; in the possession of the author	1983	Bath	OH
Collector plate	Porcelaine Etienne	Plate II; in the possession of the author	1983	Bath	OH
Quilt design	Indiana Heritage Quilts	eBay	1985	…	IN
Ben Hur Prospect (gold mine)	U.S. Bur. Mines	http://www.mindat.org/loc-88060.html	1990	San Bernadino	CA
Ben Hur Moving & Storage	Ben Hur Moving & Storage	http://benhur.com	1991	New York	NY
				Los Angeles	CA
Ben Hur T-shirts (World Cup)	Ben Hur Sports	eBay	1998	…	…
Ben Hur Dirt Kart Track	Ben Hur Speedway	http://www.benhurspeedway.net	2000	Crawfordsville	IN
Race	Harold Park Paceway	http://en.wikipedia.org/wiki/Harold_Park_Paceway	2001–8	Sydney	Australia
Playstation 2 game	Sony	http://ps2.igr.com/objects/492/492776.html	2003	…	…

TABLE 2. Chronology of Ben-Hur Items (continued)

Item	Company	Source	Date	City	State/Country
Ben Hur Water Tanker (miniature toy)	King & Country	eBay	2004	Hong Kong	China
Ben-Hur Wheat Flour	General Mills	General Mills Product Specification Sheet (2005)	2005	Minneapolis	MN
Ben Tire & Auto Service Center	Ben Tire & Auto Service Center	1300 Broadway Ave., Mattoon, IL 61938	2005	Mattoon	IL
Apartment complex	The Kaplan's Ben-Hur	2125 Yale, Houston, TX 77008	2008	Houston	TX
Ben Hur Trading (online vintage sales)	Ben Hur Trading	eBay	2008	...	TX
Ben Hur Accommodation Package	Metro Apartments on Darling Harbour	http://www.metrohotels.com.au /special/121	2010	Sydney	Australia

TABLE 2. **Chronology of Ben-Hur Items** (continued)

Item	Company	Source	Date	City	State/Country
Ben Hur Fish and Chips	Ben Hur Fish and Chips	http://www.misterwhat.co.uk/company/1547762-be-n-hur-fish-bar-edinburgh	2011	Edinburgh	Scotland
Ben Hur Mugs and Travel Mugs	CafePress	http://www.cafepress.com	2011	…	…
Apartment	…	http://www.airbnb.com/rooms/88601	2012	Rome	Italy
Ben Hur Hoodies & Sweatshirts	CafePress	http://www.cafepress.com	2012	…	…
Ben Hur Tobacco	Helens Handbags	http://helenshandbags.blogspot.com/	2012	Natick	MA
Mini Ben Hur Push-Bike 435.14	Winther	http://www.adventuretoys.co.uk/prodpage.asp?PrcdID=624	2012	…	Denmark

Acknowledgments

A book big enough, in terms of disciplinary range, to be named *Bigger than "Ben-Hur"* was of course several years in the making. We are pleased that this collection brings together all new essays from scholars in literature, theater, film, history, American studies, comparative literature, and the classics. We owe a debt of gratitude to our contributors for their generous patience and good cheer.

We would like to thank Ya'ara Notea for her excellent work as research and editorial assistant. We would also like to thank Jan Perone at the Abraham Lincoln Presidential Library, Patricia Boulos at the Boston Athenaeum, our editors Jennika Baines and Deborah Manion, series editor Robert J. Thompson, and the Syracuse University Press staff. Many thanks as well to the two anonymous readers of the manuscript for their enormously helpful suggestions.

Two institutes provided financial assistance for which we are grateful: the Israel Science Foundation (grant 866/07) and the Singapore Ministry of Education–National University of Singapore Academic Research Fund (AcRF tier 1 grant R-377-000-042-112, The Ben-Hur Event; AcRF tier 1 grant R-377-000-032-112, Flattering Letters [1880–1929]; and AcRF tier 1 grant R-377-000-037-112, Flattering Letters, Stage Two).

Notes

Foreword

1. David Mayer, "Introduction," in *Ben-Hur: A Tale of the Christ*, by Lew Wallace (Oxford and New York: Oxford Univ. Press, 1998), xv.

Introduction

1. Howard Miller, "The Charioteer and the Christ: *Ben-Hur* in America from the Gilded Age to the Culture Wars," *Indiana Magazine of History* 104, no. 2 (2008): 153–75.

2. See Neil Sinyard, "Foreword," this volume.

3. Alessandro Corio, "The Living and the Poetic Intention: Glissant's Biopolitics of Literature," *Callaloo* 36 (Fall 2013), 917.

4. Édouard Glissant, *Caribbean Discourse: Selected Essays*, trans. J. Michael Dash (Charlottesville, VA: Univ. of Virginia Press, 1989), 146.

5 John Muthyala, "Reworlding America. The Globalization of American Studies," *Cultural Critique* 47 (Winter 2001), 96.

6. Lew Wallace, *An Autobiography*, 2 vols. (New York and London: Harper & Brothers, 1906), 1:103.

7. Quoted in Robert E. Morsberger and Katharine M. Morsberger, *Lew Wallace: Militant Romantic* (New York: McGraw Hill, 1980), 291.

8. Wallace, *Autobiography*, 1:1; Irving McKee, *"Ben-Hur" Wallace: The Life of General Lew Wallace* (Berkeley and Los Angeles: Univ. of California Press, 1947), 164.

9. Victor Davis Hanson, "Lew Wallace and the Ghosts of the Shunpike," in *What Ifs? of American History: Eminent Historians Imagine What Might Have Been*, ed. Robert Cowley (New York: G. P. Putnam, 2003), 69–86; cf. John Swansburg, "The Passion of Lew Wallace," *Slate*, March 26, 2013, http://www.slate.com/articles/life/history/2013/03/ben_hur_and _lew_wallace_how_the_scapegoat_of_shiloh_became_one_of_the_best.html.

10. Wallace said that he had refashioned an existing short story into the saga of Judah Ben-Hur in reply to a challenge about his understanding of the Bible's truth-value from Robert G. Ingersoll. The latter was the most famed U.S. agnostic and a spokesman for that belief at the time. For Wallace's imprimatur, see his preface to *The First Christmas* (New York: Harper & Brothers, 1902).

11. Ferenc Morton Szasz quotes Lyman Abbott in *The Divided Mind of Protestant America, 1880–1930* (University, AL: Univ. of Alabama Press, 1982), 17.

12. Theodore Dreiser, *Dawn: An Autobiography of Early Youth* (Jaffrey, NH: Black Sparrow Press, 1998), 252.

13. Édouard Glissant, interview by Frédéric Joignot [in French], *Le Monde*, February 4, 2011, http://www.lemonde.fr/disparitions/article/2011/02/04/pour-l-ecrivain-edouard -glissant-la-creolisation-du-monde-etait-irreversible_1474923_3382.html.

14. Glissant, *Caribbean Discourse*, 91.

15. On *Ben-Hur*'s cultural impact, see Lee Scott Theisen in "'My God, Did I Set All of This in Motion?' General Lew Wallace and *Ben Hur*," *Journal of Popular Culture* 18, no. 2 (1984): 33–41.

16. Quoted in Joseph Lee Blotner, *Faulkner: A Biography* (New York: Random House, 1974), 15.

17. On the vertigo that Broadway *Ben-Hur* may have caused Lew and (perhaps even more) Sue Wallace, see Barbara Ryan, *Chronicling Ben-Hur's Rise* (Furnham, Surrey: Ashgate, forthcoming).

18. Ted Hovet Jr., "The Case of Kalem's *Ben-Hur* (1907) and the Transformation of Cinema," *Quarterly Review of Film and Video* 18 (July 2001), 296.

19. Melani McAlister, *Epic Encounters: Culture, Media, and U.S. Interests in the Middle East since 1945*, rev. ed. (Berkeley and Los Angeles: Univ. of California Press, 2005), 43–83.

20. See Gore Vidal, "Counterpunch: Gore Vidal Responds to Charlton Heston," *Los Angeles Times*, June 17, 1996, http://articles.latimes.com/1996-06-17/local/la-et-me-gore-vidal -charlton-heston-archive_1_gore-vidal-ben-hur-sam-zimbalist.

21. Jane Purcell-Guild, "Study of One Hundred and Thirty-One Delinquent Girls Held at the Juvenile Detention Home in Chicago, 1917," *Journal of the American Institute of Criminal Law and Criminology* 10 (November 1919), 461; Jane Addams's pursuit of faith as Barbara Sicherman relates it in *Well-Read Lives: How Books Inspired a Generation of American Women* (Chapel Hill, NC: Univ. of North Carolina Press, 2010), 298fn11; "All Confide in Funk," *Washington Post*, September 4, 1899; and Oakley C. Johnson, "Preventive Remedial English in the Negro Secondary School," *Journal of Negro Education* 18, no. 4 (1949): 474–83.

22. Terry Lindvall, "Silent Cinema and Religion, An Overview (1895–1930)," in *The Routledge Companion to Literature and Film*, ed. John Lyden (London and New York: Routledge, 2010), 13–31.

1. *Ben-Hur*'s and America's Rome

1. For the standard account see Robert Shalhope, "Toward a Republican Synthesis: The Emergence of an Understanding of Republicanism in American Historiography," *William and Mary Quarterly* 29, no. 1 (1972): 49–80; and Robert Shalhope, "Republicanism and Early American Historiography," *William and Mary Quarterly* 39, no. 2 (1982): 334–56.

2. For the original introduction of the concept of "classical republicanism" see Zera Fink, *The Classical Republicans: An Essay in the Recovery of a Pattern of Thought in Seventeenth-Century England* (Evanston, IL: Northwestern Univ. Press, 1962). The magisterial analysis of this creed remains J. G. A. Pocock, *The Machiavellian Moment: Florentine Political Thought and the Atlantic Republican Tradition* (Princeton, NJ: Princeton Univ. Press, 2003).

3. For changing notions of "democracy" and "republic" in eighteenth-century America see Willi Paul Adams, *The First American Constitutions: Republican Ideology and the Making of the State Constitutions in the Revolutionary Era*, trans. Rita and Robert Kimber (Lanham, MD: Rowman & Littlefield, 2001), 96–114.

4. For the ways in which the world of classical antiquity was becoming meaningful after 1750 to ever-growing numbers of North Americans see Eran Shalev, *Rome Reborn on Western Shores: Historical Imagination and the Creation of the American Republic* (Charlottesville, VA: Univ. of Virginia Press, 2009).

5. *Cato* was also the most popular play in the colonies; see Fredric M. Litto, "Addison's *Cato* in the Colonies," *William and Mary Quarterly* 23, no. 3 (1966): 431–49. For the history of Addison's *Cato* in America see also Albert Furtwangler, "*Cato* in Valley Forge," in *American Silhouettes: Rhetorical Identities of the Founders* (New Haven, CT: Yale Univ. Press, 1987), 64–84.

6. Litto, "Addison's *Cato*," 443.

7. Garry Wills believes that the play was "omnipresent in the revolutionary rhetoric in America"; Gary Wills, *Cincinnatus: Washington and the Enlightenment* (New York: Doubleday, 1984), 127. See also Carl J. Richard, *The Golden Age of the Classics in America: Greece, Rome, and the Antebellum United States* (Cambridge, MA: Harvard Univ. Press, 2009), 57–60.

8. Litto, "Addison's *Cato*," 449. Wills argues that *Cato* affected Americans both by its republican example and by the teaching of the dangers in Caesarism; Wills, *Cincinnatus*, 136.

9. Litto, "Addison's *Cato*," 444–46.

10. Furtwangler, "*Cato* in Valley Forge," 64–84.

11. Jonathan Mitchell Sewall, *A New Epilogue to Cato, Spoken at a Late Performance of That Tragedy* (Portsmouth, NH: Daniel Fowle, 1778).

12. John C. Shields, *The American Aeneas: Classical Origins of American Self* (Knoxville, TN: Univ. of Tennessee Press, 2004), 192.

13. Ibid., 174–93; Litto, "Addison's *Cato*," 447.

14. Sewall, *New Epilogue*. Capitalization in original.

15. The *New Epilogue* was not the only case in which Americans produced glossaries matching classical figures with contemporaries. The Cliosophic Society of the College of New Jersey attributed both Greek and Roman names to approximately half of their sixty-seven members between the years 1770 and 1776. See James McLachlan, "Classical Names, American Identities: Some Notes on College Students and the Classical Traditions in the 1770s," in *Classical Traditions in Early America*, ed. John William Eadie (New York: Trillium,

1976), 96–98. Another instance of such a glossary was a cipher composed by Alexander Hamilton in 1792, in which twenty-two of twenty-four code names he attributed to politicians (including the president, several ministers, and senators) were classical: Washington was Scavola, Adams was Brutus, Jefferson was Scipio, and James Madison became Tarquin. See Alexander Hamilton to Gouverneur Morris, June 22, 1792, in *The Papers of Alexander Hamilton*, ed. Jacob E. Cooke and Harold Syrett (New York: Univ. of Columbia Press, 1966), 11:546.

16. Richard, *The Golden Age*, 41–82.

17. Gordon S. Wood, *Empire of Liberty: A History of the Early Republic, 1789–1815* (New York: Oxford Univ. Press, 2009), 576.

18. Mark Noll, *America's God: From Jonathan Edwards to Abraham Lincoln* (New York: Oxford Univ. Press, 2002), 165–70.

19. Wood, *Empire of Liberty*, 581.

20. For a useful working definition of evangelicalism see David W. Bebbington, *Evangelicalism in Modern Britain: A History from the 1730s to the 1980s* (London: Routledge, 1989), 2–17; Noll, *America's God*, 208.

21. Donald M. Scott, *From Office to Profession: The New England Ministry, 1750–1850* (Philadelphia, PA: Univ. of Pennsylvania Press, 1978), 178.

22. Mark Noll, *God and Race in American Politics: A Short History* (Princeton, NJ: Princeton Univ. Press, 2009), 29–30.

23. Richard W. Fox, *Jesus in America: Personal Savior, Cultural Hero, National Obsession* (San Francisco, CA: Harper, 2004), 195, 202.

24. Henry Ward Beecher, "A Conversation about Christ," in *Sermons by Henry Ward Beecher, Plymouth Church, Brooklyn* (New York: J. B. Ford, 1869), 1:473–90, quote on 476.

25. Stephen Prothero, *America's Jesus: How the Son of God Became a National Icon* (New York: Farrar, Straus and Giroux, 2003), 56.

26. Campbell quoted in Paul C. Gutjahr, *An American Bible: A History of the Good Book in the United States, 1777–1880* (Stanford, CA: Stanford Univ. Press, 1999), 102.

27. Such attitudes were evident in the literary realm in William Ware's *Zenobia* (1836) and *Aurelian* (1838), and in the Joseph H. Ingraham biblical trilogy (1855–59) that began with *The Prince of the House of David*.

28. For the idea of decline and fall in western thought see J. G. A. Pocock, *Barbarians and Religion*, vol. 5 (Cambridge: Cambridge Univ. Press, 2001).

29. The classic statements on American republicanism, and thus on the dangers of corruption, are: Pocock, *The Machiavellian Moment*; Bernard Bailyn, *The Ideological Origins of the American Revolution* (Cambridge, MA: Belknap Press of Harvard Univ. Press, 1967); Gordon Wood, *The Creation of the American Republic, 1776–1787* (Chapel Hill, NC: Univ. of North Carolina Press, 1969); and Quentin Skinner, *Liberty before Liberalism* (Cambridge: Cambridge Univ. Press, 1998). For a general discussion on political corruption see Christopher J. Berry, *The Idea of Luxury: A Conceptual and Historical Investigation* (Cambridge: Cambridge Univ.

Press, 1994); and John Sekora, *Luxury: The Concept in Western Thought from Eden to Smollett* (Baltimore, MD: Johns Hopkins Univ. Press, 1977).

30. For the origin of republican thought in classical Rome see Skinner, *Liberty before Liberalism*.

31. Eran Shalev, "Jefferson's Classical Silence, 1774–1776: Historical Consciousness and Classical History in the Revolutionary South," in *Thomas Jefferson, the Classical World, and Early America*, ed. Peter S. Onuf and Nicholas P. Cole (Charlottesville, VA: Univ. of Virginia Press, 2011), 219–47.

32. The best exposition of this transition is in Richard, *Golden Age*, 41–82.

33. Letter from William Hooper to James Iredell, April 26, 1774, in *The Colonial Records of North Carolina*, ed. William L. Saunders (New York: AMS, 1968), 9:985.

34. John Adams, *The Political Writings of John Adams*, ed. George W. Carey (Washington, DC: Regnery, 2000), 55.

35. Shalev, *Rome Reborn on Western Shores*, 40–72.

36. The authoritative account of the civic humanistic language is Pocock's *Machiavellian Moment*. For a focused discussion of the notion of luxury see Sekora, *Luxury*.

37. Amy Kaplan, "Imperial Melancholy in America," *Raritan* 28, no. 3 (2009): 24.

38. On critics of imperialism, see Margaret Malamud, *Ancient Rome and Modern America* (New York: Wiley-Blackwell, 2008), 229–54.

2. Ben-Hur's Mother

1. Robert E. Morsberger and Katharine M. Morsberger, *Lew Wallace: Militant Romantic* (New York: McGraw Hill, 1980), 301. Susan Wallace wrote to the Harper editor: "Dear Sir, Because of inquiries of correspondents as to the *number of wives* Gen. Wallace had, I have thought best to ask you to add to the dedication of Ben-Hur, it: To the wife of my youth, who still abides with me. This with Gen. Wallace's consent" (November 24, 1884, Lew Wallace Collection, Box 5, Folder 9, Indiana Historical Society Archives, Indianapolis).

2. "Fiction and Social Science," *Century Illustrated Magazine* 29, no. 1 (November 1884): 153; "The Head of Medusa, and Other Novels," *Atlantic Monthly* 47, no. 283 (May 1881): 710–11.

3. Quoted in David Harlan, "Editorial," *Rethinking History* 9, nos. 2–3 (2005): 142.

4. The first phrase is by George Ripley, quoted in Morsberger and Morsberger, *Lew Wallace*, 293; the second is from a review in the *Christian Union*, December 8, 1880; the third is from the *Literary World*, March 26, 1881.

5. J. W. Gordon to Lew Wallace, December 21, 1880, Lew Wallace Collection, Box 4, Folder 15, Indiana Historical Society Archives, Indianapolis. A glimpse of this friend-fan is available in Richard F. Nation and Stephen E. Towne, eds., *Indiana's War: The Civil War in Documents* (Columbus, OH: Ohio Univ. Press, 2009), 91.

6. Paul A. Carter, *The Spiritual Crisis of the Gilded Age* (DeKalb, IL: Northern Illinois Univ. Press, 1971).

7. See Milette Shamir, "'Our Jerusalem': Americans in the Holy Land and Protestant Narratives of National Entitlement," *American Quarterly* 55, no. 1 (2003): 29–60.

8. Howard Miller, "The Charioteer and the Christ: *Ben-Hur* in America from the Gilded Age to the Cultural Wars," *Indiana Magazine of History* 104 (2008): 154. Paul Gutjahr also reads *Ben-Hur* in the context of the crisis between faith and modernity of its era in "'To the Heart of Solid Puritans': Historicizing the Popularity of *Ben-Hur*," *Mosaic: A Journal for the Interdisciplinary Study of Literature* 26, no. 3 (1993): 53–67.

9. Quoted in James H. Moorhead, "The Erosion of Postmillennialism in American Religious Thought, 1865–1925," *Church History* 53, no. 1 (1984): 61.

10. James H. Moorhead, "Between Progress and Apocalypse: A Reassessment of Millennialism in American Religious Thought, 1800–1880," *Journal of American History* 71, no. 3 (1984): 533.

11. See, for example, Ferenc Morton Szasz, *The Divided Mind of Protestant America, 1880–1930* (University, AL: Univ. of Alabama Press, 1982), chaps. 1–3.

12. Herman Melville, *Clarel: A Poem and Pilgrimage in the Holy Land* (Chicago: Northwestern Univ. Press, 2008), 498.

13. Quoted in Carter, *Spiritual Crisis*, 159.

14. The premillennialist narrative of Dispensationalism, for example, was popularized by individuals like Dwight L. Moody and by religious events like the "Niagara Biblical Conferences." On the growing popularity of premillennialist literature in this period, see Thomas O. Beebee, *Millennial Literatures of the Americas, 1492–2002* (Oxford: Oxford Univ. Press, 2009).

15. George Cotkin, *Reluctant Modernism: American Thought and Culture, 1880–1900* (Lanham, MD: Rowman & Littlefield, 2004), 2.

16. Quoted in Carter, *Spiritual Crisis*, 166. Carter points out that even Restorationists, such as the Disciples of Christ, tried to incorporate ideals of progress. He explains that "restoration of the conditions prevailing in the apostolic churches is both impossible and undesirable . . . the movement of the church is forward, not backward" (166–71).

17. See, for example, William R. Hutchison, *The Modernist Impulse in American Protestantism* (Cambridge, MA: Harvard Univ. Press, 1976), chap. 4.

18. Morsberger and Morsberger, *Lew Wallace*, 297–98.

19. Lew Wallace, preface to *The First Christmas* (New York: Harper & Brothers, 1902), iii–viii.

20. Ibid.

21. See, for example, Luce Irigaray, *Speculum of the Other Woman*, trans. Gillian C. Gill (Ithaca, NY: Cornell Univ. Press, 1974), 23.

22. Morsberger and Morsberger, *Lew Wallace*, 299.

23. See Miller, "Charioteer and the Christ," 155. See also Walsh's essay in this volume.

24. Franco Moretti, *The Way of the World: The Bildungsroman in European Culture* (London: Verso, 1987), 5.

25. Gregory S. Jackson, *The World and Its Witness: The Spiritualization of American Realism* (Chicago: Chicago Univ. Press, 2009), 33.

26. Mark Currie, *About Time: Narrative Fiction and the Philosophy of Time* (Edinburgh: Edinburgh Univ. Press, 2010), 88.

27. Theodore Dreiser, *Sister Carrie* (Oxford: Oxford Univ. Press, 1991), 20. Philip Fisher emphasizes the novel's theme of anticipation in *Hard Facts: Setting and Form in the American Novel* (Oxford: Oxford Univ. Press, 1985), 128–78.

28. Linda Hutcheon, "Irony, Nostalgia, and the Postmodern," Univ. of Toronto English Library, last modified January 19, 1998, http://www.library.utoronto.ca/utel/criticism /hutchinp.html#N24; the quote is from James Phillips, "Distance, Absence, and Nostalgia," in *Descriptions*, eds. Don Ihde and Hugh J. Silverman (Albany, NY: SUNY Press, 1985), 65.

29. Ian Duncan, *Modern Romance and Transformations of the Novel: The Gothic, Scott, Dickens* (Cambridge: Cambridge Univ. Press, 1992), 5.

30. Georg Lukacs, *The Historical Novel* (London: Merlin, 1962), 60. Original edition was published in Russian in 1937.

31. Including Mr. Gordon of Indianapolis, with whose letter this essay opened, and who compares *Ben-Hur* to Scott's *Ivanhoe* at the outset.

32. Lukacs, *Historical Novel*, 20.

33. This and other examples are quoted in Shamir, "'Our Jerusalem,'" 38–39.

34. Duncan, *Modern Romance and Transformations of the Novel*, 59.

35. A month after the book's publication, one reader wrote to Wallace in praise of different aspects of the novel, including the *"Chariot Race* at Antioch" (described as "almost enough to 'make an old man young'"). "[B]ut perhaps the *master scene* of the book," the letter continued, "occurs in that Chapter which describes the disentombing of Ben Hur's mother & sister. . . . The blended horror & pathos of this tremendous encounter . . . [where] the loving women, pass like ghosts or shadows by the form of the unconscious son & brother . . . electrify all observers of sensibility" (December 2, 1880, MSS II, Lew Wallace Collection, Lilly Library, Univ. of Indiana, Bloomington, emphases in the original). Similarly, another admirer counted "the searching for the mother and Tirzah at Jerusalem" and "the healing of their leprosy by Christ" among the scenes that "made a wonderful impression on me" (surprisingly, the chariot race was not one of them; ibid., March 22, 1886). Yet another reader was most touched by Tirzah's loyalty and love for her brother; she asked why "[a]fter all the terrible and unspeakable grief she had to lose the true and loving mother-heart" (ibid., March 10, 1896).

36. Nat Ward Fitz-Gerald, "Ben-Hur," pamphlet from the Lew Wallace Collection, Lilly Library, Univ. of Indiana, Bloomington.

37. Elsewhere in this volume, Ina Rae Hark notices this feminine/maternal ending and points out that Wallace has "chosen his protagonist's surname to mark him as most importantly a son [in Hebrew 'Ben'] of *Her*, of a mother."

38. See Miller, "Charioteer and the Christ," 166.

3. Retelling and Untelling the Christmas Story

1. Unsigned notice, *Washington Post*, August 8, 1894. Reprinted in "Uncle Tom's Cabin & American Culture," multimedia archive, Univ. of Virginia, 2009, http://utc.iath.virginia .edu; *The Sunday-School Library Bulletin* 3, no. 3 (1894): 13.

2. *Literary World* 52 (September 13, 1895): 185.

3. "The Winner in the Chariot Race," *The Nation* 80, no. 2069 (February 23, 1905): 149.

4. Meredith Nicholson, "Lew Wallace," *The Reader: An Illustrated Monthly* 5, no. 5 (1905): 572.

5. Lew Wallace, *The First Christmas, from "Ben-Hur"* (New York: Harper & Brothers, 1889), iv.

6. Lew Wallace, *The Boyhood of Christ* (New York: Harper & Brothers, 1889), 101. Through an agreement with Harper, James R. Osgood also published *The Boyhood of Christ* in London in 1892.

7. Anne M. Boylan, *Sunday School: The Formation of an American Institution, 1790–1880* (New Haven, CT: Yale Univ. Press, 1988), 6–9.

8. Robert H. Canary, "The Sunday School as Popular Culture," *American Studies* 9, no. 2 (1968): 10–12.

9. See Boylan, *Sunday School*, 68–73.

10. *Washington Post*, August 8, 1894. Books by women authors on the list include Susan Warner's *The Wide, Wide World* (1850), Harriet Beecher Stowe's *Uncle Tom's Cabin* (1852), Elizabeth Rundell Charles's *The Chronicles of the Schönberg-Cotta Family* (1862), Louisa May Alcott's *Little Women* (1868), and Anna Sewell's *Black Beauty* (1877), as well as twenty works by Isabella Macdonald Alden, a prolific Sunday-scholar author who wrote several young adult series for Presbyterian periodicals under the pen name "Pansy."

11. Wallace, *Boyhood*, 9.

12. Paul C. Gutjahr, *An American Bible: A History of the Good Book in the United States, 1777–1880* (Stanford, CA: Stanford Univ. Press, 1999), 118–19.

13. Boylan, *Sunday School*, 19.

14. Gutjahr, *American Bible*, 120.

15. Charles A. Briggs, "The Sunday-School and Modern Biblical Criticism," *North American Review* 158, no. 446 (1894): 65.

16. On the development of the lesson system, see Henry Frederick Cope, *The Evolution of the Sunday School* (Boston: Pilgrim, 1911), 101–28; Edwin Wilbur Rice, *The Sunday-School Movement and the American Sunday-School Union* (Philadelphia, PA: ASSU, 1917), 294–317; Boylan, *Sunday School*, 98–99.

17. Reliable numbers for Sunday-school attendance, including ASSU and denominational schools, are difficult to find for the nineteenth century. For region-by-region estimates of total Sunday-school participation in the United States for the year 1917, see Rice, *Sunday-School Movement*, 388–433.

18. On conversion in Sunday Schools, see Boylan, *Sunday School*, 133–46.

19. Ibid., 150.

20. On Sunday-school stories about missionary work, see Karen Sánchez-Eppler, "Raising Empires like Children: Race, Nation, and Religious Education," *American Literary History* 8, no. 3 (1996): 399–425.

21. Frederica Beard, *The Kindergarten Sunday-School* (Boston: Pilgrim, 1895), 55.

22. S. G. Atres, "Library References," *The Sunday School Journal* 30 (June 4, 1898): 342.

23. P. N. Peloubet and M. A. Peloubet, *Select Notes. A Commentary on the International Lessons for 1900* (Boston: Wilde, 1900), 325.

24. Edward Everett Hale, *Sunday-School Stories on the Golden Texts of the International Lessons of 1889* (Boston: Roberts Brothers, 1889), 29–31.

25. Boylan, *Sunday School*, 130. The quoted terms were introduced by a delegate at the first Chautauqua Assembly of Sunday-school teachers in 1874.

26. Lee Scott Theisen, "'My God, Did I Set All This in Motion?' General Lew Wallace and *Ben-Hur*," *Journal of Popular Culture* 18, no. 2 (1984): 35; Margaret Malamud, *Ancient Rome and Modern America* (London: Wiley-Blackwell, 2009), 140.

27. Philip E. Howard et al., *The Sunday School at Work* (London: Westminster Press, 1915), 237.

28. Paul Gutjahr, "'To the Heart of Solid Puritans': Historicizing the Popularity of *Ben-Hur*," *Mosaic: A Journal for the Interdisciplinary Study of Literature* 26, no. 3 (1993): 61.

29. On *Ben-Hur* in adult classes, see Amos R. Wells, *The Ideal Adult Class in the Sunday-School* (Boston: Pilgrim, 1912), 27.

30. For more organizational details, see Elizabeth Louisa Foote, *The Librarian of the Sunday School* (New York: Eaton, 1897).

31. Marion Lawrance, *How to Conduct a Sunday School: or, Thirty-One Years a Superinten-dent* (New York: Revel, 1905), 279.

32. W. F. Walker, "Address Delivered before the Hartford County (Conn.) Sunday-School Convention on the Choice and the Management of the Sunday-School Library," *The Sunday-School Library Bulletin* 5, no. 3 (September 1896): 10.

33. Elizabeth Louisa Foote, *Strengthening the Sunday-School Library: Hints from a Practi-cal Librarian* (Philadelphia, PA: Sunday-School Times, 1901), 8.

34. For more on Sunday-school libraries, see Boylan, *Sunday School*, 48–52.

35. Jesse Lyman Hurlbut, *Organizing and Building up the Sunday School* (Chicago: Pilgrim, 1910), 81.

36. Report by the board of managers for the Massachusetts Sabbath-School Society, quoted in A. E. Dunning, *The Sunday-School Library* (Boston: Congregational Sunday-School and Publishing Society, 1883), 18. Emphasis in the original.

37. Cope, *Evolution of the Sunday School*, 195.

38. David Mayer, "Introduction," in *Ben-Hur: A Tale of the Christ*, by Lew Wallace (Oxford and New York: Oxford Univ. Press, 1998), xix.

39. Stewart Holbrook, "Gen. Wallace and *Ben-Hur*," *New York Times Book Review*, August 6, 1944, 7. See also "Winner in the Chariot Race," 148–49; Carl Van Doren, *The American Novel: 1789–1939* (New York: MacMillan, 1940), 113–14.

40. Hurlbut, *Organizing and Building*, 81–82; Foote, *Strengthening the Sunday-School Library*, 3; Earnest DeWitt Burton and Shailer Mathews, *Principles and Ideals for the Sunday School: An Essay in Religious Pedagogy* (Chicago: Univ. of Chicago Press, 1903), 172.

41. Nicholson, "Lew Wallace," 572.

42. Prefaces appear in such American Jesus novels as Sarah Pogson Smith's *Zerah, The Believing Jew* (1837), William Ware's *Julian; or, Scenes in Judea* (1841), Joseph Ingraham's *The Prince of the House of David* (1855), and Elizabeth Stuart Phelps and Herbert D. Ward's *Come Forth!* (1890). Harriet Beecher Stowe wrote the introductory essay for her brother Charles's *Incarnation: Pictures of the Virgin and Her Son* (1849). On these and other Jesus novel prefaces, see Jefferson J. A. Gatrall, *The Real and the Sacred: Picturing Jesus in Nineteenth-Century Fiction* (Ann Arbor, MI: Univ. of Michigan Press, 2014), 30, 41, 44, 46, 52–53, 90, 95, 98, 106, 111; and Barbara Hochman, "Little Known Documents: Introductory Essay: Harriet Beecher Stowe," *PMLA* 118, no. 5 (2003): 1320–24.

43. Joseph Henry Harper, quoted in Irving McKee, *"Ben-Hur" Wallace: The Life of General Lew Wallace* (Berkeley and Los Angeles: Univ. of California Press, 1947), 169.

44. "A Story of the East," *New York Times*, November 14, 1880, 4.

45. Harriet Martineau, *Autobiography of Harriet Martineau* (London: Virago, 1983), 1:103. Her novel was published in the United States under the title *The Times of the Saviour* (Boston: Bowles, 1831). On Martineau's priority, see Jefferson J. A. Gatrall, "The Color of His Hair: Nineteenth-Century Literary Portraits of the Historical Jesus," *Novel: A Forum on Fiction* 42, no. 1 (2008): 109.

46. On the origins and development of the Jesus novel, see Gatrall, *The Real and the Sacred*, 21–61.

47. "La Croix d'Argent; ou, le Charpentier de Nazareth" appeared originally in volume 2 of Eugene Sue's twelve-volume *Les Mystères du Peuple; ou, Histoire d'une Famille de Prolétaire à travers les Ages* (1849–57). It was released separately in English translation in 1899. Petruccelli's *Les Mémoires de Judas* has been translated into Italian, German, and Portuguese, but not English.

48. Briggs, "Sunday-School and Modern Biblical Criticism," 65, 67.

49. Florence Morse Kingsley, *Titus, a Comrade of the Cross* (Chicago: Cook, 1895), iii. Courtesy of Lilly Library, Indiana Univ., Bloomington.

50. Brian Masters, *Now Barabbas Was a Robber: The Extraordinary Life of Marie Corelli* (London: Hodder, 1974), 3, 8, 130.

51. R. B. Kersher, "Modernism's Mirror: The Sorrows of Marie Corelli," in *Transforming Genres: New Approaches to British Fiction of the 1890s*, ed. Nikki Lee Manos and Meri-Jane Rochelson (New York: St. Martin's, 1994), 68. See also Jennifer K. Berenson Maclean,

"Barabbas, the Scapegoat Ritual, and the Development of the Passion Narrative," *The Harvard Theological Review*, 100, no. 3 (2007): 309–34.

52. P. N. Peloubet and M. A. Peloubet, *Select Notes. A Commentary on the International Lessons for 1904* (Boston: Wilde, 1904), 338.

53. "Winner in the Chariot Race," 149.

54. McKee, *"Ben-Hur" Wallace*, 164–65.

55. Ernest Renan, *Vie de Jésus* (Paris: Lévy Frères, 1863), 19.

56. Karl Heumann's *Jeschua von Nazara: Roman, auf die Ergebnisse der Historischen Forschung Begründet* (1888), written under the penname Paul Ador, has not been translated into English. It should be noted that Martineau wrote before Strauss and Renan's Lives of Jesus books were published.

57. Wallace, *Boyhood*, 16.

58. Ibid., 23.

59. Ibid., 35–36.

60. Renan, *Vie de Jésus*, liii, lv.

61. Thomas Hone's *The Apocryphal New Testament*, originally published in London in 1824 and frequently reissued, was a popular source for such non-canonical early Christian and medieval Gospels in the nineteenth century. For Mark Twain's reading of the Infancy Gospels to which Uncle Midas refers, see Hilton Obenzinger, *American Palestine: Melville, Twain, and the Holy Land Mania* (Princeton, NJ: Princeton Univ. Press, 1999), 198–215.

62. Wallace, *Boyhood*, 70.

63. Wallace, *Boyhood*, 47.

64. Two years previously, Wallace had himself served as the illustrator of a modern "Christmas story," namely, his wife Susan Wallace's *Ginèvra: or, The Old Oak Chest* (New York: Worthington, 1887).

65. Wallace, *Boyhood*, 90.

66. Wallace, *Boyhood*, 90–93.

67. Gatrall, "Color of His Hair," 119–20.

68. See Frederic W. Farrar, *The Life of Christ* (New York: Dutton, 1877), 1:312; Franz Delitzsch, *Ein Tag in Kapernaum* (Leipzig: Naumann, 1871), 31.

69. Charles Sanders Peirce, "On a New List of Categories," in *Peirce on Signs: Writings on Semiotic by Charles Sanders Peirce*, ed. James Hoopes (Chapel Hill, NC: Univ. of North Carolina Press, 1991), 30.

70. Charles Sanders Peirce, "What Is a Sign?" in *The Essential Peirce: Selected Philosophical Writings*, ed. Peirce Edition Project (Bloomington, IN: Indiana Univ. Press, 1998), 2:7–8.

71. "Letter of Lentulus," in *The Apocryphal New Testament*, ed. J. K. Elliott (Oxford: Clarendon, 1993), 542–43.

72. Lew Wallace, *Ben-Hur: A Tale of the Christ*, illus. by William Martin Johnson (New York: Harper & Brothers, 1892), 322. The most obvious precedent for such lush

illustrations of the Holy Land is found in the 1846 Harper & Brothers illuminated Bible, which, like the Garfield edition of *Ben-Hur*, represented one of the biggest coups in the publisher's history.

73. On Wallace's Holy Land landscapes, see also Phillip Maciak, "'A Rare and Wonderful Sight': Secularism and Visual Historiography in *Ben-Hur*," *J19: The Journal of Nineteenth-Century Americanists* (forthcoming).

74. Theisen, "'My God,'" 37.

75. Lew Wallace, *Lew Wallace: An Autobiography* (New York: Harper & Brothers, 1906), 2:932, 937.

4. Holy Lands, Restoration, and Zionism in *Ben-Hur*

1. Amy Kaplan, "Imperial Melancholy in America," *Raritan* 28, no. 3 (2009): 28.

2. Cotton Mather, *Magnalia Christi Americana; or, The Ecclesiastical History of the New-England* (1702; repr., New York: Russell & Russell, 1967), 42.

3. Carl Frederick Ehle Jr., "Prolegomena to Christian Zionism in America: The Views of Increase Mather and William E. Blackstone Concerning the Doctrine of the Restoration of Israel" (PhD diss., New York Univ., 1977), 331.

4. Elder Orson Hyde, *A Voice from Jerusalem, or a Sketch of the Travels and Ministry of Elder Orson Hyde* (Boston: Albert Morgan, 1842), 19.

5. "The Winner in the Chariot Race," *The Nation* 80, no. 2069 (February 23, 1905): 149.

6. Lew Wallace, *An Autobiography* (New York and London: Harper & Brothers, 1906), 934, 932, 936, 937.

7. Paul Gutjahr, "'To the Heart of Solid Puritans': Historicizing the Popularity of *Ben-Hur*," *Mosaic: A Journal for the Interdisciplinary Study of Literature* 26, no. 3 (1993): 60.

8. Quoted in Robert E. Morsberger and Katharine M. Morsberger, *Lew Wallace: Militant Romantic* (New York: McGraw Hill, 1980), 291.

9. Margaret Malamud, *Ancient Rome and Modern America* (Chichester, West Sussex, UK: Wiley-Blackwell, 2009), 148.

10. Susan E. Wallace, *The Land of the Pueblos* (New York: John A. Berry, 1888), 51–52.

11. "Winner in the Chariot Race," 148.

12. Blake Allmendinger, "Toga! Toga!" in *Over the Edge: Remapping the American West*, eds. Valerie J. Matsumoto and Blake Allmendinger (Berkeley, CA: Univ. of California Press, 1999), 39; J. G. Cawelti, *The Six-Gun Mystique*, 2nd ed. (Bowling Green, OH: Bowling Green Univ. Press, 1984); and Will Wright, *Six Guns and Society: A Structural Study of the Western* (Berkeley, CA: Univ. of California Press, 1975).

13. Malamud, *Ancient Rome and Modern America*, 138.

14. Ibid., 137.

15. Lew Wallace, *The Fair God or, The Last of the 'Tzins, A Tale of the Conquest of Mexico* (New York: Grosset & Dunlap, 1901), 232, 247.

16. Morsberger and Morsberger, *Lew Wallace*, 225.

17. Irving McKee, *"Ben-Hur" Wallace: The Life of General Lew Wallace* (Berkeley, CA: Univ. of California Press, 1947), 204.

18. George Eliot, *Daniel Deronda* (Edinburgh and London: William Blackwood and Sons, 1876), chap. 42.

19. Ibid.

20. William E. Blackstone, "Palestine for the Jews," in *Christian Protagonists for Jewish Restoration* (New York: Arno, 1977), 1.

21. Melani McAlister, *Epic Encounters: Culture, Media, and U.S. Interests in the Middle East, 1945–2000* (Berkeley, CA: Univ. of California Press, 2001), 56, 62.

22. Ibid., 65.

23. Ibid., 65–66.

5. "In the Service of Christianity"

1. Although the number of people who saw the play in its twenty-year run is uncertain, by 1920 the calculation of ten million people (paying $20 million) had been quoted so often that it stuck. See "Plays and Players," *Indianapolis News*, March 22, 1920, 6, courtesy of Indiana State Library (ISL) and Historical Bureau, Indianapolis, IN.

2. "Two Special Trains for Ben-Hur Show," *Sentinel Record*, December 21, 1913, 3, courtesy of Garland County Historical Society (GCHS), Hot Springs, AR. See also the *Minneapolis Tribune*, January 4, 1904; and the *Ben-Hur* Scrapbook, 1899–1926, 103, courtesy of the Billy Rose Collection, New York Public Library (hereinafter cited as "*Ben-Hur* Scrapbook"). Unless otherwise indicated, all references are to the first of the scrapbook's two volumes.

3. There is no recent treatment of the stage adaptation of *Ben-Hur*. Still useful, however, are Robert E. Morsberger and Katharine M. Morsberger, *Lew Wallace: Militant Romantic* (New York: McGraw Hill, 1980), 453–66; Irving McKee, *"Ben-Hur" Wallace: The Life of General Lew Wallace* (Berkeley, CA: Univ. of California Press, 1947), 175–88; and Howard Miller, "The Charioteer and the Christ," *Indiana Magazine of History* 104 (2008): 153–75. On the stage direction of the production see Lewis E. Shelton, "The 'Terrible' Mr. Ben Teal and the Shubert Brothers," *The Passing Show: Newsletter of the Shubert Archive* 15, no. 1 (1992): 8–14. The direct quotes in this sentence are from Stanley C. Arthur, "Horses the Real Actors in 'Ben-Hur,'" *New Orleans Item*, February 4, 1908, 48, *Ben-Hur* Scrapbook.

4. "Newark Theatre," *Elizabeth Journal*, December 10, 1907, *Ben-Hur* Scrapbook. See also "'Ben-Hur' a Triumph of Stagecraft," *Norfolk Landmark*, September 24, 1907; and "Music and Drama: 'Ben Hur,'" *Illinois Courier*, April 10, 1909, 12, Illinois State Historical Library (ISHL).

5. The best introduction to the syndicate war is Alfred L. Bernheim, *The Business of the Theater: An Economic History of the American Theater, 1750–1932* (New York: Actors' Equity Association, 1932), 40–74.

6. For an overview of the Christian opposition to the theater at the turn of the twentieth century see Alan Nielsen, "A 'Wicked, Unchristian Pastime,'" in *The Great Victorian Sacrilege:*

Preachers, Politics and 'The Passion,' 1879–1884 (Jefferson, NC and London: McFarland, 1991), 8–28; Terry Lindvall, *Sanctuary Cinema: Origins of the Christian Film Industry* (New York: New York Univ. Press, 2007), 28–36; and Benjamin McArthur, "Actors and Society: I," in *Actors and American Culture, 1880–1920* (Philadelphia, PA: Temple Univ. Press, 1984), 123–42.

7. American Tract Society, "The Immoral and Anti-Christian Tendency of the Theater," *Tract No. 32* (New York: American Tract Society, 1820), 1, 4, 5; Nielsen, *Great Victorian Sacrilege*, 3–7. A "Passion play" is a dramatic presentation of the events surrounding Jesus's last days, from his triumphal entry into Jerusalem through the Crucifixion and burial, but not including the resurrection and ascension. Protestant reformers denounced this tradition, which dated from the fourteenth century, as a distinctly Catholic form of blasphemy, in part because a human being played the role of Jesus.

8. For thorough surveys of the religious drama tradition to which *Ben-Hur* belonged, see Alice Brown, "Modern Religious Plays," *Toledo Blade*, December 10, 1907, 251, *Ben-Hur* Scrapbook; "Biblical Themes Popular Subject for Dramatization," *Columbus Dispatch*, December 1, 1907, 246–47, *Ben-Hur* Scrapbook; "'Ben Hur' in New York," *Atlantic Highland Journal*, March 14, 1907, 182, *Ben-Hur* Scrapbook; and "The Auditorium," *Chicago Chronicle*, December 2, 1906, section 5, 6, ISHL.

9. The traveling production of *Ben-Hur* closely resembled a small railroad circus, so it was inevitable that someone would call the Klaw & Erlanger play "the sacred circus." However, it was not the company's public relations team that created this phrase; it does not appear in the hundreds of Klaw & Erlanger press releases that I have seen. According to my extensive research, this phrase seems to have appeared for the first time in a local review in the *Springfield Union* titled "'Ben-Hur' Luck," April 27, 1906, 114, *Ben-Hur* Scrapbook. The reviewer wondered if "the sacred circus" travels "under the special dispensation of Providence" and then quoted verbatim a Klaw & Erlanger release in which Charles Towle discussed at length the show's amazing good fortune. But Towle never called the play "the sacred circus."

10. For example, see Charles Towle to A. L. Erlanger, September 19, 1905, Charles Towle file, Klaw & Erlanger Papers, Shubert Archive, New York, NY (hereinafter cited as "Towle file").

11. "Amusements: 'Ben-Hur,'" *Galesburg Republican Register*, April 6, 1914, 11, *Ben-Hur* Scrapbook; see also "'Ben Hur' at the Majestic Matinee and Night," *Fort Wayne Journal-Gazette*, April 23, 1914, 9, ISL.

12. "'Ben Hur' Coming Soon," *St. Paul Globe*, December 6, 1903, 70, *Ben-Hur* Scrapbook; *Decatur Review*, May 5, 1909, 4, ISHL.

13. For Wallace's recital of this experience, see "How I Came to Write 'Ben-Hur,'" in *An Autobiography* (New York and London: Harper & Brothers, 1906), 2:926–37.

14. Ibid., 1000–1001.

15. "'Ben Hur' Christmas Eve and Christmas Day at the Kempner," *Arkansas Gazette*, December 21, 1913, sections 2, 9, Arkansas History Commission and State Archive (AHC), Little Rock, AR. Brooks came up with the idea of using a ray of light while smoking in a

darkened room in his summer home on a hot afternoon. He noted that a stray beam of light had penetrated through the blind, setting the "myriads of silver specks or atoms" of dust and smoke in the room "dancing and rioting madly in a luminous trail" to a point on the floor. Surely, he mused, this "simple act of nature might be transferred to the stage" to "powerfully reflect the invisible appearance and nearness of the Messiah without any other tangible evidence" of his presence.

16. "The Art of Dramatization," *Macon Telegraph*, January 12, 1908, 12, *Ben-Hur* Scrapbook; "Dramatizing of Ben Hur," *Topeka Herald*, January 16, 1906, 7, *Ben-Hur* Scrapbook; "Music and Drama: Ben-Hur Next Week," *Illinois Daily Courier*, April 24, 1909, sections 1, 2, ISHL. William S. Young's stage play is reprinted in David Mayer, ed., *Playing out the Empire: Ben-Hur and Other Toga Plays and Films, 1883–1908: A Critical Anthology* (Oxford: Oxford Univ. Press, 1994), 189–290.

17. "The Auditorium: 'Ben Hur,'" *Sentinel Record*, December 10, 1913, 5, GCHS.

18. "'Ben-Hur,' The Play that Time Cannot Kill," *Wilmington News*, September 21, 1917, 82, *Ben-Hur* Scrapbook.

19. "Biblical Themes Popular Subject for Dramatists," *Columbus Dispatch*, December 1, 1907, 246–47, *Ben-Hur* Scrapbook.

20. "'Ben-Hur,'" *Terre Haute Tribune*, February 23, 1906, 32, *Ben-Hur* Scrapbook.

21. "Music and Drama," *Terre Haute Star*, April 15, 1904, 12; "'Ben Hur' on Sale," *Waterbury Republican*, April 13, 1904, 237; "But Three More Chances," *Utica Press*, March 5, 1904, 203; and "'Ben-Hur,'" *Portland Guide*, December 15, 1903, 3, *Ben-Hur* Scrapbook.

22. "Attendance at the Playhouses," *Nashville Banner*, February 20, 1906, 33, *Ben-Hur* Scrapbook.

23. "'Ben-Hur,'" *Portland Guide*, December 5, 1904, 68, *Ben-Hur* Scrapbook. The language in this press release recalls how Wallace described the healing of the *Ben-Hur* women in the novel: similar to the evangelical conversion experience, the healing represented an encounter with God that forever changed a person's basic being. Wallace compared the effect of the miraculous cure to "a draught of swift and happy effect"; the "planting, growing, and maturing all at once of a recollection so singular and so holy that the simple thought of it should be of itself ever after a formless yet perfect thanksgiving" (8:IV).

24. See *Omaha Bee*, September 29, 1903, 18, *Ben-Hur* Scrapbook.

25. "The Influence of the Religious Drama," *Scranton Times*, March 21, 1904, 192, *Ben-Hur* Scrapbook.

26. "'Ben Hur' To Be Given in This City," *Evansville Courier*, March 3, 1908, 65, *Ben-Hur* Scrapbook.

27. *Dayton Herald*, February 27, 1904, 166, *Ben-Hur* Scrapbook.

28. "Nearly Half a Hundred Thousand See Denver Shows Every Week," *Denver News*, October 5, 1908, 22, *Ben-Hur* Scrapbook.

29. "Klaw & Erlanger's Success 'Ben Hur' at Majestic Tonight," *Fort Wayne Journal-Gazette*, December 20, 1917, 15, *Ben-Hur* Scrapbook.

30. "'Ben-Hur' Next Week," *Norfolk Pilot*, September 21, 1907, 200, *Ben-Hur* Scrapbook.

31. *Minneapolis Tribune*, January 4, 1907, 103, *Ben-Hur* Scrapbook.

32. "Opening Performance of 'Ben-Hur,'" *Rochester Union & Advertiser*, March 16, 1906, 68; "Amusements," *Rochester Democrat*, March 16, 1906, 68, *Ben-Hur* Scrapbook.

33. "'Ben Hur' Coming Soon," *St. Paul Globe*, December 6, 1903, 70, *Ben-Hur* Scrapbook.

34. See the *Nashville American*, February 22, 1906, 33, *Ben-Hur* Scrapbook; and "'Ben Hur' Last Night," *Allentown Item*, October 8, 1907, 219, *Ben-Hur* Scrapbook.

35. "Audience Cheers Ben Hur Lustily," *Decatur Daily-Herald*, May 4, 1909, 10, ISHL; "'Ben Hur,'" *Little Rock Democrat*, December 16, 1908, 55, *Ben-Hur* Scrapbook; *Peoria Transcript*, April 18, 1911, 7, ISHL. For a brief discussion of the Kelley score for the dramatized *Ben-Hur* see Katherine Preston, "The Music of Toga Drama," in Mayer, *Playing out the Empire*, 24–25.

36. Any investigation of U.S. Protestants' turn toward visuals must begin with the work of David Morgan, especially *Protestants and Pictures: Religion, Visual Culture, and the Age of American Mass Production* (New York: Oxford Univ. Press, 1999). On church architecture, see Jeanne Halgren Kilde, *When Church Became Theater: The Transformation of Evangelical Architecture and Worship in Nineteenth-Century America* (Oxford and New York: Oxford Univ. Press, 2002).

37. See the correspondence between Wallace and David W. Cox, with whom he made the agreement, in Wallace MSS II Collection, 1849–91, Eli Lilly Library, Indiana Univ., Bloomington, IN (hereinafter cited as Wallace MSS II).

38. "Wallace and Others v. Riley Brothers, New York," *Optical Magic Lantern Journal* 7, no. 89 (1896): 166–67. For an advertisement for the Riley *Ben-Hur* set, see Lew Wallace Papers, collection 292 B13 F11, in the W. H. Smith Memorial Library, Indiana Historical Society, Indianapolis, IN. There is a copy of the epitome for the set in Wallace MSS II, 1892–99. See also the article, published without a byline, "Maps, Makeovers and Magic Lantern Slides," *INPerspective* 13, no. 4 (2007): 4–5.

39. Terry Bolton has collected a set of the Joseph Boggs Beale *Ben-Hur* slides, which can be seen at the American Magic-Lantern Theater in East Haddam, CT.

40. "Ben Hur's Majestic Spectacle," *Atlanta Georgian*, January 21, 1908, *Ben-Hur* Scrapbook; "Magnificent Is Ben Hur As Staged," *Youngstown Telegram*, March 6, 1906, 52, *Ben-Hur* Scrapbook.

41. The shaft of light was the result of a "strange twisting of commonplace things to an artistic end" that seemed to some reviewers to be, itself, a miracle. The ray of light caught the dust of the opera house from the recent chariot race and held it, "quivering so that the impression of the divine refulgence was made particularly real and living." The light "quivered and waved so that it needed no great effort of imagination to think of it" not as a stage effect, but "as an emanation from a great soul." In one of the very few irreverent reviews of the play, a Detroit critic wrote that "the presence of Christ somewhere in the wings is suggested by a beam of light, just as Tinker Bell is impersonated in 'Peter Pan,' and the impressionable people are hushed into solemn silence by the device." See *San Francisco Examiner*,

November 9, 1905, 10, *Ben-Hur* Scrapbook; and "'Ben-Hur,'" *Detroit Morning News*, April 14, 1908, 100, *Ben-Hur* Scrapbook.

42. "Amusements: 'Ben Hur,'" *Galesburg Republican Register*, March 30, 1914, 8, ISHL.

43. *Denver Times*, November 7, 1903, 24, *Ben-Hur* Scrapbook.

44. "'Ben Hur' Delights Large Audience," *Des Moines Leader*, January 12, 1904, 114, *Ben-Hur* Scrapbook.

45. "Ben Hur Wins Chariot Race," *Muncie Evening Press*, April 16, 1914, 2, *Ben-Hur* Scrapbook. See also "How the Race Is Won," *Galesburg Republican Register*, April 18, 1914, 13, ISHL. For the full-page Klaw & Erlanger article on the race, complete with a vivid illustration, see *Rock Island Argus*, April 3, 1911, 8, ISHL.

46. "'Ben Hur' Delights Large Audience," 114.

47. *Waterbury American*, April 18, 1904, 242, *Ben-Hur* Scrapbook.

48. See "Race a Thriller in Ben Hur Play," *Rock Island Argus*, April 12, 1911, 3, *Ben-Hur* Scrapbook.

49. *Des Moines Leader*, January 3, 1904, 102, *Ben-Hur* Scrapbook.

50. "Popularity of a Religious Drama," *San Francisco Chronicle*, December 1, 1903, 63, *Ben-Hur* Scrapbook.

51. See, for an excellent example, "'Ben Hur,'" *Columbia Record*, October 17, 1917, 94, *Ben-Hur* Scrapbook.

52. *Waterbury American*, April 18, 1904, 242, *Ben-Hur* Scrapbook.

53. *Spokane Statesman-Review*, January 7, 1903, 72; "'Ben-Hur,'" *Baltimore American*, October 27, 1907, 225, *Ben-Hur* Scrapbook.

54. "'Ben-Hur,'" *Rock Island Argus*, March 23, 1911, 3, ISHL.

55. "'Ben Hur' Stirs Audience," *Toledo News-Bee*, December 10, 1907, 252, *Ben-Hur* Scrapbook.

56. Towle and Cook spoke of a distinctive *Ben-Hur* audience in their reports from the road to Erlanger. See, for example, Towle to Erlanger, May 6, 1908, Towle file.

57. "Return of 'Ben Hur,'" *Kansas City News*, October 6, 1908, 25, *Ben-Hur* Scrapbook.

58. "The Making of a Playgoer," *New York Telegraph*, April 18, 1904, 241, *Ben-Hur* Scrapbook.

59. "Tonight at the Oliver," *Lincoln Star*, January 15, 1906, 5, *Ben-Hur* Scrapbook.

60. "Talks on Ben Hur," *Oakland Inquirer*, November 11, 1903, 45, *Ben-Hur* Scrapbook.

61. "Full House Saw 'Ben-Hur,'" *Chattanooga Times*, January 12, 1908, 25, *Ben-Hur* Scrapbook.

62. *Cleveland Leader*, November 9, 1907, Robinson Locke Collection, vol. 98, series 3, New York Public Library.

63. "At the Bradford Theatre: Influence of 'Ben-Hur,'" *Bradford Republican*, September 14, 1908, 115, *Ben-Hur* Scrapbook.

64. "'Ben Hur' at the Grand," *Cincinnati Commercial Tribune*, December 27, 1907, 8, *Ben-Hur* Scrapbook.

65. "Ben Hur," *Cleveland Leader*, December 3, 1907, 250, *Ben-Hur* Scrapbook.

66. *Little Rock Gazette*, March 6, 1908, 67, AHC.

67. "The Making of a Playgoer," *New York American*, April 18, 1904, 241, *Ben-Hur* Scrapbook.

68. *Kansas City Times*, January 12, 1906, 21, *Ben-Hur* Scrapbook.

69. "Theatrical Topics: At the Hippodrome," *Quincy Daily Herald*, March 27, 1914, 5, ISHL.

70. "Says Billy Sunday," *New York American*, November 6, 1916, 5, *Ben-Hur* Scrapbook, vol. 2.

71. Ibid.

72. A. L. Erlanger obituary, *New York Times*, March 8, 1930, 1–2.

6. June Mathis's *Ben-Hur*

1. "Studio News and Gossip," *Photoplay*, July 1922, 91; Kevin Brownlow, *The Parade's Gone By . . .* (New York: Ballantine, 1968), 444–45; and André Soares, *Beyond Paradise: The Life of Ramon Novarro* (Jackson, MS: Univ. of Mississippi Press, 2010), 70–71.

2. Brownlow, *The Parade's Gone By . . .* , 452–53; Soares, *Beyond Paradise*, 77; "Has Left 'Ben-Hur,'" *New York Morning Telegraph*, August 3, 1924, Robinson Locke Collection, New York Public Library for the Performing Arts; "June Mathis Signs," *New York Times*, August 25, 1924, Colleen Moore Scrapbook No. II, Academy of Motion Picture Arts and Sciences Library; and Tamar Lane, "June's Great Test," *Film Mercury*, June 19, 1925, 1–2. After being dismissed from *Ben-Hur*, Mathis signed with First National. There, she wrote screenplays for several hit comedies until, in mid-1925, she began another massive production. Originally titled *The Viennese Medley*, it was eventually released as *The Greater Glory*.

3. Brownlow, *The Parade's Gone By . . .* , 445–53; Soares, *Beyond Paradise*, 71–76.

4. T. J. Jackson Lears, *Rebirth of a Nation: The Making of Modern America, 1877–1920* (New York: HarperCollins, 2009), 275, 23–24, 129–32; Wendy Holliday, *Hollywood's Modern Women: Screenwriting, Work Culture, and Feminism, 1910–1940* (PhD diss., New York Univ., 1995), 48, 65–69.

5. Antonia Lant and Ingrid Periz, "Part Five: Introduction," in *Red Velvet Seat: Women's Writing on the First Fifty Years of Cinema* (London: Verso, 2006), 562; Katherine Lipke, "Most Responsible Job Ever Held by a Woman," *Los Angeles Times*, June 3, 1923, 13, 16.

6. Lant and Periz, "Part Five: Introduction," 560–62.

7. Ibid.

8. "Before June Mathis Sailed," *New York Morning Telegraph*, February 10, 1924, Robinson Locke Collection; Joseph Schenck, telegram to Marcus Loew, May 2, 1924, *Ben-Hur* Production File 8, Univ. of Southern California (USC). In the *Telegraph* article, Mathis states her hope of bringing *McTeague* to the screen as Frank Norris wrote it. Schenck's telegram cites Mathis's signature of approval on von Stroheim's massive script in his argument to dismiss her from *Ben-Hur*.

9. Lears, *Rebirth of a Nation*, 23–24.

10. Brownlow, *The Parade's Gone By . . .* , 445–53; Soares, *Beyond Paradise*, 71–76.

11. Karen Ward Mahar, *Women Filmmakers in Early Hollywood* (Baltimore, MD: Johns Hopkins Univ. Press, 2006), 140–41, 164, 168. Pickford co-founded United Artists with Charlie Chaplin, Douglas Fairbanks, William S. Hart, and D. W. Griffith. Other notable endeavors were Lois Weber's production company and facilities within Universal Studies and Nell Shipman's establishment of her own facilities and production company in Priest Lake, ID.

12. Ibid., 18–19.

13. June Mathis, *Ben-Hur*, unpublished screenplay (1923–24), scene 34, scene 156. The Williams process was a matte process like the one used in the completed film to show the destruction of the temple following the death of Christ. The Akeley camera was mounted on a tripod and contained a gyroscope for steady panning. (Copy of screenplay and information about cinematographic technology provided by Kevin Brownlow.)

14. Ibid., scene 1529. In an email message to the author, November 10, 2014, Kevin Brownlow wrote, "I presume Gaudio is Gaetano 'Tony' Gaudio, a very good Italian-born cameraman who shot such films as *The Temptress* with Garbo, *Secrets* with N. Talmadge, *The Racket* with Louis Wolheim. I believe he was the first cameraman on the Brabin *Ben-Hur*."

15. Mahar, *Women Filmmakers*, 82; William J. Mann, *Behind the Screen: How Gays and Lesbians Built Hollywood, 1910–1969* (New York: Penguin, 2001), 12; and Lipke, "Most Responsible," 13.

16. Mathis, *Ben-Hur*, scene 1025.

17. Ibid., scenes 851, 1630, 1722.

18. Ibid., scenes 1625 and 1624.

19. Lears, *Rebirth of a Nation*, 273, 1; June Mathis, "Harmony in Picture Making," *Film Daily*, May 6, 1923.

20. "'Hoo-doo Ring' Brings Fortune to June Mathis," *New York Telegraph*, June 17, 1917, Robinson Locke Collection; June Mathis, "Tapping the Thought Wireless," *Moving Picture World*, July 21, 1917, Robinson Locke Collection; and unpublished press release, June Mathis file, New York Public Library for the Performing Arts.

21. "The 'Million Dollar Girl,'" *Photoplay*, October 1923, 65; Soares, *Beyond Paradise*, 72.

22. Soares, *Beyond Paradise*, 73, 75.

23. Fred Niblo to Louis B. Mayer, May 20, 1924, *Ben-Hur* Production File 8, USC.

24. Brownlow, *The Parade's Gone By . . .* , 450.

25. Soares, *Beyond Paradise*, 27, 61, 72, 75.

26. Although Brabin's nearly total lack of achievement on *Ben-Hur* tarnished his reputation and produced questions about Mathis's wisdom in selecting him, he does appear to have been a talented filmmaker. In his only extant silent work, *The Raven* (1915), Brabin adapts Poe's famous poem by making it part of telling his family history. He opens with a self-reflexive shot of Poe's ancestor arriving in America: a daring choice for its archaic,

amateurish appearance. The rest of the film includes dissolves, double exposures, and other examples of almost every cinematic and editing trick available at the time.

27. "The Final Choice," *Movie Classic*, April 1924, 34; Brownlow, *The Parade's Gone By* . . . , 452.

28. Niblo to Louis B. Mayer, May 20, 1924; Emily W. Leider, *Dark Lover: The Life and Death of Rudolph Valentino* (New York: Farrar, Straus and Giroux, 2003), 116; Liam O'Leary, *Rex Ingram: Master of the Silent Cinema* (London: BFI, 1993), 107; and Dwinelle Beuthall, "Which Road Leads to Happiness?" *Motion Picture Magazine*, December 1926, 120.

29. Jonathan Rosenbaum, *Greed* (London: BFI, 1993), 25.

30. "Clever Salt Lake Child," *Salt Lake Tribune*, July 14, 1901, 14; "June Mathis," Employee Biography Sheet, Goldwyn, November 29, 1922, June Mathis clippings file, USC; and Christine Gledhill, ed., *Home Is Where the Heart Is: Studies in Melodrama and the Woman's Film* (London: BFI, 1987).

31. June Mathis to Laura Mary Mathis, undated copy from Barbara Madson Basich, niece of June Mathis. This letter to her sister, possibly written from her New York hospital room in March 1927, where she faced surgery just three months before her death, reads: "Laura Dear, Just a line to let you know that I love you, in case anything happens. Love Bal, he will look out for you—Here too is a line for George telling him I love him and also Sam—we have all been so close—Love—June."

32. Lears, *Rebirth of a Nation*, 57.

33. Mathis, *Ben-Hur*, note on page 1 before scene 1; scenes 1–60; and scene 1722.

34. Ruth Scodel, "The 1925 *Ben-Hur* and the 'Hollywood Question,'" in *The Ancient World in Silent Cinema*, eds. Pantelis Michelakis and Maria Wyke (Cambridge: Cambridge Univ. Press, 2013), 320, 329.

35. Mathis, *Ben-Hur*, scene 1722.

36. Scodel, "The 1925 *Ben-Hur*," 319.

7. Getting Judas Right

1. On the complicated production history of the film, see Kevin Brownlow, *The Parade's Gone By* . . . (Berkeley, CA: Univ. of California Press, 1968), 386–414.

2. cf. Thomas J. Slater's discussion in this volume of June Mathis's quite distinct use of beyond-the-frame light.

3. Supersessionism is the theological notion that Christianity has replaced Judaism. In its most virulent, imperialistic form, this theology asserts that there is no reason for the continued existence of Judaism.

4. The film contains more Jesus material than D. W. Griffith's *Intolerance: Love's Struggle through the Ages* (1916), which is now often discussed as a Jesus film.

5. Like almost all Jesus films, *Ben-Hur* relies on the harmonization of materials selected from the four canonical Gospels. Among the Gospels, the infancy-to-Passion pattern appears only in Matthew and Luke. That the 1925 film ends without a resurrection

scene connects it most closely to Mark, which also ends with a claim about Jesus's future rather than a "sighting" of him. The film's overall depiction of Jesus as a transcendent, divine figure (or a symbol of such) is most akin to that of John or of various gnostic Gospels.

6. The earliest Jesus films were Passion plays. Marc Klaw and Abraham Erlanger, who produced the Broadway *Ben-Hur*, also produced and showed the first Passion play film, *The Höritz Passion Play*, in the United States in 1897. Erlanger was also involved in the production of the 1925 *Ben-Hur*. On silent Jesus films, see Roland Cosandey, André Gaudreault, and Tom Gunning, eds., *Une Invention du Diable? Cinéma des Premiers Temps et Religion/An Invention of the Devil? Religion and Early Cinema* (Sainte-Foy, Québec, Canada: Les Presses de L'Université Laval, 1992); Jeffrey L. Staley and Richard Walsh, *Jesus, the Gospels, and Cinematic Imagination* (Louisville, KY: Westminster John Knox, 2007), 6–32; David J. Shepherd, *The Bible on Silent Film: Spectacle, Story and Scripture in the Early Cinema* (Cambridge: Cambridge Univ. Press, 2013), Kindle edition; and David J. Shepherd, ed., *The Silents of Jesus in the Cinema (1897–1927)* (London: Routledge, forthcoming).

7. Shepherd, *Bible on Silent Film*, chap. 1.

8. See Staley and Walsh, *Jesus, the Gospels, and Cinematic Imagination*, 6–16; and Shepherd, *Silents of Jesus*. As several essays in the latter demonstrate, it is difficult to say exactly what scenes an early Jesus film contains because films were sold, not rented, to exhibitors, and producers marketed new scenes to add to old films or new versions of old films. The exhibitor could also cut and paste at will. Lawrence Marston's *The Star of Bethlehem* (1912) deserves separate mention because it concentrates on the infancy rather than on the Passion.

9. Wallace repeatedly ascribes feminine or "womanly" traits to Christ. Lew Wallace, *Ben-Hur: A Tale of the Christ* (New York: Harper & Brothers, 1901), 7:V, 8:VI, 8:VII.

10. Biblical films are famous for cinematic and ideological conservatism. See Shepherd, *Bible on Silent Film*. Parenthetical references here and throughout the essay are to the films' DVD chapters (Warner Home Video DVDs).

11. The Technicolor distinguishes the Jesus material, although its effectiveness has been challenged. Brownlow (*The Parade's Gone By . . .* , 411) says it is aesthetically offensive, like a neon sign in church.

12. Olcott and Griffith's films also end before the resurrection, although Griffith's has an apocalyptic finale in which heavenly peace descends to end the history of intolerance. On *Ben-Hur*'s bland, non-creedal Christianity, see Ruth Scodel, "The 1925 *Ben-Hur* and the 'Hollywood Question,'" in *The Ancient World in Silent Cinema*, ed. Pantelis Michelakis and Maria Wyke (Cambridge: Cambridge Univ. Press, 2013), 320.

13. Cecil B. DeMille's *The Ten Commandments* (1923) also climaxes with the healing of a leprous woman. The film's hero, who stands in for Jesus, welcomes his errant love interest back into the light and she is miraculously cured. Among other Jesus films, the healing of lepers is prominent only in Pier Paolo Pasolini's *Il Vangelo Secondo Matteo* (1964).

14. cf. Scodel, "1925 *Ben-Hur*," 319–20.

15. The hallowing of the family is quite common in U.S. cinema. For a discussion of this hallowing in D. W. Griffith's films, see Richard Walsh, "Griffith's Talismanic Jesus: *Intolerance* and *The Birth of a Nation*," in Mayer, *Silents of Jesus*. The Klaw & Erlanger *Ben-Hur* climaxes similarly because it ends with the healing of the Hur women as Jesus approaches Jerusalem. The 1959 film cuts repeatedly back and forth between the women's healing and the Crucifixion so that the stories have a kind of joint climax. The blood and water that run from the cross into the world are the film's climactic, although not final, visual whereas the climax of Wallace's novel is the revelation of the divine Christ. The novel's last half speaks repeatedly of the coming king and then shows Jesus in his Passion. Jesus speaks for the first time in the novel at his arrest to ask "whom seek ye?" and to assert divinely "I am he" (8:VIII). The "I am" echoes in Ben-Hur's memory at the cross as does Jesus's "I am the resurrection and the life" (8:IX).

16. For an enlightening comparison of cup/water motifs in the novel, the 1959 film, and the Gospel of John, see Larry J. Kreitzer, *The New Testament in Fiction and Film: On Reversing the Hermeneutical Flow* (Sheffield, UK: Sheffield Academic, 1993), 44–66.

17. The table, background, and triad grouping of the disciples resemble Da Vinci's painting, although the individual "triad" groups are not exact copies. For a painting that places Judas on the viewer's side of the table, see Domenico Ghirlandaio's *Last Supper* (1480), "Art and the Bible," accessed October 3, 2014, http://www.artbible.info/art/last-supper .html.

18. See, for example, Judith Buchanan, "Gospel Narratives on Silent Film," in *The Cambridge Companion to Literature on Screen*, ed. Deborah Cartmell and Imelda Whelehan (Cambridge: Cambridge Univ. Press, 2007), 55.

19. See Vivian Sobchack, "Embodying Transcendence: On the Literal, the Material, and the Cinematic Sublime," *Material Religion* 4, no. 2 (2008): 194–203. Sobchack identifies two other ways in which film depicts the sacred: (1) transcendence in immanence locates the sacred in the material world; and (2) negative transcendence imagines a sacred "other" wholly beyond human ken and semiotics, which is therefore inexpressible materially, except by awareness of a gap or opening in the material world. This description slightly alters Sobchack's labels. Her analysis builds on that of Paul Schrader in *Transcendental Style in Film: Ozu, Bresson, Dreyer* (Berkeley, CA: Univ. of California Press, 1972). He denounces the biblical epics' typical depiction of the sacred (Sobchack's symbolic transcendence) in favor of Sobchack's negative transcendence. For an analysis of the cinematic depiction of the sacred in terms of different comparative religion scholars' views of the sacred, see Richard Walsh, *Reading the Gospels in the Dark: Portrayals of Jesus in Film* (Harrisburg, PA: Trinity Press International, 2003), 187–89.

20. Docetic Christology asserts that Christ is a wholly spiritual being who only appears to take on human form. Orthodox Christology asserts that Jesus Christ is both fully human and fully divine (spiritual). Johannine is a scholarly designation for New Testament materials associated with the apostle John: the Gospel of John, 1–3 John, and Revelation.

21. For example, one might see these allusive visuals as symbols of one's own sacred tradition or simply as things of historical, cultural import. Note again the non-dogmatic character of the film's final words.

22. On this depiction of Jesus in early silent films, see Charles Keil, "*From the Manger to the Cross*: The New Testament Narratives and the Question of Stylistic Retardation," in Cosandey, Gaudreault, and Gunning, *Une Invention du Diable?* 112–20. On this practice as the general pattern of Jesus films, see Walsh, *Reading the Gospels in the Dark*, 34–39, and "Griffith's Talismanic Jesus." For Shepherd (*Bible on Silent Film*, chaps. 8–9), biblical stories in the silent film era are typically spectacles, not stories. The story is provided by invented subplots or by parallel modern stories. For Bruce Babington and Peter William Evans in *Biblical Epics: Sacred Narrative in the Hollywood Cinema* (Manchester: Manchester Univ. Press, 1993, 179–83), *Ben-Hur*'s marginal depiction of Christ and the focus on awed faces emphasizes faith "in things unseen" (and undefined to create the largest possible acceptance by the audience). Faith then becomes the only remaining "miracle." cf. John 20:29–31.

23. The victorious nature of Niblo's final scene depends on cultural assumptions about the telos of the family and on the historical awareness that Christianity ultimately triumphed over Rome. Christian/Roman epics generally depend on these assumptions too.

24. On the history of Judas portrayals, see Kim Paffenroth, *Images of the Lost Disciple* (Louisville, KY: Westminster John Knox, 2001); Susan Gubar, *Judas: A Biography* (New York: W. W. Norton, 2009); and Richard Walsh, *Three Versions of Judas* (London: Equinox, 2010).

25. See, for example, Mark 14:20–21; Luke 22:3; John 6:70–71, 13:2, 27. For discussion, see Walsh, *Three Versions*, 22–50.

26. For discussion, and exceptions, see Walsh, *Three Versions*, 120 50; Walsh, "The Gospel According to Judas: Myth and Parable," in *The Bible in Film—The Bible and Film*, ed. Cheryl J. Exum (Leiden, the Netherlands: Brill, 2006), 37–53; and Walsh, "Gospel Judases: Interpreters at Play in Mythic Fields," *Postscripts: The Journal of Sacred Texts and Contemporary Worlds* 2, no. 1 (2006): 29–46. Shepherd (*Bible on Silent Film*, chap. 4) finds Armand Bour's *Le Baiser de Judas* (1908) a sympathetic portrayal of Judas's remorse. He also calls it the first Judas film.

27. Paffenroth, *Images of the Lost Disciple*, 144.

28. Hyam Maccoby, *Judas Iscariot and the Myth of Jewish Evil* (New York: Free Press, 1992), 25–29, 146–54. Maccoby argues that the traditional Christian Judas is nothing but a Christian name, construct, or myth that blatantly reflects Christian supersessionism. On Judas as Christian myth-making, see Walsh, *Three Versions*, 151–62.

29. See Thomas De Quincey, "Judas Iscariot," in *The Collected Writings of Thomas De Quincey*, ed. David Mason (London: A & C Black, 1897), 8:177–206.

30. Political aims motivate at least in part the Judases of Robert Wiene's *I.N.R.I.* (1923), Cecil B. DeMille's *The King of Kings* (1927), Nicholas Ray's *King of Kings* (1961), Norman Jewison's *Jesus Christ Superstar* (1973), Franco Zeffirelli's *Jesus of Nazareth* (1977), Martin Scorsese's *The Last Temptation of Christ* (1988), Roger Young's *Jesus* (1999), Raffaele Mertes's *Judas* (2001),

and Charles Robert Carner's *Judas* (2004). On the motivation of cinematic Judases, see Adele Reinhartz, *Jesus of Hollywood* (Oxford: Oxford Univ. Press, 2007), 151–77; and Walsh, *Three Versions*, 141–50.

31. For a fuller discussion, see Walsh, *Reading the Gospels*, 121–46; Staley and Walsh, *Jesus, the Gospels, and Cinematic Imagination*, 33–42; and Walsh, *Three Versions*, 113–19.

32. An earlier European example is the Judas in Robert Wiene's *I.N.R.I.* (1923).

33. This part of the film's finale resembles the apocalyptic but non-violent arrival of the heavenly kingdom in Griffith's *Intolerance*. The apocalyptic finale of *The Birth of a Nation* is more violent.

34. For the pattern and *Ben-Hur*'s deviation see Babington and Evans, *Biblical Epics*, 177–79, 194–97.

35. For a discussion of supersession in the *Ben-Hur* tradition, see Babington and Evans, *Biblical Epics*, 194–97.

36. Hebrew Bible epics chart similar transformations. See, for example, Noah's movement from vengeance (judgment) to love in Darren Aronofsky's *Noah* (2014). For an argument that a *lex talionis*/love dichotomy does indicate Christian supersessionism in Griffith's 1916 *Intolerance* and in DeMille's 1923 *Ten Commandments*, see Shepherd, *Bible on Silent Film*, chaps. 6, 8.

37. For an argument for subtle supersession in the 1959 *Ben-Hur* film, see Adele Reinhartz, *Bible and Cinema: An Introduction* (London: Routledge, 2013), 98–101.

38. See Scodel, "1925 *Ben-Hur*," 313–29. She discusses the film's possible relationship to various "Jewish" issues of the day (e.g., immigration, Zionism).

39. The 1959 film makes this ethical dichotomy more blatant. See also Hilton Obenzinger's essay in this volume.

40. The allusive visualization of Jesus may imply a lofty Christology that would be difficult for Jewish monotheists to accept, but the film's sacred and Jesus's precise relationship to it remain at the level of suggestion and symbolism.

41. For Babington and Evans (*Biblical Epics*, 16, 99), the epics dramatize the conflict between religion and secularism in the twentieth-century United States, but they also reach some kind of détente because the epics must be all things to all viewers. The epics also replay U.S. values (e.g., individualism, freedom, rationalism) if not the story of heroic U.S. "everypersons" or the U.S. founders. On the latter, see Michael Wood, *America in the Movies*, 2nd ed. (New York: Columbia Univ. Press, 1989); and Gilles Deleuze, *Cinema 1: The Movement Image*, trans. Hugh Tomlinson and Barbara Habberjam (Minneapolis, MN: Univ. of Minnesota Press, 1997). For discussions of more specific modern topics that fascinate the biblical epic, see Gerald E. Forshey, *American Religious and Biblical Spectaculars* (Westport, CT: Praeger, 1992); and Reinhartz, *Bible and Cinema*, 17–107.

42. For a discussion of similar "constructions" of religion in recent cinema dealing with the historical era of early modernity, see Richard Walsh, "The Cinematic Construction of Early Modern Religions," *Reformation* 18, no. 1 (December 2013): 134–47.

43. On modernity's complicated relationship to the spiritual—seen positively when it refers to individual subjectivity and increasingly negatively when it refers to (a possibly oppressive) transcendent "other"—see Walsh, *Three Versions*, 108–19, 131–50.

44. Babington and Evans, *Biblical Epics*, 190. They also find implicit critiques of a too puritanical Christian superego in this gendering or in the epic's "feminine" values (202–205).

45. cf. the scene in the later *King of Kings* in which Judas stands in the street alone, holding a rock almost used to stone the adulteress, while the narrator intones that Judas must choose between a messiah of war and one of peace (16).

46. One can distinguish between *imitatio Christi* stories and Christ-figure stories. See Theodore Ziolkowski, *Fictional Transfigurations of Jesus* (Princeton, NJ: Princeton Univ. Press, 1972). For the fuzziness of such categories, see Richard Walsh, "A Beautiful Corpse: Fiction and Hagiography in *Son of Man*," in *Son of Man: An African Jesus Film*, eds. Richard Walsh, Jeffrey L. Staley, and Adele Reinhartz (Sheffield, UK: Sheffield Phoenix, 2013), 192–94.

47. But Jesus is clearly the stronger figure. He successfully gives Judah water despite brutal Roman opposition (18), whereas Judah fails in his attempt to do the same on the Via Dolorosa (58). At other points, the 1959 film more closely parallels Judah and Jesus. For example, Balthasar mistakes Judah for Jesus (29). More importantly, this Judah rejects his Roman citizenship, declaring, "I am Judah Ben-Hur" in a scene before Pilate that recalls Jesus's "I am" before the high priest (see Mark 14:62). Although the 1959 film does not present Jesus's trial scene, its Pilate does tell Judah to be wary of crucifying himself (54).

48. Do the parallels suggest that Judah's "resurrection" from the galleys stands in for Jesus's resurrection, which is absent from the film, and imply that Jesus's story, like Judah's, does not end in "certain death?" Is this another instance in which Judah's story takes over the Gospel story?

49. Griffith's *Intolerance* multiplies similar suffering Christ figures to include the oppressed hordes of all history. See Walsh, "Griffith's Talismanic Jesus." *Intolerance* reflects prewar pacifism. Does the 1925 *Ben-Hur* reflect postwar distaste over war's violence and its effects? See Michael Williams, *Film Stardom, Myth and Classicism: The Rise of Hollywood's Gods* (Basingstoke, Hampshire, UK and New York: Palgrave Macmillan, 2012), 113–41. To expand on the Christ or Gospel parallels, Judah has his own triumphal entry into Jerusalem, on a white horse in contrast to Jesus's black donkey (30–31), and his own Sermon on the Mount addressed to his gathered legions (31, contrast 19).

50. Incidentally, the film does not include Jesus's adoption as son of God either (see, e.g., Matt. 3:17). Therefore, does Judah's adoption as son of Rome take over this Gospel moment too (18)? It seems significant that the scene of Judah's triumph, like many of the Jesus scenes, is in Technicolor.

51. Note that Reimarus's account of the political/spiritual dichotomy differs dramatically from that of De Quincey. See Albert Schweitzer, *The Quest of the Historical Jesus*, trans. W. Montgomery (Minneapolis, MN: Augsburg Fortress, 2001); and H. S. Reimarus, *Fragments*, ed. Charles Talbert, trans. Ralph S. Fraser (Chico, CA: Scholars, 1985).

52. Later historians, beginning with Albert Schweitzer, congratulate themselves on finding a more Jewish (and apocalyptic) Jesus. On the modern construction of scholarly identity transpiring in the construction of this Jewish Jesus, which may still involve elements of supersessionism, see Walsh, *Three Versions*, 115–19; William Arnal, *The Symbolic Jesus: Historical Scholarship, Judaism and the Construction of Identity* (London: Equinox, 2005); and James G. Crossley, *Jesus in an Age of Terror: Scholarly Projects for a New American Century* (London: Equinox, 2008).

8. Take Up the White Man's Burden

1. John Buchan, *Sick Heart River* (London: Hodder & Stoughton, 1941).

2. Geza Vermes, *Jesus and the World of Judaism* (London: SCM, 1983), 1. See also Richard Walsh's essay in this volume.

3. Graham Greene, "The Last Buchan," in *Collected Essays* (Harmondsworth, Middlesex, UK: Penguin, 1969), 167–69; and Suzanne McCarthy, "Sick Heart River," *Suzanne's Bookshelf* (blog), June 11, 2007, http://powerscourt.blogspot.co.il/2007/06/sick-heart-river.html.

4. Buchan, *Sick Heart River*, 181. Subsequent references to this novel are parenthetical.

5. Jefferson J. A. Gatrall, "The Color of His Hair: Nineteenth-Century Literary Portraits of the Historical Jesus," *Novel: A Forum on Fiction* 42, no. 1 (2009): 113, 116. See also Shawn Kelley, *Racializing Jesus: Race, Ideology, and the Formation of Modern Biblical Scholarship* (London and New York: Routledge, 2002); Jeffrey S. Siker, "Historicizing a Racialized Jesus: Case Studies in the 'Black Christ,' the 'Mestizo Christ,' and White Critique," *Biblical Interpretation* 15 (2007): 26–53; and Ella Shohat, "Sacred Word, Profane Image: Theologies of Adaptation," in *A Companion to Literature and Film*, eds. Robert Stam and Alessandra Raengo (London: Oxford Univ. Press, 2004): 23–45.

6. Gertrude Himmelfarb, *Victorian Minds* (New York: Alfred A. Knopf, 1968), 249.

7. Susannah Heschel quotes Renan in "From Jesus to Shylock: Christian Supersessionism and 'The Merchant of Venice,'" *Harvard Theological Review* 99, no. 4 (2006): 417; John Buchan, *Memory Hold-the-Door* (London: Hodder & Stoughton, 1941), 102.

8. See "Mixed Blood Aided White Geniuses," *New York Times*, February 18, 1907, 4; Gatrall, "Color of His Hair," 122.

9. "Literature---Art---Science," *Chicago Daily*, November 27, 1880, 9; George D. Burton, "What We Get from It," *New York Times*, April 9, 1898, RB245; S. C. de Soissons, "Still 'Quo Vadis,'" *New York Times*, April 9, 1898, RB244.

10. Maria Wyke, "Silent Laughter and the Counter-Historical: Buster Keaton's *Three Ages* (1923)," in *The Ancient World in Silent Cinema*, eds. Pantelis Michelakis and Maria Wyke (Cambridge: Cambridge Univ. Press, 2013), 295–96.

11. Thomas J. Slater, "June Mathis's *Ben-Hur*: A Tale of Corporate Change and the Decline of Women's Influence in Hollywood"; Richard Walsh, "Getting Judas Right: The 1925 *Ben-Hur* as Jesus Film and Biblical Epic"; both in this volume.

12. David Cannadine, "John Buchan: A Life at the Margins," *American Scholar* 67 (Summer 1998): 2. I refer to a New York financier to track remarks like Cannadine's; however, my interest in race makes it relevant that Frances Galliard is a Quebecois who has lapsed from the Roman Catholic training of his childhood. Weak doctrinal training leaves him vulnerable to Lew Frizel but not stuck at the backwoodsman's brutish miscomprehension of God's truth. This authorial decision hints that Catholics are less equipped than Calvinists to ponder the Bible's teachings as independently as Sir Edward must while he treks. The implication is that the Scot's Christianity is more manly, more modern, and "whiter."

13. David Daniell, *The Interpreter's House: A Critical Assessment of John Buchan* (London: Nelson, 1975), 159. For *Sick Heart*'s categorization by the British humor magazine *Punch*, see http://www.johnbuchansociety.co.uk.

14. For a defense of Buchan against the anti-Semitism accusation, see the extended version of Roger Kimball, "'Realism Coloured by Poetry': Rereading John Buchan," *The New Criterion*, September 2003, http://www.newcriterion.com/articles.cfm/-ldquo-Realism -coloured-by-poetry-rdquo--rereading-John-Buchan-1688.

15. Ruth Scodel, "The 1925 *Ben-Hur* and the 'Hollywood Question,'" in Michelakis and Wyke, *Ancient World in Silent Cinema*, 320.

16. "More American Notes," *Free Church of Scotland Monthly*, March 2, 1891, 69; and "Books That Should Be Read," *Irish Presbyterian*, February 1, 1895.

17. The cartoon by Rea Irvin, first published April 25, 1936, can be found occasionally on eBay.

18. Helen Jay, "The Best Books for Children," *Ladies' Home Journal* 9 (January 1892): 18.

19. Booth Tarkington, "Lew Wallace," in *There Were Giants in the Land: Twenty-Eight Historic Americans as Seen by Twenty-Eight Contemporary Americans* (Washington, DC: U.S. Department of the Treasury, 1942): 75–83.

20. See Heschel, "From Jesus to Shylock," 419.

21. "Influence of Fiction," *St. Paul Daily News*, October 7, 1889, 2.

22. Edmund Gosse, "The Best Books," *Lippincott's Monthly Magazine* 68 (December 1901): 739.

23. "Chronicle and Comment: The Late General Wallace," *Bookman*, April 1905, 116; Rupert Hughes, "No Greatest," *New York Times*, August 29, 1915, SM9.

24. Lew Wallace, *An Autobiography* (New York and London: Harper & Brothers, 1906), 952.

25. See "Gen. Lew Wallace: A Talk with the Gallant Soldier and Author of 'Ben Hur,'" *Atchison Daily Globe*, July 13, 1887; and M. B. Schrader, "Stage Favorites," *New York Times*, February 23, 1902, 30.

26. Robert E. and Katharine Morsberger quote the 1903 letter in *Lew Wallace: Militant Romantic* (New York: McGraw Hill, 1980), 239. This letter's date suggests influence from the show via attendance or seeing photos of its handsome leading man.

27. Buchan had done his research: every seven years, the Dene group known to Europeans as "Hares" because of their reliance on rabbit, suffered famine when the rabbit population dropped. Buchan exhibits prejudice, all the same, when *Sick Heart* equates the Hares' malaise with superstition. It would be more accurate to say that this reaction to a dearth of rabbit represents generations of experience that predate weapons powerful enough to bring down the moose and caribou that keep the Hares alive under Sir Edward's gun-toting supervision. Comparable is his use of alpine skills to save Lew.

28. Buchan fans reading this scene may recall a Richard Hannay tale, *Mr. Standfast* (1919), that describes a tense scene of winter climbing to effect a rescue. The comparison is to Sir Edward's credit but Lew Frizel's detriment.

29. Daniel Gorman discusses Buchan's belief in Britannic identity in *Imperial Citizenship: Empire and the Question of Belonging* (Manchester and New York: Manchester Univ. Press, 2006), 78.

30. Janet Adams Smith, *John Buchan: A Biography* (London: Rupert Hart-Davis, 1965), 466.

9. The Erotics of the Galley Slave

1. Algernon Charles Swinburne, "Hymn to Proserpine (After the Proclamation in Rome of the Christian Faith)" (1866), Representative Poetry Online, I.35, http://rpo.library.utoronto.ca/poems/hymn-proserpine

2. Georges Bataille, *Erotism: Death and Sensuality*, trans. Mary Dalwood (San Francisco: City Lights, 1957), 120–21.

3. Swinburne, "Hymn to Proserpine," II.43–44.

4. Bataille, *Eroticism*, 90; and Richard Rambuss, *Closet Devotions* (Durham, NC: Duke Univ. Press, 1998), 26.

5. Andrea Dworkin, *Intercourse* (1987; repr., New York: Basic Books, 2006); Charles Darwent, "Arrows of Desire: How Did St Sebastian Become an Enduring, Homo-erotic Icon?" *Independent*, February 10, 2008, http://www.independent.co.uk/arts-entertainment/art/features/arrows-of-desire-how-did-st-sebastian-become-an-enduring-homoerotic-icon-779388.html; and Richard A. Kaye, "'A Splendid Readiness for Death': T. S. Eliot, the Homosexual Cult of St. Sebastian, and World War I," *Modernism/Modernity* 6, no. 2 (1999): 109.

6. Rambuss, *Closet Devotions*, 65.

7. In 2004, Mel Gibson's *The Passion of the Christ* demonstrated that such anxieties can be misplaced as audiences shift with time. Although *The Passion of the Christ* depicted Jesus's injuries in such a graphic manner that the film could almost qualify for the subgenre of "torture porn," church groups of all denominations embraced it wholeheartedly; it earned more than $370 million at the domestic box office.

8. Laura Mulvey, "Visual Pleasure and Narrative Cinema," *Screen* 16, no. 3 (1975): 6–18.

9. See Mary Anne Doane, "Film and the Masquerade: Theorizing the Female Spectator," *Screen*, 23, no. 3–4 (1982): 74–87; and Linda Williams, "When the Woman Looks," in

Re-Vision: Essays in Feminist Film Criticism, ed. Mary Ann Doane, Patricia Mellencamp, and Linda Williams (Washington, DC: American Film Institute, 1983), 83–99.

10. Kaja Silverman, *Male Subjectivity at the Margins* (London: Routledge, 1992), 3.

11. Steve Neale, "Masculinity as Spectacle: Reflections on Men and Mainstream Cinema," *Screen* 24, no. 6 (1983): 2–17.

12. See Ina Rae Hark, "Animals or Romans: Looking at Masculinity in *Spartacus*," in *Screening the Male: Exploring Masculinities in Hollywood Film*, ed. Steven Cohan and Ina Rae Hark (London: Routledge, 1993), 151–72; Ina Rae Hark, "Tortured Masculinity: Gendering Jesus in *The Robe*," *Quarterly Review of Film and Television* 18, no. 2 (2001): 117–28; and Merle K. Peirce, "Transgressive Masculinities in Selected Sword and Sandal Films" (master's thesis, Rice Univ., 2009).

13. Steven Cohan, *Masked Men: Masculinity and the Movies in the Fifties* (Bloomington, IN: Indiana Univ. Press, 1997).

14. Gordon Thomas, "Getting It Right the Second Time: Adapting *Ben-Hur* for the Screen," *Bright Lights Film Journal* (May 2006), http://www.brightlightsfilm.com/52/benhur .htm. See also Howard Miller's essay in this volume.

15. Gore Vidal, *Palimpsest: A Memoir* (New York: Penguin, 1996), 304–306.

16. Thomas, "Getting It Right the Second Time." Wyler emphasizes Heston's height, broad shoulders, and aquiline profile so insistently that Judah does seem to be offered up for erotic engagement. Especially in crowd scenes, amidst shorter and far less impressive extras, he is naturally the figure to whom all eyes turn.

17. Gary Devore, "'I'M QUEER!' 'No! I'M QUEER!' Hollywood Homosexuality and Roman Epic Films," *Popular Culture Review* 10, no. 1 (1999): 129–30; for a countervailing opinion see Peter Richards, "Whose Hur?" *Film Comment* 35, no. 2 (1999): 41.

18. Thomas, "Getting It Right the Second Time." See also Richard Walsh's essay in this volume.

19. That Arrius becomes a liminal figure in the film's representations of masculinity is signaled by the fact that he is the only major male character who spends no time in Judea. This allows him to escape the choice between allegiance to the emperor or to Christ. Arrius stands as the best Rome can do to produce a good man, but that best is not good enough in the film's moral economy. Thus, Judah on his path to salvation must repudiate both Arrius's name and his authority, even though he continues to honor the man himself.

20. Although the filmmakers would never intentionally include such a blasphemous notion, this pattern implicates God the father, who is willing to send his only begotten son to suffering and death to achieve the goal of redeeming humankind from original sin.

21. For instance, much is made of Judah's receipt of Arrius's family ring, which parallels the gift of Esther's ring after he frees her. Eventually he returns Arrius's ring and reclaims his name as Judah Ben-Hur: a divorce, as it were.

22. Melani McAlister, *Epic Encounters: Culture, Media, and U.S. Interests in the Middle East since 1945*, 2nd ed. (Berkeley, CA: Univ. of California Press, 2005), 78.

23. History has, however, confirmed the sheik's point of view. Although violent revolution often only replaces one dominant power with another, to wait for change until all people embrace the God that is "in every man" (as the film phrases it) is to become complicit with the oppressor's earthly aims. Oppressors may lose out in the afterlife, but they cause extensive misery to the living, whom faith instructs not to rise up against tyranny. That nominally Christian conquerors have cynically used conversion to pacify populations they wish to keep in servitude is an inconvenient truth that *Ben-Hur* rushes past.

10. Challenging a Default *Ben-Hur*

1. See Jon Solomon, "The Early Dramatic Productions: Tableau and Pantomime." Unpublished manuscript.

2. I have deliberately chosen the Arabic word *intifada* ("the shaking off") to describe Palestinian resistance to the Israeli occupation, first in 1987–93 and again in 2000–2005, because Judah is drawn into a similar resistance movement and, for the three years he spends recruiting, training, and equipping a rebel army, assumes the role of resistance leader.

3. The most recent (2010) television miniseries, produced by the Alchemy Television Group from a script written by Alan Sharp, was directed by Steve Shill. This production substitutes Athene, "a Greek courtesan," for Iras.

4. 1 Kings 10:14.

5. On surrogate paternity in the novel, see Ina Rae Hark's essay in this volume.

6. Cesti were boxers who fought in brutal hand-to-hand combat in the arena. The term is taken from the gloves (*cestus*) these gladiators wore.

7. William S. Young, *Ben-Hur*, VI:1. Never published and transcribed from the 1898 licensing script in the Lord Chamberlain's Collection in the British Library, the text of Young's *Ben-Hur* may be found in David Mayer's *Playing out the Empire, Ben Hur and Other Toga Plays and Films, 1883–1908* (Clarendon Press of Oxford Univ. Press, 1994), 189–290.

8. See, in particular, Alexander Dumas, fils, *La Dame aux Camélias* (novel 1849, play 1852) and *Le Demi-monde* (1855). Also Émile Augier, *Le Mariage d'Olympe* (1853) and Théodore Barriere, *Les Filles de Marbre* (1853).

9. Bara's major "vamp" films were *Under Two Flags* (1916) and *Cleopatra* (1917).

10. The Devadasi were another of Wallace's anachronisms. He was thinking of a caste in southern India in which girls were dedicated to a temple and served as ritual prostitutes. For an account of the Daphne resort located on the outskirts of Antioch, see Edward Gibbon, *The History of the Decline and Fall of the Roman Empire* (London: Strahan & Cadell, 1777), 3:342–44.

11. The Misenum coast contained the villas of Rome's wealthiest residents. Wallace implies a further irony in Iras's suicide: she is raddled, impoverished, and defeated, and the waters of Misenum are her last luxury.

12. The Kalem Studios' version of *Ben-Hur*, with William S. Hart repeating his stage role of Messala, was the subject of a legal case brought before New York's Federal District

Court by Klaw & Erlanger and Wallace's publisher, Harper & Brothers. The complainants accused Kalem of turning their drama into a "low spectacle." In a 1911 decision, this complaint was upheld. The film was ordered to be destroyed but, fortunately, copies survived. The case has become the basis for federal legislation preventing unauthorized use of copyrighted materials.

11. Coda

1. See Walter Lietzen, ed., *Ben Hur Lodge No. 322 A. F. & A. M., 1890–1990* (Kansas City, KS: Record Publications, 1989), ix, 5.

Selected Bibliography of Ben-Hur Scholarship

This list is meant to be neither exhaustive nor all inclusive. Rather, it offers an overview of the major scholarship about *Ben-Hur* and its adaptations originating from a variety of academic disciplines. Although the earliest entries we include date to the 1940s, the bibliography reflects the growing interest in the *Ben-Hur* tradition since 1990.

Allitt, Patrick. "The American Christ." *American Heritage* 39, no. 7 (1988): 128–38.

Allmendinger, Blake. "Toga! Toga!" In *Over the Edge: Remapping the American West*, edited by Valerie J. Matsumoto, 32–49. Berkeley, CA: Univ. of California Press, 1999.

Apostolos-Cappadona, Diane. "The Art of 'Seeing': Classical Painting and *Ben-Hur*." In *Image and Likeness: Religious Visions in American Film Classics*, edited by John R. May, 104–15. New York: Paulist, 1991.

Babington, Bruce, and Peter William Evans. "The Poetics of the Roman/Christian Epic." In *Biblical Epics: Sacred Narrative in the Hollywood Cinema*, 177–205. Manchester: Manchester Univ. Press, 1993.

Ben-Ari, Nitsa. "The Double Conversion of *Ben-Hur*: A Case of Manipulative Translation." *Target: International Journal of Translation Studies* 14, no. 2 (2002): 263–301.

Brownlow, Kevin. "The Heroic Fiasco: *Ben-Hur*." In *The Parade's Gone By . . .* , 385–414. Berkeley and Los Angeles: Univ. of California Press, 1968.

Buchanan, Judith. "Gospel Narratives on Silent Film." In *The Cambridge Companion to Literature on Screen*, edited by Deborah Cartmell and Imelda Whelehan, 47–60. Cambridge: Cambridge Univ. Press, 2007.

Connolly, Joy. "Crowd Politics: The Myth of the 'Populus Romanus.'" In *Crowds*, edited by Jeffrey T. Schnapp and Matthew Tiews, 77–96. Stanford, CA: Stanford Univ. Press, 2006.

Devore, Gary. "'I'M QUEER!' 'No, I'M QUEER!' Hollywood Homosexuality and Roman Epic Films." *Popular Culture Review* 10, no. 1 (1999): 127–38.

Forshey, Gerald E. *American Religious and Biblical Spectacles*. Media and Society Series. Westport, CT: Praeger, 1992.

Gatrall, Jefferson J. A. "The Color of His Hair: Nineteenth-Century Literary Portraits of the Historical Jesus," *Novel: A Forum on Fiction* 42, no. 1 (2009): 109–30.

Gutjahr, Paul. *An American Bible: A History of the Good Book in the United States, 1777–1880*. Stanford, CA: Stanford Univ. Press, 1999.

———. "'To the Heart of Solid Puritans': Historicizing the Popularity of *Ben-Hur*." *Mosaic: A Journal for the Interdisciplinary Study of Literature* 26, no. 3 (1993): 53–68.

Hannington, Luke. "Melodrama Made Good: Ennoblement by Deletion in Edgar Stillman Kelley's Score to *Ben-Hur*." *Journal of Film Music* 5, no. 1–2 (2012): 49–56.

Hanson, Victor Davis. "Lew Wallace and the Ghosts of the Shunpike." In *What Ifs? of American History: Eminent Historians Imagine What Might Have Been*, edited by Robert Cowley, 69–86. New York: G. P. Putnam, 2003.

Harap, Louis. "Religious Poetry and Fiction." In *The Image of the Jew in American Literature: From Early Republic to Mass Immigration*, 135–88. 2nd ed. Philadelphia, PA: Jewish Publication Society of America, 1978.

Heszer, Catherine. "Ben-Hur and Ancient Jewish Slavery." In *A Wandering Galilean: Essays in Honour of Seán Freyne*, edited by Zuleika Rodgers, Margaret Daly-Denton, and Anne Fitzpatrick McKinley, 121–39. Leiden: Brill, 2009.

Hickman, Roger. "The Ben-Hur Legacy." *Journal of Film Music* 5, no. 1–2 (2012): 41–48.

Holbrook, Stewart. "Gen. Wallace and *Ben-Hur*." *New York Times Book Review*, August 6, 1944.

Hovet, Theodore Richard Jr. "The Case of Kalem's *Ben-Hur* (1907) and the Transformation of Cinema." *Quarterly Review of Film and Video* 18, no. 3 (2001): 283–94.

———. "Realism and Spectacle in *Ben-Hur* (1880–1959)." PhD diss., Duke Univ., 1996.

Jackson, Gregory S. "A Game Theory of Evangelical Fiction." *Critical Inquiry* 39, no. 3 (2013): 451–85.

Joshel, Sandra R., Margaret Malamud, and Donald T. McGuire Jr. *Imperial Projections: Ancient Rome in Modern Popular Culture*. Baltimore, MD: Johns Hopkins Univ. Press, 2001.

Junkelmann, Marcus. "On the Starting Line with Ben-Hur." In *Gladiators and Caesars: The Power of Spectacle in Ancient Rome*, edited by Eckart Köhne, Cornelia Ewiglebe, and Ralph Jackson, translated by Anthea Bell, 86–102. Berkeley and Los Angeles: Univ. of California Press, 2000.

Kaplan, Amy. "Imperial Melancholy in America." *Raritan* 28, no. 3 (2009): 13–31.

——. "Romancing the Empire: The Embodiment of American Masculinity in the Popular Historical Novel of the 1890s." *American Literary History* 2, no. 4 (1990): 659–90.

Kreitzer, Joseph L. *The New Testament in Fiction and Film: On Reversing the Hermeneutical Flow.* Ithaca, NY: Cornell Univ. Press, 1993.

Leskovar, Darja Mazi. "*Ben-Hur* in Slovenian: Translations of an American Novel about Multicultural Issues." *Acta Neophilologica* 44, no. 1–2 (2011): 35–45.

Lifson, Amy. "Ben-Hur: The Book that Shook the World." *Humanities* 30, no. 6 (2009): 15–19.

Maciak, Philip. "'A Rare and Wonderful Sight': Secularism and Visual Historiography in *Ben-Hur,*" *J19: The Journal of Nineteenth-Century Americanists* (forthcoming).

Malamud, Margaret. *Ancient Rome and Modern America.* New York: Wiley-Blackwell, 2008.

Mayer, David. *Playing out the Empire: Ben Hur and Other Toga Plays and Films, 1883–1908.* Oxford: Clarendon Press of the Oxford Univ. Press, 1994.

McAlister, Melani. "'Benevolent Supremacy': The Biblical Epic at the Dawn of the American Century, 1947–1960." In *Epic Encounters: Culture, Media, and U.S. Interests in the Middle East since 1945,* 43–83. 2nd ed. Berkeley, CA: Univ. of California Press, 2005.

McKee, Irving. *"Ben-Hur" Wallace: The Life of General Lew Wallace.* Berkeley and Los Angeles: Univ. of California Press, 1947.

Miller, Howard. "The Charioteer and the Christ: *Ben-Hur* in America from the Gilded Age to the Culture Wars." *Indiana Magazine of History* 104, no. 2 (2008): 153–75.

Morsberger, Robert E., and Katharine M. Morsberger. *Lew Wallace: Militant Romantic.* New York: McGraw Hill, 1980.

Murphy, Geraldine. "Ugly Americans in Togas: Imperial Anxiety in the Cold War Hollywood Epic." *Journal of Film and Video* 56, no. 3 (2004): 3–19.

Paul, Joanna. "'The Biggest Epic Yet': Spectacle and *Ben-Hur.*" In *Film and the Classical Epic Tradition,* 213–50. Oxford: Oxford Univ. Press, 2013.

Pentz-Harris, Marcia L., Linda Seger, and R. Barton Palmer. "Screening Male Sentimental Power in *Ben-Hur.*" In *Nineteenth-Century American Fiction on Screen,* edited by R. Barton Palmer, 106–32. Cambridge: Cambridge Univ. Press, 2007.

Reinhartz, Adele. "Swords, Sandals, and Christianity." In *Bible and Cinema: An Introduction,* 83–108. Oxon and New York: Routledge, 2013.

Reynolds, David S. *Faith in Fiction: The Emergence of Religious Literature in America.* Cambridge, MA: Harvard Univ. Press, 1981.

Richards, Peter. "Whose Hur?" *Film Comment* 35, no. 2 (1999): 38–42.

Russell, James. "Exhilaration and Enlightenment in the Biblical Bestseller: Lew Wallace's *Ben-Hur,* a Tale of Christ." In *Must Read: Rediscovering American Bestsellers: From Charlotte Temple to the Da Vinci Code,* edited by Sarah Churchwell and Thomas Ruys Smith, 153–73. London: Continuum, 2012.

Ryan, Barbara. "One Reader, Two Votes: Retooling Fan Mail Scholarship." In *The History of Reading, Volume 3: Methods, Strategies, Tactics,* edited by Rosalind Crone and Shafquat Towheed, 66–79. Basingstoke, Hampshire and New York: Palgrave Macmillan, 2011.

———. "Teasing out Clues, Not Kooks: *The Man Nobody Knows* and *Ben-Hur.*" *Reception: Texts, Readers, Audiences, History* 5, no. 1 (2013): 9–23.

Scodel, Ruth. "The 1925 *Ben-Hur* and the 'Hollywood Question.'" *The Ancient World in Silent Cinema,* edited by Pantelis Michelakis and Maria Wyke, 313–29. Cambridge: Cambridge Univ. Press, 2013.

Shelton, Lewis E. "The 'Terrible' Mr. Ben Teal and the Shubert Brothers." *The Passing Show: Newsletter of the Shubert Archive* 15, no. 1 (1992): 8–14.

Slater, Thomas J. "The Vision and the Struggle: June Mathis's Work on *Ben-Hur* (1922–24)." *Post Script: Essays in Film and the Humanities* 28, no. 1 (2008): 63–78.

Smylie, James H. "The Hidden Agenda in *Ben-Hur.*" *Theology Today* 29, no. 3 (1972): 294–304.

Solomon, Jon. "The Classical Sources of Lew Wallace's *Ben-Hur.*" *International Journal of the Classical Tradition* 22, no. 1 (2015): 29–75.

———. "Erato: The New Testament and Tales of the Christ." In *The Ancient World in the Cinema,* 117–224. New Haven, CT and London: Yale Univ. Press, 2001.

———. "Fugitive Sources, *Ben-Hur,* and the Popular Art 'Property.'" *RBM: A Journal of Rare Books, Manuscripts, and Cultural Heritage* 9, no. 1 (2008): 67–78.

———. "The Kalem *Ben-Hur* (1907)." *The Ancient World in Silent Cinema,* edited by Pantelis Michelakis and Maria Wyke, 189–204. Cambridge: Cambridge Univ. Press, 2013.

———. "The Music of Ben-Hur." *Syllecta Classica* 23, no. 1 (2012): 153–78.

Squires, L. Ashley. "The Wealthiest Man in the Empire: *Ben-Hur* as Model of Evangelical Political Engagement." *Arizona Quarterly: A Journal of American Literature, Culture, and Theory* 69, no. 1 (2013): 23–46.

Theisen, Lee Scott. "'My God, Did I Set All of This in Motion?' General Lew Wallace and *Ben Hur.*" *Journal of Popular Culture* 18, no. 2 (1984): 33–41.

Thomas, Gordon. "Getting It Right the Second Time: Adapting *Ben-Hur* for the Screen." *Bright Lights Film Journal* 52 (May 2006; revised June 4, 2014). http://www.brightlightsfilm.com/52/benhur.htm.

Tuszynski, Susan. "A Cold War Cautionary Tale: Heterosexuality and Ideology in William Wyler's *Ben-Hur.*" *Journal of Popular Film and Television* 34, no. 3 (2006): 116–22.

Wallace, Lew. *An Autobiography*. New York and London: Harper & Brothers, 1906.

Williams, Michael. "*Ben-Hur: A Tale of the Christ* (1925) and the Idolisation of Ramon Novarro." In *Film Stardom, Myth, and Classicism: The Rise of Hollywood's Gods*, 113–43. Basingstoke, UK and New York: Palgrave Macmillan, 2013.

———. "The Idol Body: Stars, Statuary, and the Classical Epic." *Film and History: An Interdisciplinary Journal of Film and Television Studies* 39, no. 2 (2009): 39–48.

Winchell, Mark Royden. "Racing for Glory: Fred Niblo's *Ben-Hur* (1926) and William Wyler's *Ben-Hur* (1959)." In *God, Man, and Hollywood: Politically Incorrect Cinema from "The Birth of a Nation" to "The Passion of the Christ,"* 61–76. Wilmington, DE: ISI Books, 2008.

Winkler, Martin M. "The Roman Empire in American Cinema after 1945." *The Classical Journal* 93, no. 2 (December 1997–January 1998): 167–96.

Contributors

JEFFERSON J. A. GATRALL earned a PhD in Comparative Literature at Columbia University and is Associate Professor of Russian at Montclair State University. He is the co-editor of *Alter Icons: The Russian Icon and Modernity* (2010) and a special issue of the journal *arcadia* on identity and community (2008). He has published articles on Chekhov, Tolstoy, Dostoevsky, Proust, and Lew Wallace. He is the author of *The Real and the Sacred: Picturing Jesus in Nineteenth-Century Fiction* (2014).

INA RAE HARK is Distinguished Professor Emeritus in the English Department at the University of South Carolina. Her publications include the books *Screening the Male: Exploring Masculinities in Hollywood Film* (co-editor, 1993), *The Road Movie Book* (co-editor, 1997), *American Cinema of the 1930s* (editor, 2007), *Star Trek* (2008), and *Deadwood* (2012), as well as numerous articles on film and television studies.

DAVID MAYER is Emeritus Professor of Drama and Research Professor at the University of Manchester. He studies British and American popular entertainment of the nineteenth and early twentieth century. His recent writing explores links between the Victorian stage and early motion pictures. He is co-founder of The Victorian and Edwardian Stage on Film Project and a contributing member to The (D. W.) Griffith Project, which was developed by Le Giornate del Cinema Muto, Pordenone, the British Film Institute, and the U.S. Library of Congress. His books include *Harlequin in His Element: English Pantomime, 1806–1836* (1968), *Henry Irving and "The Bells"* (1984), *Playing out the Empire: "Ben-Hur" and other Toga-Plays and Films* (1994), and *Stagestruck Filmmaker: D. W. Griffith and the American Theatre* (2009). In 2012 he received the Distinguished Scholar Award from the American Society for Theatre Research. A Guggenheim Fellow, he has also received research fellowships from Yale and Harvard Universities, the Harry Ransom Humanities Research Center, the Leverhulme Trust, and the British Academy.

HOWARD MILLER is Distinguished Teaching Professor Emeritus in the Departments of History and Religious Studies at the University of Texas, Austin. The author of "The Charioteer and the Christ: 'Ben-Hur' in America from the Gilded Age to the Culture Wars" (2008), he is working on a book-length study of *Ben-Hur* and its impact on U.S. culture from its publication in 1880 to the present.

HILTON OBENZINGER writes fiction, poetry, history, and criticism, and is Associate Director of the Chinese Railroad Workers in North America Project at Stanford University. He has published eleven books; most relevant among them to the present collection is *American Palestine: Melville, Twain, and the Holy Land Mania* (1999).

BARBARA RYAN earned her PhD from the University of North Carolina at Chapel Hill. An Associate Professor in the University Scholars Programme at the National University of Singapore, she is the author of *Love, Wages, Slavery* (2006) and a co-editor of *Reading Acts* (2002). Ryan is currently working on a book-length study of *Ben-Hur*'s reception before the first feature-length film was made in 1925.

ERAN SHALEV is Associate Professor and Chair of the History Department at Haifa University. He is the author of *Rome Reborn on Western Shores: Historical Imagination and the Creation of the American Republic* (2009) and of *American Zion: The Old Testament as a Political Text from the Revolution to the Civil War* (2013).

MILETTE SHAMIR is Associate Professor in the Department of English and American Studies at Tel Aviv University. Her publications include *Inexpressible Privacy: The Interior Life of Antebellum American Literature* (2006) and *Boys Don't Cry? Rethinking Narratives of Masculinity and Emotion in the U.S.* (co-editor, 2002). Her present research is on American biblical orientalism in the postbellum period.

NEIL SINYARD is Emeritus Professor of Film Studies at the University of Hull. He is a prolific film scholar and critic whose long list of books includes, most recently, *Filming Literature: The Art of Screen Adaptation* (2013) and *A Wonderful Heart: The Films of William Wyler* (2013).

THOMAS J. SLATER is Professor of English at Indiana University of Pennsylvania where he teaches film studies, literature, and composition. He has published several essays on the work of June Mathis and other women in silent film, including Alla Nazimova, Lois Weber, Marion Fairfax, and Corrine Griffith. He continues to explore the life and work of Mathis in preparation for a full manuscript.

JON SOLOMON is Robert D. Novak Professor of Western Civilization and Culture and Professor of the Classics and of Cinema Studies at the University of Illinois at Urbana-Champaign. He has published numerous books and anthologies, including a revised and expanded edition of his *The Ancient World in the Cinema* (2001) and *Ancient Worlds in Film and Television* (2013). He is now completing a study of *Ben-Hur* as the prototype of popular literary properties and commercial success.

RICHARD WALSH is Professor of Religion and Co-Director of the Honors Program at Methodist University. His research interests include critical theory and biblical reception. His publications include *Mapping Myths of Biblical Interpretation* (2001), *Reading the Gospels in the Dark* (2003), *Finding St. Paul in Film* (2005), and *Three Versions of Judas* (2010). He is also co-editor of *Son of Man: An African Jesus Film* (2013, with Jeffrey L. Staley and Adele Reinhartz) and *Borges and the Bible* (2015, with Jay Twomey).

Index